Politics of liberation

This book explores various forms of oppression that plague contemporary society. Through the analyses and reflections of theorists and social activists – including Paulo Freire himself – *Politics of Liberation* brings together under a common project of human liberation critical voices from around the globe – from Mexico, Guatemala, Britain, Canada, Brazil, Argentina, Australia, New Zealand and the United States.

The contributors argue that Freire's work offers an avenue out of the malaise of contemporary politics and culture. They situate Freire *temporally* in relation to moments of modernity and postmodernity; *culturally* and *existentially* in relation to the First and Third Worlds and the standpoint of indigenous peoples; *politically* in terms of his attention to the range of sites and dimensions of oppression and their relatedness; and *intellectually* in relation to the eclectic range of theories on which he draws.

The book is a response to the current global crisis of solidarity among progressive and dissident intellectuals, educators and cultural workers. It is a crisis that challenges educators and activists to transcend narrow ethnic, cultural, religious and nationalist particularisms but without recourse to transcendental narratives which make universal claims to truth. Freire's work addresses ways of resisting forms of oppression as they are produced in the context of First-World and Third-World social and cultural sites through Freirean-based liberational strategies that build upon forms of solidarity without positing universalist claims.

The book will be required reading for anyone interested in liberation and especially for scholars and students of sociology, education and politics.

Peter L. McLaren is Associate Professor at the Graduate School of Education, University of California at Los Angeles. **Colin Lankshear** is Associate Professor in the School of Language and Literacy Education, and Director of Literacy Studies Education, Queensland University of Technology.

Politics of liberation

Paths from Freire

**Edited by Peter L. McLaren
and
Colin Lankshear**

London and New York

First published 1994
by Routledge
11 New Fetter Lane, London EC4P 4EE

Simultaneously published in the USA and Canada
by Routledge
29 West 35th Street, New York, NY 10001

Typeset in Times by
NWL Editorial Services, Langport, Somerset

Printed and bound in Great Britain by
Mackays of Chatham PLC, Chatham, Kent

British Library Cataloguing in Publication Data
A catalogue record for this book is available from the British Library.

Library of Congress Cataloging in Publication Data
Politics of liberation: paths from Freire / [edited by] Peter McLaren
and Colin Lankshear; with a foreword by Donaldo Macedo and an
afterword by Joe Kincheloe.
p. cm.
Includes bibliographical references and index.
1. Freire, Paulo, 1921– . 2. Liberty. 3. Popular education –
Philosophy. 4. Critical pedagogy. I. McLaren, Peter, 1948– .
II. Lankshear, Colin.
HM271.P63 1993   93–825
123'.5 – dc20   CIP

ISBN 0–415–09126–8 (hbk)
ISBN 0–415–09127–6 (pbk)

To Paulo Freire,
to my wife, Jenny,
and to the memory of Laurie McDade, who was killed in an
automobile accident shortly after she was invited
to contribute to this volume.
Her important scholarship will be sorely missed by those who
dream of liberation and struggle to make freedom happen.

Peter L. McLaren

To Paulo Freire, Michele Knobel and Maxine Greene,
and to Eric Braithwaite and Jack Shallcrass.

Colin Lankshear

'This impressive volume, edited by a Canadian and a New Zealander who have had considerable experience working in Latin America, offers a unique and important contribution to liberatory pedagogy and the development of a theory of political praxis. McLaren and Lankshear continue to work at the leading edge of the critical analyses of education and its relationship to culture, society, and social power. More than an exploratory exegesis of my work, *The Politics of Liberation* challenges and extends some of my ideas in ways that are always provocative, and often filled with insights that will prove to be critically important if we are to keep the politics of liberation alive in this age of global capitalism and postmodern cultures.'

Paulo Freire

Contents

Notes on contributors   ix

Preface
Donaldo Macedo   xiii

Acknowledgements   xix

Introduction
Peter L. McLaren and Colin Lankshear   1

1 **Freire and a feminist pedagogy of difference**
   Kathleen Weiler   12

2 **Critical thought and moral imagination: peace education
   in Freirean perspective**
   Marguerite and Michael Rivage-Seul   41

3 **Conscientization and political literacy: a British encounter
   with Paulo Freire**
   Ian Lister   62

4 **Toward liberatory mathematics: Paulo Freire's epistemology
   and ethnomathematics**
   Marilyn Frankenstein and Arthur B. Powell   74

5 **Twenty years after *Pedagogy of the Oppressed*: Paulo Freire
   in conversation with Carlos Alberto Torres**
   Carlos Alberto Torres and Paulo Freire   100

6 **Conscientization and social movements in Canada: the relevance
   of Paulo Freire's ideas in contemporary politics**
   Peter Findlay   108

7 **Freire – present and future possibilities**
   Edgar González Gaudiano and Alicia de Alba   123

8 Critical literacy, feminism, and a politics of representation
   Jeanne Brady   142

9 Politics, praxis and the personal: an Argentine assessment
   Adriana Puiggrós   154

10 Education and hermeneutics: a Freirean interpretation
   Michael Peters and Colin Lankshear   173

11 Postmodernism and the death of politics: a Brazilian reprieve
   Peter L. McLaren   193

   Afterword
   Joe L. Kincheloe   216

   Name index   219
   Subject index   223

Contributors

Jeanne Brady is Assistant Professor of Education at Pennsylvania State University. Her interests are feminist pedagogy and cultural studies. She is the author of the forthcoming book, *Schooling Young Children: Feminism and Literacy for Empowerment* (SUNY Press).

Alicia de Alba is an educational researcher based in the Centre for University Studies at the National Autonomous University of Mexico. Currently studying for her PhD in Education, she has published numerous articles in national and international journals and is the author of two books: *Curriculum: crisis, mito y perspectivas* and *Evaluación Curricular*.

Peter Findlay taught social policy at Carleton University in Ottawa, Canada, where he was Director of the School of Social Work. He is now active internationally as a consultant in social development in Asia, Africa and Eastern Europe, having previously worked on social welfare planning in Sri Lanka, South Africa and Zimbabwe.

Marilyn Frankenstein is Chair of the Department of Applied Language and Mathematics at the College of Public and Community Service, University of Massachusetts, Boston. Author of *Relearning Mathematics* (Free Association Books 1989), she taught mathematics to high school students and adults in New York City and New Jersey for more than twenty years. With Arthur Powell she is editing a collection of articles on Ethnomathematics and writing a criticalmathematics education text. She is a co-founder of the Criticalmathematics Educators Group, a member of the *Radical Teacher* editorial collective, and serves on the community board of the Boston Algebra in Middle Schools Project.

Paulo Freire currently devotes most of his time to writing and lecturing, but still teaches occasionally at the Pontificia Universidade Católica de São Paulo, and at the Universidade de Campinas in the state of São Paulo. He has written many books and articles on pedagogy for liberation, his best-known works including

Pedagogy of the Oppressed, Education for Critical Consciousness, Pedagogy in Process and *The Politics of Education.* His most recent books are *Educação na cidade* and *Pedagogia da esperanza.* Among many honors accorded him are the UNESCO Peace Prize in 1986 and the Organization of American States Simon Rodriguez prize in education in 1992.

Edgar González Gaudiano is Professor of Environmental Education at the National Autonomous University of Mexico, and National Director for Environmental Education in Mexico. A member of the Board of the North American Association for Environmental Education, he has recently completed his PhD in Education. He has contributed numerous articles in national and international journals and books, and is co-author/co-editor of *El Campo de Curriculum* in two volumes.

Joe L. Kincheloe is Professor of Education at Florida International University in Miami. He has written extensively on critical postmodernism and its relation to educational issues. He is the author of nine books including *Teachers as Researchers: Qualitative Paths to Empowerment* and *Toil and Trouble: Good Work, Smart Workers, and the Integration of Academic and Vocational Education.*

Colin Lankshear is Director of the research concentration in Literacy Studies in Education at the Queensland University of Technology. Most of his published work is in the politics of literacy and education. His books include *Literacy, Schooling and Revolution* and (with Peter McLaren) *Critical Literacy: Politics, Praxis and the Postmodern.*

Ian Lister is Professor of Education at the University of York, England. In the 1970s he was Research Director of the UK National Programme for Political Literacy. In the 1980s he worked for Human Rights Education. His present interests include educational reform, alternatives to conventional schools, and education for a better future.

Donaldo Macedo is Associate Professor of English and Director of the Bilingual and English as a Second Language Graduate Studies Program at the University of Massachusetts at Boston. He has published extensively in the areas of linguistics, language acquisition, literacy and Creole studies. He co-authored with Paulo Freire *Literacy: Reading the Word and the World* (Bergin and Garvey). His latest work includes *Cultural Literacy for Stupidification* (forthcoming).

Peter L. McLaren formerly held the positions of Renowned Scholar-in-Residence, and Director of the Center for Education and Cultural Studies, in the School of Education and Allied Professions at Miami University of Ohio. He is presently Associate Professor, Graduate School of Education, University of California, Los Angeles. He has served as educational correspondent for a teacher's union in his native Canada, and since 1985 has been active in urban educational reform in the United States. Author of numerous books on critical educational theory, he lectures extensively in Latin America and Europe, and co-edits two publication series dealing with critical social theory and critical pedagogy (with Henry Giroux for SUNY Press, and Joe Kincheloe for Westview Press).

Michael Peters is a Senior Lecturer in the Department of Education, University of Auckland, New Zealand. His research interests are in the areas of educational philosophy, poststructuralism and the modernity/postmodernity debate. He has contributed to a number of edited collections and a wide range of international journals.

Arthur B. Powell is a member of the editorial board of *Radical Teacher*. With John Volmink and Marilyn Frankenstein he edits the Criticalmathematics Educators Group newsletter. He is Associate Professor at Rutgers University-Newark and Chair of the Academic Foundations Department. His research interests include the use of graphing calculators for visualizing functions and writing for enabling students to make sense of mathematics.

Adriana Puiggrós is Professor of Argentine and Latin American Education at the University of Buenos Aires. She directed a collaborative project which involved universities from several Latin American countries investigating alternative pedagogies and educational prospects in the subcontinent. Her books include *Imperialism and Education in Latin America*, *Democracy and Authoritarianism in Argentinian and Latin American Pedagogy*, and *Popular Education in Latin America*.

Marguerite and Michael Rivage-Seul are both teachers at Berea College in Kentucky. Peggy is a philosopher of education. She holds an undergraduate diploma from Central Michigan University, and graduate degrees from the School for International Training and the University of Kentucky. Peggy's area of specialization is in the pedagogy of Paulo Freire, with whom she studied in Brazil in 1984.

A former Catholic priest, Mike teaches general studies and religion. He is a moral theologian who specializes in liberation theology. Peggy and Mike spent the 1992–93 academic year as 'invited researchers' at the *departamento ecuménico de investigaciones* (DEI) in San José, Costa Rica. DEI plans to translate and publish the Rivage-Seuls' forthcoming *Imagining World War III: A Conceptual Spirituality for the New World Order*.

Carlos Alberto Torres is Associate Professor in the Graduate School of Education at the University of California, Los Angeles. A recognized authority on Paulo Freire's thought, he has taught in universities in Argentina, Mexico, Canada and the United States. He has written numerous articles and books on nonformal education, sociology of education, comparative education and critical pedagogy. These include *The Politics of Nonformal Education in Latin America* and *The Church, Society and Hegemony: A Critical Sociology of Religion in Latin America*.

Kathleen Weiler teaches in the Education Department of Tufts University. She is the author of *Women Teaching for Change* and co-editor of three collections, *Rewriting Literacy*, *What Schools Can Do*, and *Feminism and Social Justice in Education: International Perspectives*. She is currently at work on a history of women teachers in California. This work has been supported by the Bunting Institute, the Spencer Foundation and the National Endowment for the Humanities.

Preface

Donaldo Macedo

As the capitalist 'banking model' of education generates greater and greater failure, many liberal and neo-liberal educators are looking to Paulo Freire's pedagogy as an alternative. No longer can it be argued that Freire's pedagogy is appropriate only in Third-World contexts. For one thing, we are experiencing a rapid Third Worldinization of North America where inner cities resemble more and more the shantytowns of the Third World with a high level of poverty, violence, illiteracy, human exploitation, homelessness and human misery. The abandonment of our inner cities and the insidious decay of their respective infrastructures, including their schools, makes it very difficult to maintain the artificial division between the First World and the Third World. It is just as easy to find Third Worldness in the First World inner cities as it is to discover First World opulence in the oligarchy in El Salvador, Guatemala and within many other Third-World nations. The Third Worldinization of the North American inner cities has also produced large-scale educational failures that have created minority student drop-out rates from 50 percent in the Boston Public Schools to over 70 percent in larger metropolitan areas like New York City.

Against this landscape of educational failure, conservative educators, by and large, have recoiled in an attempt to salvage the status quo and contain the 'browning' of America. These conservative educators have attempted to re-appropriate the educational debate and to structure the educational discourse in terms of competition and privatization of schools. The hidden curriculum of the proposed school privatization movement consists of taking resources from poor schools that are on the verge of bankruptcy to support private or well-to-do schools. Private school choice is only private to the degree that it generates private profit while being supported by public funds. What is rarely discussed in the North American school debate is that public schools are part of the fabric of any democratic society. In fact, conservative educators fail to recognize that a democratic society that shirks its public responsibility is a democracy in crisis. A society that equates for-profit privatization with democracy is a society with confused priorities. A democratic society that falsely believes, in view of the Savings and Loan debacle and the Wall Street scandals, for example, that quality, productivity, honesty and efficiency can be achieved only through for-profit privatization is a society that displays both an intellectual and ethical bankruptcy of ideas. If we follow the line of argument that 'private' is best, we should once again consider Jack Beaty's question: 'Would we set up a private Pentagon to improve our public defense establishment?' (Beaty 1992). Would private-is-best logic eradicate the on-going problems in the military that range from rampant sexual harassment to payment of over six hundred dollars for a toilet seat and billions for planes that don't fly? Most Americans would find the privatization of the Pentagon an utter absurdity claiming a national priority for a strong defense. Instead of dismantling public education further, I believe we should make it a national public priority. I would also contend that the safeguarding of our democracy rests much more on the creation of an educated smart citizenry than on the creation of smart bombs.

In contrast to the market notion of school reform in the United States, many liberal and neo-liberal educators have rediscovered Freire as an alternative to the conservative domestication education that equates free market ideology with democracy. Part of the problem with some of these pseudo-critical educators is that, in the name of liberation pedagogy, they reduce Freire's leading ideas to a method. According to Stanley Aronowitz, the North American fetish for method has allowed Freire's philosophical ideas to be 'assimilated to the prevailing obsession of North American education, following a tendency in all human and social sciences, with methods – of verifying knowledge and, in schools, of teaching, that is, transmitting knowledge to otherwise unprepared students' (Aronowitz 1993: 8). This fetish for method works insidiously against adhering to Freire's own pronouncement against the importation and exportation of methodology. In a long conversation I had with him about this issue he said: 'Donaldo, I don't want to be imported or exported. It is impossible to export pedagogical practices without re-inventing them. Please, tell your fellow American educators not to import me. Ask them to recreate and rewrite my ideas.'

Freire's leading ideas concerning the act of knowing transcend the methods for which he is known. In fact, according to Linda Bimbi, 'the originality of Freire's work does not reside in the efficacy of his literacy methods, but, above all, in the originality of its content designed to develop our consciousness' as part of a humanizing pedagogy (cited in Gadotti 1989: 32). According to Freire, 'a humanizing education is the path through which men and women can become conscious about their presence in the world. The way they act and think when they develop all of their capacities, taking into consideration their needs, but also the needs and aspirations of others' (Freire and Frei Betto 1985: 14–15).

With that said, why is it that some educators, in their attempt to cut the chains of oppressive educational practices, blindly advocate for the dialogical model, creating, in turn, a new form of methodological rigidity laced with benevolent oppression – all done under the guise of democracy with the sole purpose that it is for your own good? Many of us have witnessed pedagogical contexts in which you are implicitly or explicitly required to speak, to talk about your experience as an act of liberation. We have all been at conferences where the speaker is chastised because he or she failed to locate himself or herself in history. In other words, he or she failed to give primacy to his or her experiences in addressing issues of critical democracy. It does not matter that the speaker had important and insightful things to say. This is tantamount to dismissing Marx because he did not entrance us with his personal lived-experiences.

The appropriation of the dialogical method as a process of sharing experiences is often reduced to a form of group therapy that focuses on the psychology of the individual. Although some educators may claim that this process creates a pedagogical comfort zone, in my view it does little beyond making the oppressed feel good about his or her own sense of victimization. In other words, the sharing of experiences should not be understood in psychological terms only. It invariably requires a political and ideological analysis as well. That is, the sharing of experiences must always be understood within a social praxis that entails both reflection and political action. In short, it must always involve a political project with the objective of dismantling oppressive structures and mechanisms.

This overdose of experiential celebration that characterizes some strands of critical pedagogy offers a reductionist view of identity and experience within, rather than outside, the problematics of power, agency and history. By over-indulging in the legacy and importance of their respective voices and experiences, these educators often fail to move beyond a notion of difference structured in polarizing binarisms and uncritical appeal to the discourse of experience (Giroux, in press). For this reason, they invoke a romantic pedagogical mode that exoticizes lived experiences as a process of coming to voice. By refusing to link experiences to the politics of culture and critical democracy, these educators reduce their pedagogy to a form of middle-class narcissism. On the one hand, the dialogical method provides the participants with a group therapy space for stating their grievances and, on the other hand, it offers the educator or facilitator a safe pedagogical zone to deal with his or her class guilt.

By refusing to deal with the issue of class privilege, the pseudo-critical educator dogmatically pronounces to empower students, to give them voices. These educators are even betrayed by their own language. Instead of creating pedagogical structures which would enable oppressed students to empower themselves, they paternalistically proclaim: 'We need to empower students.' This position often leads to the creation of what I call literacy and poverty pimps to the extent that, while proclaiming to empower students, they are in fact strengthening their own privileged position.

The following example will clarify my point. A progressive colleague of mine who had been working with me in a community-based literacy project betrayed her liberal discourse to empower the community when one of the agencies we work with solicited my help to write a math literacy proposal for them. I agreed and welcomed the opportunity. One of my goals is to develop structures so that community members and agencies can take their own initiative and chart their own course thus eliminating the need for our continued presence and expertise. In other words, our success in creating structures so that community members empower themselves rests on the degree to which our presence and expertise in the community are no longer necessary because community members have acquired their own expertise, thus preventing a type of neo-colonialism.

When my colleague heard about the math literacy proposal she was reticent but did not show outward opposition. However, weeks later, when she learned that the community-based math literacy grant I was writing with the community members competed with our own university-based proposal which was designed to provide literacy training to community members, my colleague reacted almost irrationally. She argued that the community agency that had written the math literacy grant did not follow a democratic process in that it had not involved her in the development of the grant. A democratic and participatory process in her view referred to the condition that community action needed to include her, this despite the fact that she is not a member of the particular community the math literacy grant was designed to serve. Apparently, in her mind, one can be empowered as long as the empowerment does not encroach on the 'expert's' privileged, powerful position. This is a position of power designed to paternalistically empower others.

When I pointed out the obvious ideological contradictions in my colleague's behavior, her response was quick, aggressive and almost automatic. 'I'll be very mad if they get their proposal and we don't get ours.' It became very clear to me that my colleague's real political commitment to the community hinged on the extent to which her 'expert' position remained unthreatened. That is, the literacy 'expert', do-gooder, anti-establishment persona makes sure that his or her privileged position within the establishment as an anti-establishment 'expert' is never absorbed by empowered community members.

It is this colonizer, paternalistic attitude that led this same colleague to pronounce publicly, at a major conference, that community people don't need to go to college because they know so much more than do members of the university community, thus there is little that the university can teach them. While making such public statements this colleague was busily moving from the inner city to an affluent suburb, making sure that her children attend better schools.

A similar attitude emerged in a recent meeting to develop a community–university relationship grant proposal. During the meeting a liberal white professor rightly protested the absence of community members in the committee. However, in attempting to valorize the community knowledge base, she rapidly fell into a romantic paternalism by stating that the community people knew much more than the university professors and that they should be invited to come to teach us rather than we teaching them. This position not only discourages community members from having access to the cultural capital from which these professors have benefitted greatly but it also disfigures the reality context which makes the university cultural capital indispensable for any type of real empowerment. It also smacks of a false generosity of paternalism which Freire aggressively opposes:

The pedagogy of the oppressed animated by authentic humanism (and not humanitarianism) generously presents itself as a pedagogy of man. Pedagogy which begins with the egoistic interests of the oppressors (an egoism cloaked in the false generosity of paternalism) and makes of the oppressed the objects of its humanitarianism, itself maintains and embodies oppression. It is an instrument of dehumanization.

(Freire 1990: 39)

The paternalistic pedagogical attitude represents a middle-class narcissism that gives rise to pseudo-critical educators who are part of the same instrumentalist approach to literacy they claim to renounce. The instrumentalist approach to literacy does not only refer to the goal of providing readers who meet the basic requirements of our contemporary society as proposed by conservative educators. Instrumentalist literacy also includes the highest level of literacy through disciplinary specialism and hyper-specialization. Pseudo-critical educators are part of this latter form of instrumentalist literacy to the extent that they reduce Freire's dialogical method to a form of specialism. In other words, both the instrumentalist literacy for the poor in the form of a competency-based skill banking approach, and the highest form of instrumentalist literacy for the rich acquired through the university in the form of professional specialization, share one common feature: they both prevent the development of critical thinking which enables one to read the world critically and to understand the reasons and linkages behind the facts. The instrumentalist approach to literacy, even at the highest level of specialism (including method as a form of specialism) functions to domesticate the consciousness via a constant disarticulation between the reductionistic and narrow reading of one's field of specialization and the reading of the universe within which one's specialism is situated. This inability to link the reading of the word with the world, if not combated, will further exacerbate already feeble democratic institutions and the unjust asymmetrical power relations that characterize the hypocritical nature of contemporary democracies. At the lowest level of instrumentalist literacy a semi-literate reads the word but is unable to read the world. At the highest level of instrumental literacy achieved via specialization, the semi-literate is able to read the text of his or her specialization but is ignorant of all other bodies of knowledge that constitute the world of knowledge. This semi-literate specialist was characterized by Ortega y Gasset as a 'learned ignoramus'. That is to say, 'he is not learned, for he is formally ignorant of all that does not enter into his speciality; but neither is he ignorant, because he is a "scientist" and "knows" very well his own tiny portion of the universe' (Ortega y Gasset 1932: 112).

Because the 'learned ignoramus' is mainly concerned with his or her tiny portion of the world disconnected from other bodies of knowledge, he or she is never able to relate the flux of information so as to gain a critical reading of the world. A critical reading of the world implies, according to Freire, 'a dynamic comprehension between the least coherent sensibility of the world and a more coherent understanding of the world' (Freire and Macedo 1987:131). This implies, obviously, the ability, for example, of medical specialists in the United States who have contributed to a great technological advancement in medicine to understand and appreciate why over 30 million Americans do not have access to this medical technology and why we still have the highest infant mortality rate in comparison to other developed nations.

I want to end this preface by proposing an anti-method pedagogy that refuses the rigidity of models and methodological paradigms. The anti-method pedagogy forces us to view dialogue as a form of social praxis so that the sharing of experiences is informed by reflection and political action. Dialogue as social praxis 'entails that recovering the voice of the oppressed is the fundamental condition for human emancipation' (Aronowitz 1993: 18). The anti-method pedagogy also frees us from the beaten path of certainties and specialisms. It rejects the mechanization of intellectualism. In short, it calls for the illumination of Freire's leading ideas that will guide us toward the critical road of truth, toward the reappropriation of our endangered dignity, toward the reclaiming of our humanity. No one could argue more pointedly against reducing dialogue and problem-posing to a mere method than Freire himself:

> Problem posing education is revolutionary futurity. Hence, it is prophetic . . . Hence it corresponds to the historical nature of man. Hence it affirms men as beings who transcend themselves . . . Hence it identifies with the movement which engages men as beings aware of their incompletion – an historical movement which has its point of departure, its subjects and its objective.
>
> (cited in Aronowitz 1993: 11–12).

The anti-method pedagogy not only adheres to Freire's view of education as revolutionary futurity, it also celebrates the eloquence of Antonio Machado's poem: *'Cominante no hay camino, se hace el camino al andar.'* Traveler, there is no road, the road is made as one walks.

REFERENCES

Aronowitz, S. (1993) 'Paulo Freire's radical democratic humanism' in P. McLaren and P. Leonard, eds., *Paulo Freire: A Critical Encounter*, London: Routledge.
Beaty, J. (1992) *The Boston Globe*, 14 August.
Freire, P. (1990) *Pedagogy of the Oppressed*, New York: Continuum.
Freire, P. and Frei Betto (1985) *Essa Escola Chamada Vida*, São Paulo: Atica.
Freire, P. and Macedo, D. (1987) *Literacy: Reading the Word and the World*, South Hadley, MA: Bergin & Garvey Publishers.
Gadotti, M. (1989) *Convite a Leitura de Paulo Freire*, São Paulo: Editora Scipione.
Giroux, H. (in press). 'The politics of difference and multiculturalism in the era of the Los Angeles uprising', in *Journal of the Midwest Modern Language Association*.
Ortega y Gasset, J. (1932) *The Revolt of the Masses*, New York: W.W. Norton & Company, Inc.

Acknowledgements

We acknowledge, with thanks, the continuing support of Chris Rojek. Anne Gee's contribution to this book is also greatly appreciated.

To Jenny McLaren and Michele Knobel, who have given much to this and other projects, we say thank you.

We are also especially grateful to Tania McGilchrist and Ali Murdoch for their assistance in preparing the typescript, as well as to the Faculty of Education, Massey University, for providing generous administrative support to this work.

Introduction

Peter L. McLaren and Colin Lankshear

Oppression, and the yearning to escape and rise above it, has been an abiding fact of human life down the ages. Oppression has assumed different tangible forms and been experienced by myriad groups at the hands of varying forces across time and space. But throughout and everywhere oppression has been experienced as a constraint to living more fully, more humanly: constraint born of social contingencies of power; of discursive regulation through interested and contrived social practices carried out so as to privilege some at the expense of others.

This has remained constant whether we think of the children of Israel making their way through the wilderness; the struggles of slaves against their Egyptian or Roman or, in more recent times, colonial masters; the plight of repressed sects under religious regimes; the misery of the urban child or peasant-turned-proletarian at the dawn of industrial capitalism; women in practically every society during recorded history; the Palestinians in their struggle to secure a homeland; indigenous peoples of the colonized Third World and emergent colonies of the 'developed' world; people of color in colonial and post-colonial settings; those whose sexuality defies conventional norms; or those making their way in all parts of the world in 'New Times' who wonder what control over their lives remains to them.

The dilemma is constant whether we think in terms of humans possessing some Kantian capacity for self-authorship, a potential for self-creation through really free labor in Marx's sense, an emancipatory interest as Habermas would have it, or an ontological vocation which can be impeded in ways identified by Freire.

Moreover, oppression retains this same sense in the age of the decentered subject and multiple subjectivities. All that vary across time and space are the specific objects of oppression, conceptions of what it means to live more humanly and more fully, and the contingent arrangements within which people enact and maintain discourses which diminish the humanity of others.

Oppression and its negation – liberation or emancipation – have necessarily been conceived and theorized in different ways according to local and temporal variables. In all cases, however, the urgent and ontological quest for liberation, for the right to live humanly as fully as possible, remains unchanged. Indeed, the need continually to reconceptualize and 'retheorize' oppression and liberation, to understand them more deeply, is an essential aspect of our existence as conscious critical beings who would be free.

In recent times the theme of oppression and liberation has been associated closely with the theory and practice of Paulo Freire. Ever since Freire's work first 'broke' in English with the publication of *Pedagogy of the Oppressed* readers and commentators, theorists and pedagogues, reflectors and activists, have pondered how far a pedagogy forged in the Latin Third World applies to the everyday routines, relations, and institutions of the First. Despite the 'developed' Western European roots of Latin American colonization, which, notwithstanding five hundred years of subsequent local history, have left an indelible imprint on the face of life in the Latin subcontinent, surely the profound differences between nations and realities of the metropolitan centre and those of the periphery militate against any easy or direct appropriation of Freirean pedagogy across these worlds.

This remains a legitimate question, and in this volume Carlos Alberto Torres elicits Freire's up-to-the-moment response. Yet what, perhaps, was not so well recognized back in the early 1970s was the extent to which the centre itself was in the throes of major – possibly *epochal* – change: deep structural change that would impact increasingly on being and consciousness, on the myriad routines of daily life, and that sooner or later would force a radical rethinking of oppression and liberation within the First World itself and a thoroughgoing reconceptualizing of relations between the First and Third Worlds. Moreover, these same processes of change were also, finally, to impact upon the Second World residing behind the Iron Curtain, changing its face in previously unimaginable ways and forcing its accommodation within a new world order.

For if the early 1970s brought Freire and the pedagogy of the oppressed, it also brought Alain Touraine, Daniel Bell, and other early, theoretically worked-through warning bells of New Times: post-industrialism, post-Fordism, the age of information, the end of ideology, even 'the end of history'.

In what probably remains the best succinct broad sweep of New Times, Stuart Hall (1991) identifies key changes impinging directly on contemporary experience and imposing the need to conceive and theorize anew the politics of oppression and liberation.

Changes within post-industrialism have revolutionized work practices, restructured entire workforces and 'feminized' work to new levels. Intensified multinational activity has brought a new international division of labor which, among other things, puts First World unskilled labor in competition for low wages with Third World workers, and vastly increases the vulnerability of illiterate and otherwise 'undereducated' citizens in societies like our own. At the same time major developments in product diversification create, simultaneously, new possibilities for identity formation and manipulated consumer 'choice'.

These changes establish new parameters of oppressive practices. They also, however, have complex implications for factors bearing on politics and pedagogies of liberation: notably, our constructions of identity, subjecthood, and the dialectic between subjective and objective dimensions of socio-cultural change. Specifically, Hall notes the trends toward greater fragmentation and pluralism, the weakening of older collective solidarities and block identities and the emergence of new identities associated with greater work flexibility, the maximization of individual choices through personal consumption.

(ibid.: 58)

The 'down side' of this is that social victims are less often gathered together in one place and with a shared recognition of their situation than in earlier times. Interestingly, the welfare state has played a contradictory role here. It has acted to mitigate poverty in various ways, but has also had the effect of weakening awareness of deprivation, bestowing on 'clients' the common role only of beneficiary. The contemporary condition, then, is not one of large numbers of people aware of shared or overlapping deprivation who might mobilize and create effective political demands, as in the nineteenth century and the Great Depression. It is more one of fragmentation and separation (Lankshear and Levett 1992).

While New Times operate 'out there' to change the conditions of our lives, they also work 'in here' on our *selves*. Lines of continuity that previously lent stability to our social identities have been weakened, though not broken, by 'modern environments and experiences [cutting] across all boundaries of geography and ethnicity, of class and nationality, of religion and ideology' (Berman 1982, cited in Hall 1991).

This has forced a rethinking of the self and the stress laid in modernist thought on objective as opposed to subjective conditions of experience and change. Objective conditions were for a long time 'in the saddle', with privileged explanatory power invested in 'objective contradictions', 'impersonal structures' and the 'processes that work "behind men's [sic] backs"'(ibid.: 59).

Strong overtones of 'the objective conditions of oppression' run through Freire's work, although the subjective and the subject were always in evidence – not exactly, however, the subject currently enjoying celebrated elaboration within discourses of 'the Post'. Freire's object of oppression and ideological domination, his subject of the humanizing praxis of liberation, was rather more the collective or generalized *oppressed* (Luke and Walton 1993). While never approximating to the aberrant extremes of crude accounts of the great Marxist subject of history – the proletariat – Freire's subject was typically more collective than individual, more unified and coherent than multiple and decentered. This said, however, it must be noted that in his conception of individuals who could be both oppressed (e.g., in the public domain) and oppressors (e.g., in the private domain), who live as incomplete beings constantly in a process of becoming, and who harbour profoundly contradictory beliefs and aspirations, we find notions that resonate with the distinctively postmodern conception of the subject that follows. Certainly it is a much shorter step from Freire's account of human subjects to contemporary views of the subject and self than it is from the classical liberal humanist view.

The discourses of New Times, however, march to a different tune from that which sounded at the dawn of *Pedagogy of the Oppressed* and Freire's other earlier works. The individual subject has assumed much greater importance in accounts of political and historical experience and process. Not only has the individual subject

> become more important, [but] our models of 'the subject' have altered. We can no longer conceive of 'the individual' in terms of a whole and completed ego or autonomous 'self'. The 'self' is experienced as more fragmented and incomplete, composed of multiple 'selves' or identities in relation to the different social worlds we inhabit, something of a history 'produced' in process.
>
> (ibid.: 58–9)

This demise of the unified, autonomous self of modernity and liberal humanism has been accompanied, relatedly, by a fall from favor of the grand narratives of rationality, progress and development, which, far from merely providing the cornerstones of modernist political theory, also largely underwrote projects of political change.

We are faced too with new ways of understanding forms of oppression as they are produced in the context of our postmodern society. Iris Marion Young (1992) offers a detailed typology of oppression that is worth summarizing.[1] She argues, rightly in our view, that the meaning of oppression has shifted from the practice of colonial domination and conquest. That is, it can no longer be thought simply to be an evil perpetrated by others, as the exercise of tyranny by a ruling group. Young has substantially redefined the term to designate 'the everyday practices of a well-intentioned liberal society' (ibid.: 175–6) and 'systemic and structural phenomena that are not necessarily the result of intentions of a tyrant' (ibid.). In other words, 'oppressions are systematically reproduced in major economic, political, and cultural institutions' (ibid.: 176) and are part of the basic fabric of social life. In Young's view, oppression can exist even in the absence of overt discrimination, the latter term referring to an individualist concept that links discrimination to an identifiable agent. Oppression, rather, is related to 'unconscious assumptions and reactions of well-meaning people in ordinary interactions, media and cultural stereotypes, and structural features of bureaucratic hierarchy and market mechanisms, the normal ongoing processes of everyday life' (ibid.: 177).

Oppression disempowers groups – and here Young warns us not to think of groups simply as aggregates in which group membership is linked to a simple set of attributes. Rather, group membership means that one finds oneself as a member of a group in the sense that one's identity 'is defined in relation to how others identify him or her, and they do so in terms of groups that always already have specific attributes, stereotypes, and norms associated with them, in reference to which a person's identity will be formed' (ibid.: 178). The oppression of a group does not mean that there is a correlating oppressor group, which is not to suggest that individuals do not intentionally harm others.

Young explicates what she refers to as 'five faces of oppression' that affect groups in North America such as women, blacks, Chicanos, Puerto Ricans, most

Spanish-speaking Americans, Native Americans, Jews, lesbians, gay men, Arabs, Asians, old people, working-class people, poor people, and physically or mentally impaired people.

1 *Exploitation*, notes Young, is a form of domination in which the labor of working-class groups is transferred to benefit the wealthy, reproducing and causing class divisions and relations of inequality. For instance, women are exploited as wage workers and also in the sphere of domestic labors; additionally, women undergo forms of gender oppression in the workplace and within the wider structure of patriarchy. Race, as well as class and gender, is also a structure of oppression. Blacks and Latinos are oppressed by capitalist superexploitation in a segregated labor market where skilled, high-paying and unionized jobs are primarily the preserve of whites.

2 *Marginalization* refers to groups which constitute the growing 'underclass' of people who suffer material deprivation, and are confined to lives of unemployment and 'expelled from useful participation in social life' (ibid.: 186). Often marginalized groups are racially marked, and this includes groups both in Third World and in Western capitalist countries – 'blacks or Indians in Latin America, blacks, East Indians, Eastern Europeans or North Africans in Europe' (ibid.). Marginalized people are often positioned by the dominant culture in relations of dependency where they are excluded from equal citizenship rights. Even if they are materially comfortable, these groups may be oppressed on the basis of their marginal status; for instance, senior citizens who suffer from feelings of uselessness, boredom, and lack of self-worth.

3 *Powerlessness* deals with structures of social division, such as social status. More specifically, it describes 'the lives of people who have little or no work autonomy, exercise little or no creativity or judgement in their work, have no technical expertise or authority, express themselves awkwardly, especially in public or bureaucratic settings, and do not command respect' (ibid.: 189). Young here refers to the cultures of professionals and non-professionals, which, of course, are linked to the division between mental and manual labor. She refers specifically to the norms of respectability in our society and the ways in which such norms privilege 'professional' dress, speech, tastes and demeanor – and the way this privilege appears in the dynamics of racism and sexism.

4 *Cultural imperialism*, according to Young, refers to 'the universalization of one group's experience and culture and its establishment as the norm' (ibid.: 191). The dominant cultural group exercises its power by bringing other groups under the measure of its domination. Consequently, the dominant groups construct the differences of subordinate groups as lack and negation in relation to their privileging norms. For instance, 'the difference of women from men, Native Americans or Africans from Europeans, Jews from Christians, homosexuals from heterosexuals, or workers from professionals becomes reconstructed as deviance and inferiority' (ibid.). Victims of cultural

imperialism live their oppression by viewing themselves from the perspective of the way others view them: a phenomenon known as 'double consciousness'. Young writes:

> The dominant culture's stereotyped, marked, and inferiorized images of the group must be internalized by group members at least to the degree that they are forced to react to behaviors of others that express or are influenced by those images . . . This consciousness is double because the oppressed subject refuses to coincide with these devalued, objectified, stereotyped visions of herself or himself. The subject desires recognition as human, capable of activity, full of hope and possibility, but receives from the dominant culture only the judgement that he or she is different, marked, or inferior.
>
> (ibid.: 192)

Cultural imperialism, Young notes, involves the paradoxical experience of being invisible while simultaneously being positioned as different. It is the process of being defined by both dominant and subordinate cultures.

5   *Violence* involves the fear of systematic and legalized oppression. For instance, systematic violence is directed at members of particular groups simply because they belong to those specific groups. Young notes that in US society women, blacks, Asians, Arabs, gay men, and lesbians live under threats of xenophobic, random, and unprovoked attacks, as do Jews, Puerto Ricans, Chicanos, and other Spanish-speaking Americans inhabiting certain regions. This form of violence is also 'legitimate' because most white people find it a common occurrence and do little to punish the offenders. In our view, this could be seen clearly in the beating of Rodney King by Los Angeles police in 1992.

Liberation politics has had to chart difficult seas in recent years. Besides those complications already identified by Hall, it has had to face a gamut of post-structuralist challenges focusing on text, meaning, and the 'textualizing of the reader'. Seemingly, at times, the prospects for conceiving any viable politics against oppression were down to zero. Indeed, even the challenge of effecting a meaningful sense and practice of *citizenship* within the 'enormous expansion of "civil society" caused by the diversification of the different worlds in which men and women can operate' (Hall 1991: 63) and the institutional upheaval of the current moment of transition, capped by the radical restructuring of the welfare state, has proved daunting and, often, confusing.

There have, of course, been temporary lapses into 'postmodern excesses' of perceived powerlessness and cynicism. These, however, have prompted politically committed responses entirely in keeping with the spirit of the vision and project to which Freire has devoted his work. McLaren (in press) has discussed the new strands of resistance and oppositional postmodernism that offer a serious challenge to those 'ludic' varieties of postmodernism that attempt simply to uncover the undecidability and contingency of representations.

In addition, feminist critics have identified a range of concerns associated with extreme versions of decentering text and/or subject. Mascia-Lees, Sharpe and Cohen, for example, pose a crucial issue for social theory:

> Once one articulates an epistemology of free play in which there is no inevitable relationship between signifier and signified, how is it possible to write an ethnography that has descriptive force? Once one has no metanarratives into which the experience of difference can be translated, how is it possible to write any ethnography [that has potential to inform a politics of liberation]?
>
> (1989: 27)

Again, feminists, among others, have also noted how in its assault on the classic figure of Western humanism – the rational, unified, non-contradictory, and self-determining individual – poststructuralist discourse has erased the suffering, bleeding, breathing subject of history. Poststructuralism's infatuation with the dancing signifier whose meaning is always ephemeral, elusive, dispersed, and mutable, and the emphasis which it places on textualizing the reader as an intricate composition of an infinite number of codes or texts (cf. Barthes 1975), can be subversive of its potentially empowering and transformative agenda. Knowledge can be depotentiated and stripped of its emancipatory possibilities if it is acknowledged only as a form of textualization. Moreover, such a facile treatment of discourse can lead to the subject's encapsulation in the membranes of his or her rationalizations, leading to a soporific escape from the pain and sensations of living, breathing, human subjects. As Alan Megill warns:

> All too easy is the neglect or even the dismissal of a natural and historical reality that ought not to be neglected or dismissed . . . For if one adopts, in a cavalier and single-minded fashion, the view that everything is discourse or text or fiction, the realia are trivialized. Real people who really died in the gas chambers at Auschwitz or Treblinka become so much discourse.
>
> (1985: 345)

Clearly there is danger in assuming a literal interpretation of Derrida's 'there is nothing outside of the text'. We are faced with the postmodern 'loss of affect' which occurs when language attempts to 'capture the "ineffable" experience of the Other' (Yudice 1988: 225). We risk textualizing gender, denying sexual specificity, or treating difference as merely a formal category with no empirical and historical existence.

Moreover, this resistance extends, mercifully, beyond *theory* and into the 'real world'. And with this, as Hall reminds us, comes the possibility of a larger and richer politics than envisaged previously. Far from a situation where there is no resistance to 'the system', we find

> a proliferation of new points of antagonism, new social movements of resistance organized around them, and, consequently, a generalization of 'politics' to

spheres which hitherto the left assumed to be apolitical; a politics of the family, of health, of food, of sexuality, of the body. What we lack is any overall map of how these power relations connect and of their resistances. Perhaps there isn't, in that sense, one 'power game' at all – more a network of strategies and powers and their articulations – and thus a politics that is always positional.

(1991: 63; see also McLaren, in press)

If this is so, it may be that from time to time we nonetheless need 'props' to help us sustain a sense of overall political focus and purpose, even though we accord these props provisional status only: a metanarrative to which we ascribe provisional authority; an arch of social dreaming (McLaren 1992); a reminder of struggles and politics that have inspired through their achievements; a sense that perhaps, in the end, there *is* some common humanity that makes the wishful hope for a world without oppression at least provisionally coherent. In such moments, people throughout the world continue to find Paulo Freire's testimony and vision more than sufficient to sustain.

Freire's internationally celebrated praxis began in the late 1940s and continued unabated in Brazil until 1964, when he was arrested. He was imprisoned by the military government for 70 days and exiled for his work in the National Commission of Popular Culture and in the National Plan of Literacy Training, of which he had served as coordinator. Freire's sixteen years of exile were tumultuous and productive times: a five-year stay in Chile as a UNESCO consultant with the Chilean Agrarian Reform Corporation, specifically the Reform Training and Research Institute; an appointment in 1969 to Harvard University's Center for Studies in Development and Social Change; a move to Geneva, Switzerland, in 1970 as consultant to the Office of Education of the World Council of Churches, where he developed literacy programs for Tanzania and Guinea-Bissau that focused on the re-Africanization of their countries; the development of literacy programs in some post-revolutionary former Portuguese colonies, such as Angola and Mozambique; assisting the governments of Peru and Nicaragua with their literacy campaigns; the establishment of the Institute of Cultural Action in Geneva in 1971; a brief return to Chile after Salvador Allende was assassinated in 1973, provoking General Pinochet to declare Freire a subversive; and his eventual return to Brazil in 1980 to teach at the Pontificia Universidade Católica de São Paulo and the Universidade de Campinas in São Paulo. These events were accompanied by numerous works, most notably *Pedagogy of the Oppressed, Cultural Action for Freedom*, and *Pedagogy in Process: Letters to Guinea-Bissau*. In more recent years (1989–91), Freire has worked as Secretary of Education of São Paulo, continuing his radical agenda of literacy reform for the people of that city.

To the lingering questions of the relevance and applicability of Freire's Third World pedagogy within First World settings and wider issues of relations between these worlds – many of which have been complicated by new meanings attaching to the notion of Third Worlds operating with the First and recent developments in post-colonial theory – we must add others of recent origin.

At this twist-point in our intellectual and political history, *Politics of Liberation* offers a collection of works, mediated by the landmark contribution of Paulo Freire, focused on precisely these themes. Almost uniquely within its genre, it brings voices from Freire's world into collaboration with voices from our own.

Donaldo Macedo's Preface forcefully articulates the danger of domesticating Freire's pedagogy by treating it as a methodology.

In Chapter 1 Kathleen Weiler addresses possibilities and problems of experience in a pedagogy of liberation. Drawing on examples of feminist pedagogy she suggests the need for a vision of liberatory pedagogy that acknowledges contradictory positions of oppression within classroom situations. Often critical of shortcomings in Freire's approach, but always on the same side, Weiler identifies three areas of concern raised in feminist pedagogy that offer clues to enriching and expanding Freirean initiatives.

Marguerite and Michael Rivage-Seul next turn the tables on the question of the applicability of Freire's pedagogy to First World settings by evaluating the use of a North American pedagogy of critical thinking in strife-torn Guatemala. They analyze a Philosophy for Children program developed to teach about democracy and compare it against a Freirean model employed in São Paulo, Brazil. The considerable risks involved in the Guatemalan exercise in 'technology transfer' are brought home forcefully.

In Chapter 3 Ian Lister assesses attempts to apply a broadly Freirean philosophy and pedagogy within British schools in terms of three movements for political education – the Programme for Political Education from the mid-1970s, new movements and human rights education in the early 1980s, and current concerns to develop citizenship education. Lister identifies some major problems arising empirically out of the British initiatives and points to the high stakes involved in current debates about the kind of citizenship education appropriate for a complex, developed, multicultural society in an increasingly interdependent world.

Marilyn Frankenstein and Arthur Powell consider Freire's epistemology in relation to understanding more fully how people think mathematically in order to promote mathematical knowledge more effectively and to reclaim the hidden and distorted histories of the contributions made by all cultures to mathematics. They argue that Freire's epistemology informs the theoretical basis of ethnomathematics and advocate further inquiry into the links between mathematic knowledge and cultural and political action.

Carlos Alberto Torres interviews Paulo Freire against a backdrop of Freire's role as Secretary of Education for the municipality of São Paulo and from the perspective of twenty years' distance from the original publication of *Pedagogy of the Oppressed*. In the course of elaborating his current views on a diverse range of themes, Freire assesses the prospects of contributing to overcoming present-day problems in Brazilian education from his position as Secretary of Education, and addresses the conditions under which the political philosophy underlying his work could be applied successfully to teacher training within First World systems.

In Chapter 6 Peter Findlay illustrates the use of Freirean approaches to the politics of social movements in Western countries by reference to Canada. Within an account of the Canadian political structure, struggles over the Free Trade Agreement with the United States, and the progress of various 'post-socialist' initiatives, Findlay advances a Freirean analysis of popular social movements. He concludes by showing how Freire's pedagogical approach sheds light on two important dilemmas facing these new movements.

Edgar González Gaudiano and Alicia de Alba situate Freire's work within a neo-Marxist perspective, drawing comparisons between the struggles of Mexican and Brazilian indigenous peoples. They consider the potential of Freire's work for building counter-hegemonic movements among oppressed Latin American groups, underscoring the fact that this work cannot be appreciated fully outside of the legacy of Latin American intellectual life. The chapter ends with a plea for fuller and more equal cultural contact between the diverse cultures that populate the 'global village' as a condition of the new perspective that will be needed to address the challenges of the next century.

In Chapter 8 Jeanne Brady explores some of the points at which a critique of Freire's work informs the development of conceptions and practices of literacy integral to building a thriving multicultural democratic society. She focuses on arguments advanced from feminist and post-colonial perspectives, and assesses their significance for an approach to literacy that helps us name and transform ideological and social conditions impeding the practice of a critical citizenship informed by democratic principles and grounded in hope.

Adriana Puiggrós responds to questions put by Peter McLaren. In the course of analyzing the emergence of Latin American education systems, with particular reference to education in her native Argentina, she considers the difficulties facing the acceptance of Freire's work in the subcontinent and assesses the strengths and weaknesses of his work, particularly in relation to her own work as a politically committed academic.

In the penultimate chapter Michael Peters and Colin Lankshear approach current interest in text by reference to recent developments in hermeneutics stemming from the work of Hans-Georg Gadamer. They discuss the differences that stand between Freire and Gadamer and note the points at which Freire moves beyond Gadamer to propose a critical hermeneutics linking interpretation and action in a philosophy aimed at promoting revolutionary social change.

Peter McLaren discusses Freire's politics of liberation in the light of current debates in the social sciences over modernism and postmodernism. While Freire's politics of liberation shares many traits with modernist forms of Marxist humanism, McLaren argues that it nevertheless avoids in important ways the debilitating aspects of 'master narratives'. He concludes that Freire's emancipatory praxis can serve as an important – and urgent – alternative to current 'ludic' or 'spectral' forms of postmodern social theory.

In the Afterword, Joe Kincheloe engages Freire's work from the standpoint of an epistemology of self and social empowerment, describing it as a form of 'synergism' constructed at the intersection of a modernist ethics and a critical postmodernism. For Kincheloe, the contributions in this volume are situated as an attempt to reinvent praxis in the light of the recent revolution in critical social theory. Such a reinvention, Kincheloe warns, cannot take place if we forget the 'children of the damned'. Freire's work is invoked as both a conceptual and an ethical antidote to such forms of social amnesia.

NOTE

1 This summary of Young's typology also appear in Peter McLaren, *Life in Schools*, 2nd edition, New York: Longman (in press).

REFERENCES

Barthes, R. (1975) *S/Z*, London: Cape.
Berman, M. (1982) *All That Is Solid Melts into Air: The Experience of Modernity*, New York: Simon and Schuster.
Freire, P. (1972) *Pedagogy of the Oppressed*, Harmondsworth: Penguin.
Hall, S. (1991) 'Brave new world', *Socialist Review* 21, 1, 57–64.
Lankshear, C. and Levett, A. (1992) 'New times and literacies that matter'. Keynote Address to the Australian Council for Adult Literacy annual conference, University of Sydney, 9–11 October.
Luke, A. and Walton, C. (1993) 'Teaching and assessing critical reading' in T. Husen and T. Postlethwaite, eds, *International Encyclopedia of Education*, 2nd edition, London: Pergamon Press.
McLaren, P. (1992) 'Critical pedagogy: constructing an arch of social dreaming and a doorway to hope', *Journal of Education* 173, 1, 9–34.
—— (in press) 'Multiculturalism and the postmodern critique: towards a pedagogy of resistance and transformation', *Cultural Studies* 7, 1, 118–46.
—— (in press) 'White terror', *Strategies*.
Megill, A. (1985) *Prophets of Extremity*, Berkeley: University of California Press.
Young, I.M. (1992) 'Five faces of oppression' in T.E. Wertenberg, ed., *Rethinking Power*, Albany, NY: State University of New York Press.
Yudice, G. (1988) 'Marginality and the ethics of survival' in A. Ross, ed., *Universal Abandon?*, Minneapolis: University of Minnesota Press.

Chapter 1

Freire and a feminist pedagogy of difference

Kathleen Weiler

INTRODUCTION

We are living in a period of profound challenges to traditional Western epistemology and political theory. These challenges, couched in the language of postmodernist theory and in post-colonialist critiques, reflect the rapid trans-formation of the economic and political structure of the world order – the impact of transnational capital, the ever more comprehensive integration of resources, labor and markets, the pervasiveness of media and consumer images. The interdependent world system is based on the exploitation of oppressed groups; but that system at the same time calls forth oppositional cultural forms which give voice to the conditions of subaltern groups. White male bourgeois dominance is being challenged by people of color, women, and other oppressed groups, who assert the validity of their own knowledge and demand social justice and equality in numerous political and social struggles. In the intellectual sphere, this shifting world system has led to a shattering of Western metanarratives, and to the variety of stances of postmodernist and cultural identity theory. A major theoretical challenge to traditional Western knowledge systems is emerging from feminist theory, which has been increasingly influenced by both postmodernist and cultural identity theory. Feminist theory, like other contemporary approaches, validates difference, challenges universal claims to truth, and seeks to create social transformation in a world of shifting and uncertain meanings.

In education, these profound shifts are evident on two levels: first, at the level of practice, as excluded and formerly silenced groups challenge dominant approaches to learning and to definitions of knowledge; and second, at the level of theory, as modernist claims to universal truth are called into question (e.g. Giroux 1991; Cherryholmes 1988; Giroux and Simon 1989; Britzman, forthcoming). These challenges to accepted truths have been raised not only to the institutions and theories that defend the status quo, but also to the critical or liberatory pedagogies that emerged in the 1960s and 1970s. Feminist educational critics, like other theorists influenced by postmodernism and theories of difference, want to retain the vision of social justice and transformation that underlies liberatory pedagogies; but they find that the claims to universal truths and assumptions of a collective experience of oppression of liberatory pedagogies do not adequately address the realities of their own confusing and often tension-filled classrooms. This consciousness of the inadequacy of classical liberatory pedagogies has been particularly true for feminist educators, who are acutely aware of the continuing force of sexism and patriarchal structures and the power of race, sexual preference, physical ability and age to divide teachers from students and students from one another.

Paulo Freire is without question the most influential theorist of critical or liberatory education. His theories have profoundly influenced literacy programs throughout the world and what has come to be called critical pedagogy in the United States. His theoretical works, particularly *Pedagogy of the Oppressed*, provide classic statements of liberatory or critical pedagogy based on universal claims of truth. Feminist pedagogy as it has developed in the United States provides an historically situated example of a critical pedagogy in practice. Feminist conceptions of education are similar to Freire's pedagogy in various ways; feminist educators often cite Freire as the educational theorist who comes closest to the approach and goals of feminist pedagogy (see Culley and Portuges 1985a).[1] Both feminist pedagogy as it is usually defined and Freirean pedagogy rest upon visions of social transformation; underlying both are certain common assumptions concerning oppression, consciousness, and historical change. Both pedagogies assert the existence of oppression in people's material conditions of existence and as a part of consciousness; both rest on a view of consciousness as more than a sum of dominating discourses, but as containing within it a critical capacity, what Gramsci called 'good sense'; both thus see human beings as subjects and actors in history and hold a strong commitment to justice and a vision of a better world, of the potential for liberation. These ideas have powerfully influenced teachers and students in a wide range of educational settings, both formal and informal.

But in action, the goals of liberation or opposition to oppression have not always been easy to understand or achieve. As universal goals, these ideals do not address the specificity of people's lives; they do not directly analyze the contradictions between conflicting oppressed groups or the ways in which a single individual can experience oppression in one sphere while being privileged or oppressive in another. Feminist and Freirean teachers are in many ways engaged in what de Lauretis (1984: 178) has called 'shifting the ground of signs', challenging accepted meanings and relationships that occur at what she calls 'political or more often micropolitical' levels; groupings which 'produce no texts as such, but by shifting the "ground" of a given sign . . . effectively intervene upon codes of perception as well as ideological codes'. But in attempting to challenge dominant values and to 'shift the ground of signs', feminist and Freirean teachers raise conflicts for themselves and their own students, who themselves are historically situated and whose own subjectivities are often contradictory and in process. These conflicts have become increasingly clear as both Freirean and feminist pedagogies are put into practice. Attempting to implement these pedagogies without acknowledging the conflict not only of divided consciousness, what Lorde (1984: 123) calls 'the oppressor within us', but also the conflicts among groups trying to work together to name and struggle against oppression – among teachers and students in classrooms, or among political groups working for change in very specific areas – can lead to anger, frustration, and a retreat to safer or more traditional approaches. The numerous accounts of the tensions of trying to put liberatory pedagogies into practice demonstrate the need to re-examine the assumptions of the classic texts of liberatory pedagogy and to consider the various issues that have arisen in attempts at critical and liberatory classroom practice (e.g. Ellsworth 1989, Berlak 1989, Britzman 1990).

As a white feminist writing and teaching from the traditions of both critical pedagogy and feminist theory these issues are of particular concern to me. In this chapter I examine and critique the classic liberatory pedagogy of Paulo Freire, particularly as it is presented in *Pedagogy of the Oppressed*, his most famous and influential text. I then examine the development and practice of feminist pedagogy, which emerged in a particular historical and political moment in the United States, and which, as a situated pedagogy, provides an example of some of the difficulties of putting these ideals into practice, and suggest at the same time some possible theoretical and practical directions for liberatory pedagogies in general. I argue that an exploration of the conflicts and concerns that have arisen for feminist teachers attempting to put into practice their versions of a feminist pedagogy can help enrich and re-envision Freirean goals of liberation and social progress. This emerging pedagogy does not reject the goals of justice, the end of oppression, and liberation, but frames them more specifically in the context of historically defined struggles and calls for the articulation of interests and identity on the part of the teacher and theorist as well as the student. This approach questions whether the oppressed cannot also act as oppressors, and challenges the idea of a commonality of oppression. It raises questions about common experience as a source of knowledge, the pedagogical authority of the teacher, and the nature of political and pedagogical struggle.

THE PEDAGOGY OF PAULO FREIRE

Freire's pedagogy developed in particular historical and political circumstances of neo-colonialism and imperialism. As is well known, Freire's methods developed originally from his work with peasants in Brazil and later in Chile and Guinea-Bissau.[2] Freire's thought thus needs to be understood in the context of the political and economic situation of the Third World. In Freire's initial formulation, oppression was conceived in class terms and education was viewed in the context of peasants' and working people's revolutionary struggles. Equally influential in Freire's thought and pedagogy was the influence of radical Christian thought and the revolutionary role of liberation theology within Latin America. As is true for other radical Christians in Latin America, Freire's personal knowledge of extreme poverty and suffering challenged his deeply felt Christian faith grounded in the ethical teachings of Jesus in the Gospels. Freire's pedagogy is thus founded on a moral imperative to side with the oppressed that emerges from both his Christian faith and his knowledge and experience of suffering in the society where he grew up and lived. Freire has stated repeatedly that his pedagogical method cannot simply be transferred to other settings, but that each historical site requires the development of a pedagogy appropriate to that setting (Freire and Shor 1987). In his most recent work he has also addressed sexism and racism as systems of oppression that need to be considered as seriously as class oppression. Nonetheless, Freire is frequently read neither in the context of the specific settings in which his work developed nor with these qualifications in mind. His most commonly read text still is his first book to be published in English, *Pedagogy of the Oppressed*. In this classic text Freire presents the epistemological basis for his pedagogy and discusses the concepts of oppression, conscientization, and dialogue that are at the heart of his pedagogical project, both as he enacted it in settings in the Third World and as it is appropriated by radical teachers in other settings.

Freire organizes his approach to liberatory pedagogy in terms of a dualism between the oppressed and the oppressors and between humanization and dehumanization. This organization of thought in terms of opposing forces reflects Freire's own experiences of literacy work with the poor in Brazil, a situation in which the lines between oppressor and oppressed were clear. For Freire, humanization is the goal of liberation; it has not yet been achieved, nor can it be achieved so long as the oppressors oppress the oppressed. That is, liberation and humanization will not occur if the roles of oppressor and oppressed are simply reversed. If oppression is to be realized, new relationships among human beings must be created:

> Because it is a distortion of being more fully human, sooner or later being less human leads the oppressed to struggle against those who made them so. In order for this struggle to have meaning, the oppressed must not, in seeking to regain their humanity (which is a way to create it), become in turn oppressors of the oppressors, but rather restorers of the humanity of both.
>
> (Freire 1971: 28)

The struggle against oppression leading to humanization is thus utopian and visionary. As Freire says elsewhere, 'to be utopian is not to be merely idealistic or impractical but rather to engage in denunciation and annunciation' (Freire 1985: 57). By 'denunciation' Freire refers to the naming and analysis of existing structures of oppression; by 'annunciation', he means the creation of new forms of relationships and being in the world as a result of mutual struggle against oppression. Thus Freire presents a theoretical justification for a pedagogy that aims to critique existing forms of oppression and to transform the world and thus create new ways of being (humanization).

Radical educators throughout the world have used *Pedagogy of the Oppressed* as the theoretical justification for their work. As an eloquent and impassioned statement for the need for and possibility of change through reading the world and the word, there is no comparable contemporary text. But when we look at *Pedagogy of the Oppressed* from the perspective of recent feminist theory and pedagogy, certain problems arise that may reflect the difficulties that have sometimes occurred when Freire's ideas are enacted in specific settings. The challenges of recent feminist theory do not imply the rejection of Freire's goals for what he calls a pedagogy for liberation; feminists certainly share Freire's emphasis on seeing human beings as subjects and not the objects of history. A critical feminist re-reading of Freire, however, points to ways in which the project of Freirean (like that of feminist) pedagogy can be enriched and re-envisioned.

From a feminist perspective, *Pedagogy of the Oppressed* is now striking in its use of the male referent, a usage that was universal in the 1960s when this book was written.[3] Much more troublesome is the failure to define terms such as 'humanization' more specifically in terms of men and women, black and white, or other forms of socially defined identities. The assumption of *Pedagogy of the Oppressed* is that in struggling against oppression the oppressed will move toward true humanity. But this leaves unaddressed the forms of oppression experienced by different actors, the possibility of struggles among people oppressed differently by different groups – what Cameron McCarthy (1988) calls nonsynchrony of oppression. It also presents humanization as a universal, without considering the various definitions this may bring forth from people of different groups. When Freire speaks of the oppressed needing to fight the tendency to become 'sub-oppressors', he means that the oppressed have only the pattern of oppression before them as a way of being in a position other than the one they are in. As Freire writes, 'Their ideal is to be men; but for them, to be men is to be oppressors. This is their model of humanity' (1971: 30). What is troubling here is not just the use of 'men' for human beings, but that the model of oppressor implied here is one based on the immediate oppressor of men, in this case, bosses over peasants or workers. What is not addressed is the possibility of simultaneous contradictory positions of oppression and dominance – that the man oppressed by the boss could at the same time oppress his wife, for example, or the white woman oppressed by sexism exploit the black woman. By framing his discussion in such abstract terms, Freire fails to address the contradictions and tensions within social settings in which overlapping forms of oppression exist.

This reliance on the abstractly oppressed raises difficulties as well in Freire's use of experience as the means of acquiring a radical literacy, 'reading the world and the word'. At the heart of Freire's pedagogy is Freire's insistence that all people are subjects and knowers of the world. Their political literacy will emerge from their reading of the world; that is, their own experience. This reading will lead to collective knowledge and action. But what if that experience is divided? What if different truths are discovered in reading the world from different positions? For Freire, education as the practice of freedom 'denies that men are abstract, isolated, independent, and unattached to the world ... Authentic reflection considers neither abstract men nor the world without men, but men in their relations with the world' (ibid.: 69). But implicit in this vision is the assumption that when the oppressed perceive themselves in relation with the world, they will act together collectively to transform the world and to move toward their own humanization. The nature of their perception of the world and their oppression is implicitly assumed to be uniform for all the oppressed. The possibility of a contradictory experience of oppression among the oppressed is absent. As Freire says:

> Accordingly, the point of departure must always be with men in the 'here and now', which constitutes the situation within which they are submerged, from which they emerge, and in which they intervene. Only by starting from this situation – which determines their perception of it – can they begin to move.
>
> (ibid.: 73)

The assumption again is that the oppressed, these men, are submerged in a common situation of oppression, and that their shared knowledge of that oppression will lead them to collective action.

Central to Freire's pedagogy is the practice of conscientization, the coming to a consciousness of oppression and the commitment to end that oppression. Conscientization is based on this common experience of oppression. It is through this reading of the world that the oppressed will come to knowledge. The role of the teacher in this process is to instigate a dialogue between teacher and student based on their common ability to know the world and to act as subjects in the world. But the question of the authority and power of the teacher, particularly those forms of power based on the teacher's subject position as raced, classed, and gendered, etc., is not addressed by Freire. There is, again, the assumption that the teacher is 'on the same side' as the oppressed and that as they engage together in dialogue about the world they will uncover the same reality, the same oppression, and the same liberation. In *Pedagogy of the Oppressed* the teacher is presented as a generic man, whose interests will be with the oppressed as they mutually discover the mechanisms of oppression. The subjectivity of the Freirean teacher is in this sense what Spivak (1988) refers to as 'transparent'. In fact, of course, teachers are not abstract, but are raced, classed, gendered individuals of particular ages, abilities, etc. The teacher will be seen and heard by students not as an abstraction, but as a particular person with a certain defined history and relationship to the world.

In a later book, Freire argues that the teacher 'has to assume the necessary authority which he or she must have, without going beyond it, in order to destroy it, by becoming authoritarian' (Freire and Shor 1987: 91). Freire asserts thus the reality of the teacher's authority:

> The educator continues to be different from the students, but, and now for me this is the central question, the difference between them, if the teacher is democratic, is his or her political dream is a *liberating* one, is that he or she cannot permit the necessary difference between the teacher and the students to become 'antagonistic'.
>
> (ibid.: 93)

In this passage Freire acknowledges the power of the teacher by virtue of the structural role of 'teacher' within a hierarchical institution, and, under the best of circumstances, by virtue of the teacher's greater experience and knowledge. But Freire does not go on to investigate what the other sources of 'antagonism' in the classroom might be. However much he provides a valuable guide to the use of authority of the liberatory teacher, he never addresses the question of other uses of power held by the teacher, by virtue of race, gender or class, that might lead to 'antagonisms'. Without naming these sources of tension, it is difficult to address or build upon them to challenge existing structures of power and subjectivities. Without recognizing more clearly the implicit power and limitations of our position as teachers, calls for a collective liberation or opposition to oppression slide over the surface of the tensions of teachers and students as subjects with conflicting interests and histories and with different kinds of knowledge and power.

A number of questions are thus left unaddressed in *Pedagogy of the Oppressed*. How are we to situate ourselves in relation to the struggles of others? How are we to address our own contradictory positions of oppressors and oppressed? Where are we to look for liberation when our collective 'reading of the world' reveals contradictory and conflicting experiences and struggles? The Freirean vision of the oppressed as undifferentiated and the source of unitary political action, the transparency of the subjectivity of the Freirean teacher, and the claims of universal goals of liberation and social transformation fail to provide the answers to these questions.

Calling into question the universal and abstract claims of *Pedagogy of the Oppressed* is certainly not to argue that Freire's pedagogy should be rejected or discarded. The ethical stance of Freire in terms of praxis and his articulation of people's worth and ability to know and change the world are an essential basis for radical pedagogies in opposition to oppression. Freire's thought illuminates the central question of political action in a world increasingly without universals. Freire, like liberation theologians such as Sharon Welch, positions himself on the side of the oppressed; he claims the moral imperative to act in the world. As Peter McLaren has commented in reference to Freire's political stand: 'The task of liberating others from their suffering may not emerge from some transcendental fiat, yet it nevertheless compels us to affirm our humanity in solidarity with victims' (McLaren 1986: 399). But in order better to seek the affirmation of our own humanity and to seek to end suffering and oppression, I am arguing for a more situated theory of oppression and subjectivity and for the need to consider the contradictions of such universal claims of truth or process.

In the next section I explore feminist pedagogy as an example of a situated pedagogy of liberation. Like Freirean pedagogy, feminist pedagogy is based on assumptions of the power of consciousness raising, the existence of oppression and the possibility of ending it, and the desire for social transformation. But in its historical development, feminist pedagogy has revealed the shortcomings that emerge in the attempt to enact a pedagogy that assumes a universal experience and abstract goals. In the attempt of feminist pedagogy to address these issues, a more complex vision of a liberatory pedagogy is being developed and explored.

FEMINIST PEDAGOGY, CONSCIOUSNESS RAISING AND WOMEN'S LIBERATION

Feminist pedagogy in colleges and universities has developed in conjunction with the growth of women's studies and what is inclusively called the new scholarship on women. These developments within universities – the institutionalization of women's studies as programs and departments and the challenge to existing canons and disciplines by the new scholarship on women and by feminist theory – are reflected in the classroom teaching methods that have come to be termed loosely 'feminist pedagogy'. Defining exactly what feminist pedagogy means in practice, however, is difficult. It is easier to describe various methods used in specific women's studies courses and included by feminist teachers claiming the term 'feminist pedagogy' than it is to provide a coherent definition.[4] But common to the claims of feminist teachers is the goal of providing students with the skills to continue political work as feminists after they have left the university. Nancy Schniedewind makes a similar claim for what she calls 'feminist process', what she characterizes as 'both a feminist vision of equalitarian personal relations and societal forms and the confidence and skills to make their knowledge and vision functional in the world' (1987: 29).

The pedagogy of feminist teachers is based on certain assumptions about knowledge, power, and political action that can be traced beyond the academy to the political activism of the women's movement of the 1960s. While women's studies at the university level have come to encompass a wide variety of political stances and theoretical approaches, feminist pedagogy continues to echo the past struggles of its origins and to retain a vision of social activism; virtually all women's studies courses and programs at least partially reflect this critical oppositional and activist stance, even within programs by now established and integrated into the bureaucratic structures of university life. As Linda Gordon points out:

> Women's studies did not arise accidentally, as the product of someone's good idea, but was created by a social movement for women's liberation with a sharp critique of the whole structure of society. By its very existence, women's studies constitutes a critique of the university and the body of knowledge it imparts.
>
> (1975: 559)

Despite tensions and splits within feminism at a theoretical level and in the context of women's studies programs in universities, the political commitment of women's liberation that Gordon refers to continues to shape feminist pedagogy. Thus, like Freirean pedagogy, feminist pedagogy is grounded in a vision of social change. And like Freirean pedagogy, feminist pedagogy rests on truth claims of the primacy of experience and consciousness that are grounded in historically situated social change movements. Key to understanding the methods and epistemological claims of feminist pedagogy is an understanding of the origins of feminist pedagogy in more grass-roots political activity, particularly in the consciousness-raising groups of the women's liberation movement of the late 1960s and early 1970s.

Consciousness-raising groups began to form more or less spontaneously in northern and western cities in late 1967 among white women who had been active in the civil rights and new left movements.[5] In a fascinating parallel to the rise of the women's suffrage movement out of the abolitionist movement in the nineteenth century, these activist and politically committed women came to apply the universal demands for equality and justice of the civil rights movement to their own situation as women.[6] While public actions, such as the Miss America protest of 1968, mass meetings, and conferences were organized in this early period, the unique organizational basis for the women's liberation movement was small groups of women who came together for what came to be known as consciousness-raising. Early consciousness-raising groups, based on friendships and common political commitments, focused on discussion of shared experiences of sexuality, work, family, and participation in the male-dominated left political movement. Consciousness raising focused on collective political change rather than individual therapy. The groups were unstructured and local; they could be formed anywhere and did not follow formal guidelines, but used the same sorts of methods because the methods addressed common problems. As one woman remembers the first meeting of what became her consciousness-raising group:

> The flood broke loose gradually and then more swiftly. We talked about our families, our mothers, our fathers, our siblings; we talked about our men; we talked about school; we talked about 'the movement' (which meant new left men). For hours we talked and unburdened our souls and left feeling high and planning to meet again the following week.
>
> (Nancy Hawley, cited in ibid.: 205)

Perhaps the clearest summary of consciousness-raising from this period can be found in Kathie Sarachild's essay, 'Consciousness-raising: a radical weapon' (1975). In this article Sarachild, a veteran of the civil rights movement in the south and a member of Redstockings, one of the earliest and most influential women's groups, presents an account that is both descriptive and proscriptive.[7] She makes clear that consciousness-raising arose spontaneously among small groups of women and that she is describing and summarizing a collective process that can be used by other groups of women. Fundamental to Sarachild's description of consciousness-raising is its grounding in the need for political action. She describes the emergence of the method of consciousness-raising among a group of women who considered themselves radicals, in the sense of demanding fundamental changes in society. As Sarachild comments:

We were interested in getting to the roots of problems in society. You might say we wanted to pull up weeds in the garden by their roots, not just pick off the leaves at the top to make things look good momentarily. Women's liberation was started by women who considered themselves radical in this sense.

(1975: 144)

A second fundamental aspect of consciousness-raising is the reliance on experience and feeling. According to Sarachild, the focus on examining women's own experience came from a profound distrust of accepted authority and truth. These claims about what was valuable and true accepted existing assumptions about women's 'inherent nature' and 'proper place'. In order to call those truths into question (truths we might now call hegemonic and that Foucault, for example, would tie to structures of power), women had nowhere to turn except to their own experienced lives. Thus Sarachild describes the process in her group:

In the end the group decided to raise its consciousness by studying women's lives by topics like childhood, jobs, motherhood, etc. We'd do any outside reading we wanted to and thought was important. But our starting point for discussion, as well as our test of the accuracy of what any of the books said, would be the actual experience we had in these areas.

(ibid.: 145)

The last aspect of consciousness raising was a common sharing of experience in a collective, leaderless group. As Michelle Russell points out, this sharing is similar to the practice of 'testifying' in the black church, and depends upon openness and trust in the group (1983). The assumption underlying this sharing of stories was that there was commonality among women; as Sarachild puts it, 'we made the assumption, an assumption basic to consciousness-raising, that most women were like ourselves – not different' (1975: 147).

The model for consciousness raising among Redstockings, as was true for other early groups, came from the experiences of many of the women as organizers in the civil rights movement in the south. Sarachild, for example, cites the example of the Student Non-violent Coordinating Committee and quotes Stokely Carmichael in arguing for the need for people to organize to understand their own conditions of existence and to fight their own struggles. Other sources cited by Sarachild include the nineteenth-century suffragist Ernestine Rose, Mao Tsetung, Malcolm X, and the practice of 'speaking bitterness' in the Chinese Revolution described by William Hinton in *Fanshen*. Both the example of the civil rights movement and the revolutionary tradition of the male writers that provided the model for early consciousness raising supported women's commitment to political action and social change.[8] As Sarachild comments:

We would be the first to dare to say and do the undareable, what women really felt and wanted. The first job now was to raise awareness and understanding, our own and others' – awareness that would prompt people to organize and to act on a mass scale.

(1975: 145)

Thus consciousness raising shared the assumptions of earlier revolutionary traditions, that understanding and theoretical analysis were the first steps to revolutionary change and that neither was adequate alone; theory and practice were intertwined as praxis. As Sarachild puts it, 'Consciousness-raising was seen as both a method for arriving at the truth and a means for action and organizing' (ibid.: 147). What was original in consciousness raising, however, was its emphasis on experience and feeling as the guide to theoretical understanding, an approach that reflected the realities of women's socially defined subjectivities and the conditions of their lives. Irene Peslikis, another member of Redstockings, wrote, 'When we think of what it is that politicizes people it is not so much books or ideas but experience' (Peslikis 1970: 339).

While Sarachild and other early feminists influenced by a left political tradition explored the creation of theory grounded in women's feelings and experiences, they never lost the commitment to social transformation.[9] In their subsequent history, however, consciousness raising and feminist pedagogy did not always retain this political commitment to action. As the women's movement expanded to reach wider groups of women, consciousness raising tended to lose its commitment to revolutionary change. This seems to have been particularly true as the women's movement affected women with a less radical perspective and with little previous political involvement. Without a vision of collective action and social transformation, consciousness raising held the possibility of what Berenice Fisher calls 'a diversion of energies into an exploration of feelings and "private" concerns to the detriment of political activism' (Fisher 1980: 22; see also hooks 1989). The structureless and local nature of consciousness raising groups only reinforced these tendencies toward a focus on individual rather than collective change. The one site in which the tradition of consciousness raising did find institutional expression was in academia, in the growth of women's studies courses and programs stimulated by the new scholarship on women.

The first women's studies courses reflecting the growth of the women's movement in what has come to be called the second wave of feminism were taught in the late 1960s (Boxer 1988: 71). In 1970 Paul Lauter and Florence Howe founded The Feminist Press, an important outlet for early feminist scholarship and the recovery of lost texts by women writers.[10] In 1977 the founding of the National Women's Studies Association provided a national organization, journal and annual conferences that gave feminists inside and outside of academia a forum for exchanging ideas and experiences. By the late 1980s respected journals such as *Signs* and *Feminist Studies* were well established and women's studies programs and courses were widespread (if not always supported enthusiastically by administrations) in colleges and universities.[11] At the same time feminist research and theory, what has come to be called 'the new scholarship on women', put forth a profound challenge to traditional disciplines.[12]

The growth of women's studies programs and feminist scholarship thus provided an institutional framework and theoretical underpinning for feminist pedagogy – the attempt to express feminist values and goals in the classroom. But while feminist scholarship has presented fundamental challenges to traditional androcentric knowledge, the attempt to create a new pedagogy modeled on consciousness raising has not been as successful or coherent a project. Serious challenges to the goal of political transformation through the experience of feminist learning have been raised in the attempt to create a feminist pedagogy in the academy. The difficulties and contradictions that have emerged in the attempt to create a feminist pedagogy in traditional institutions like universities raise serious questions for all liberatory pedagogies and echo some of the problems raised by the unitary and universal approach of *Pedagogy of the Oppressed*. But in engaging these questions feminist pedagogy suggests new directions that can enrich Freirean and other pedagogies of liberation.

Feminist pedagogy has raised three areas of concern that I think are particularly useful in this regard. The first of these concerns the role and authority of the teacher; the second addresses the epistemological question of the source of knowledge and truth claims in personal experience and feeling; the last, emerging from challenges of women of color and postmodern feminist theorists, raises the question of difference. The challenges of women of color and of postmodern feminist theory have led to a shattering of the unproblematic and unitary category 'woman' as well as the assumption of the inevitable unity of 'women'. Instead, these theorists have increasingly emphasized the importance of recognizing difference as a central category of feminist pedagogy. These theoretical challenges to the unity of both 'woman' and 'women' have in turn called into question the authority of women as teachers and students in the classroom, the epistemological value of both feeling and experience, and the nature of political strategies for enacting feminist goals of social change. I turn next to an exploration of these key issues of authority, experience, feeling, and difference within feminist pedagogy and theory.

THE ROLE AND AUTHORITY OF THE TEACHER

In many respects, the feminist vision of the teacher's authority echoes the Freirean image of the teacher who both is a joint learner with students and holds authority by virtue of greater knowledge and experience. But as we have seen, Freire fails to address the various forms of power held by teachers depending on their race, gender, and the historical and institutional setting in which they work. In the Freirean account, they are in this sense 'transparent'. In the actual practice of feminist pedagogy, the issues of difference, positionality, and the need to recognize the implications of subjectivity or identity for teachers and students have become central. Moreover, the question of authority in institutional settings makes problematic the possibility of achieving the collective and non-hierarchical vision of early consciousness-raising groups within university classrooms.

The basic elements of these early groups – an emphasis on feeling, experience, sharing, and a suspicion of hierarchy and authority – continue to influence feminist pedagogy in academic settings. But the institutionalized nature of women's studies in the hierarchical and bureaucratic structure of academia creates tensions that run counter to the original commitment to praxis in such groups. Early consciousness-raising groups were homogeneous, antagonistic to authority, with a commitment to political change that had emerged directly from the civil rights and new left movements. Feminist pedagogy within academic classrooms addresses hetero-geneous groups of students within a competitive and individualistic culture in which the teacher holds institutional power and responsibility (even if she may want to reject that power) (Friedman 1985). As bell hooks comments, 'The academic setting, the academic discourse [we] work in, is not a site known for truthtelling' (1989: 29). The very success of feminist scholarship has meant the development of a rich theoretical tradition with deep divisions and opposing goals and methods. Socialist feminism, liberal feminism, radical feminism, postmodernist feminism all approach issues from quite different perspectives.[13] Thus the source of the teacher's authority as a 'woman' who can call upon a common woman's knowledge is called into question, at the same time as the feminist teacher is 'given' authority by virtue of her role within the hierarchical structure of the university.

The question of authority in feminist pedagogy seems to be centered on two different conceptions. The first refers to the institutionally imposed authority of the teacher within a hierarchical university structure. The teacher in this role must give grades, is evaluated by administrators and colleagues in terms of expertise in a body of knowledge, and is expected to take responsibility for meeting the goals of an academic course as it is understood within the wider university. This hierarchical structure is clearly in opposition to the collective goals of a common women's movement and is miles from the early, structureless consciousness-raising groups in which each woman was an expert in her own life. Not only does the university structure impose this model of institutional authority, but students themselves expect it. As Barbara Davis comments: 'The institutional pressure to [impart knowledge] is reinforced by the students' well-socialized behaviour. If I will tell them "what I want", they will deliver it. They are exasperated with my efforts to depart from the role of dispenser of wisdom' (1983: 91). Feminist educators have attempted to address this tension between their ideals of collective education and the demands of the university by a variety of expedients: group assignments and grades, pass/fail courses, and such techniques as self-revelation and the articulation of the dynamics of the classroom (e.g. Torton Beck 1983).

Another aspect of institutionalized authority, however, is the need for women to *claim* authority in a society that denies it to them. As Culley and Portuges have pointed out, the authority and power of the woman feminist teacher is already in question from many of her students precisely because she is a woman:

> As women, our own position is precarious, and the power we are supposed to exercise is given grudgingly, if at all. For our own students, for ourselves, and for our superiors, we are not clearly 'us' or 'them'. The fact of class, of race,

of ethnicity, of sexual preference – as well as gender – may cut across the neat divisions of teacher/student.

(1985b: 12; see also 1985c)

Thus the issue of institutional authority raises the contradictions of trying to achieve a democratic and collective ideal in a hierarchical institution, but it also raises the question of the meaning of authority for feminist teachers whose right to speak or to hold power is itself under attack in a patriarchal (and racist, homophobic, classist and so on) society. The question of asserting authority and power is a central concern to feminists precisely because as women they have been taught that taking power is inappropriate. From this perspective, the feminist teacher's acceptance of authority becomes in itself liberating to herself and to her students. It becomes a claim to authority on her own value as a scholar and teacher in a patriarchal society that structurally denies or questions that authority as it is manifest in the organization and bureaucracy of the university. Women students, after all, are socialized to be deferential and both men and women students are taught to accept male authority. It is instructive for them to see women assert authority.

But this use of authority will lead to positive social change only if that teacher is working also to empower students themselves in a Freirean sense.[14] As Susan Friedman argues:

> What I and other women have needed is a theory of feminist pedagogy consistent with our needs as women operating at the fringes of patriarchal space. As we attempt to move on to academic turf culturally defined as male, we need a theory that first recognizes the androcentric denial of *all* authority to women and, second, points out a way for us to speak with an authentic voice not based on tyranny.

(1985: 207)

These concerns lead to a conception of authority and power in a positive sense, both in terms of women asserting authority as women and in terms of valuing intellectual work and the creation of theory as a means of understanding and thus changing the world.

The authority of the intellectual raises issues for women in the academy that are similar to those faced by other democratic and collective political movements. There is a contradiction between the idea of a women's movement including all women and a group of what Berenice Fisher calls 'advanced women' (1980: 22). For feminists who question the whole tradition of androcentric thought, there is deep suspicion of women who take a position as 'experts' who will translate and interpret other women's experiences. Fisher articulates these tensions well:

> Who are intellectuals in relation to the women's movement? ... Are intellectuals sorts of leaders, sage guides, women who give voice to or clarify a broader urge toward social change? Is intellectual work essentially elitist, a matter of mere privilege to think, to write, to create? Is it simply a patriarchal mode of gaining and maintaining power, a way of negating women's everyday

experience, a means of separating some women from the rest of the 'community'?

(1989: 202)

Fisher argues that feminist intellectuals are struggling with these questions in their scholarship, teaching, and roles within the universities and the wider women's movement. She does not reject the authority of the feminist intellectual, but she also does not deny the need to address and clarify these contradictions. She, like Charlotte Bunch, is an embodiment of this attempt to accept both the authority and the responsibility of the feminist intellectual who is creating theory.

In terms of feminist pedagogy, the authority of the feminist teacher as intellectual and theorist finds expression in the goal of making students themselves theorists of their own lives, by interrogating and analyzing their own experience. In an approach very similar to Freire's concept of conscientization, this strategy moves beyond the naming or sharing of experience to the creation of a critical understanding of the forces which have shaped that experience. This process of theorizing is itself antithetical to traditional views of women. As Charlotte Bunch points out, traditionally

> Women are supposed to worry about mundane survival problems, to brood about fate, and to fantasize in a personal manner. We are not meant to think analytically about society, to question the way things are, to consider how things could be different. Such thinking involves an active, not a passive, relationship to the world.

(1983: 156)

Thus feminist educators like Fisher and Bunch accept their authority as intellectuals and theorists, but they consciously attempt to construct their pedagogy to recognize and encourage the capacity of their students also to theorize and recognize their own power.[15] This is not a conception of authority in the institutional terms of a bureaucratized university system, but an attempt to claim the authority of theorist and guide for students who are themselves potential theorists.

Feminist concerns about the authority of the feminist teacher address questions of classroom theory and practice ignored by Freire in his formulation of the teacher and student as two 'knowers' of the world, or his assertion that the liberatory teacher should acknowledge and claim authority but not authoritarianism. The feminist exploration of authority is much richer and addresses more directly the contradictions between goals of collectivity and hierarchies of knowledge. Feminist teachers are conscious of the power of various subject positions as much greater than is represented in Freire's 'transparent' liberatory teacher. An acknowledgement of the realities of conflict and tensions based on contradictory political goals as well as the meaning of historically experienced oppression for both teachers and students leads to a pedagogy that respects difference as significant not just for students, but for teachers as well.

EXPERIENCE AND FEELING AS SOURCES OF KNOWLEDGE

As feminists explore the relationship of authority, theory, and political action, they raise questions about the categories and truth claims underlying both consciousness raising and feminist pedagogy. These claims rest on the categories of experience and feeling as guides to theoretical understanding and political change. Basic to the Freirean method of conscientization is the belief in the ability of all people to be knowers and to read both the word and the world. In Freirean pedagogy it is through the interrogation of their own experiences that the oppressed will come to an understanding of their own power as knowers and creators of the world; this knowledge will contribute to the transformation of their world. In consciousness raising groups and in feminist pedagogy in the university a similar reliance on experience and feeling has been fundamental to the development of a feminist knowledge of the world that can be the basis for social change. Underlying both Freirean and early feminist pedagogy is an assumption of a common experience as the basis for political analysis and action. Both experience and feeling were central to consciousness raising and remain central to feminist pedagogy in academia; they are claimed as a kind of 'inner knowing', shaped by society, but at the same time containing an oppositional quality. Feeling is looked to as a guide to a deeper truth than that of abstract rationality. Experience, which is interpreted through ideologically constructed categories, also can be the basis for an opposition to dominant schemes of truth, if what is experienced runs counter to what is set forth and accepted as 'true'. Feminist educators, beginning with women in the early consciousness-raising groups, have explored both experience and feeling as sources of knowledge, and both deserve closer examination.

In many ways feeling or emotion has traditionally been seen as a source of women's knowledge about the world. As we have seen, in the early consciousness-raising groups feelings were looked to as the source of a 'true' knowledge of the world for women living in a society that denied the value of their perceptions. Feelings or emotion were seen as a way of testing accepted claims of what is universally true of human nature or specifically true of women. Such claims as Freud's theory of penis envy, for example, were challenged by women first because this theoretical description of women's psychology did not match women's feelings about their own lives. As feminist pedagogy has developed, with a continued emphasis on the function of feelings as a guide to knowledge about the world, feelings or emotions have been seen as links between a kind of inner truth or inner self and the outside world – including ideology, culture, and other discourses of power.[16] However, as feminist educators have explored the uses of feeling or emotion as a source of knowledge, several difficulties have become clear.

First of all, there is a danger that the expression of strong emotion can be simply cathartic and can in fact serve to deflect the need for action to address the underlying causes of that emotion. Moreover, it is not clear how to distinguish among a wide range of emotions as the source of political action. At a more theoretical level, there are contradictions involved in claiming that the emotions are a source for knowledge and at the same time arguing that they are manipulated and shaped by dominant discourses. Both consciousness-raising groups and feminist theorists have asserted the social construction of feelings and their manipulation by the dominant culture; at the same time, they look to feelings as a source of truth. Berenice Fisher points to the contradiction implicit in these claims:

> In theoretical terms, we cannot simultaneously claim that all feelings are socially conditioned and that some feelings are 'true'. We would be more consistent to acknowledge that society only partly shapes our emotions, leaving an opening where we can challenge and change the responses to which we have been socialized. That opening enables the consciousness-raising process to take place and gives us the space in which to reflect on the new emotional responses that our process evokes.
>
> (1987: 48)

In this formulation, Fisher seems to be arguing for a kind of Gramscian 'good sense', a locus of knowing in the self that is grounded in feeling as a guide to theoretical understanding. Feelings are thus viewed as a kind of cognition – a source of knowledge.

Perhaps the most eloquent argument for feelings as a source of oppositional knowledge is found in the work of Audre Lorde. Lorde, a black lesbian feminist theorist and poet, writes from the specificity of her own socially defined and shaped life. For her, feeling is the source of poetry, a means of knowing that challenges white, Western, androcentric epistemologies. She specifically ties her own feelings as a black woman to a non-Western way of knowing. As she writes:

> As we come more into touch with our own ancient, non-european conscious-ness of living as a situation to be experienced and interacted with, we learn more and more to cherish our feelings, to respect those hidden sources of power from where true knowledge and, therefore, lasting action comes.
>
> (1984: 57)

Lorde is acutely aware of the ways in which the dominant society shapes our sense of who we are and what we feel. As she points out: 'within living structures defined by profit, by linear power, by institutional dehumanization, our feelings were not meant to survive' (ibid.: 34). Moreover, Lorde is conscious of the oppressor within us: 'For we have, built into all of us, old blueprints of expectation and response, old structures of oppression, and these must be altered at the same time as we alter the living conditions which are the result of those structures' (ibid.: 123). But although Lorde does not deny what she calls 'the oppressor within', she retains a belief in the power of deeper feeling to challenge the dominant definitions of truth and to point the way to an analysis that can lead to an alternative vision:

As we begin to recognize our deepest feelings, we begin to give up, of necessity, being satisfied with suffering and self-negation, and with the numbness which so often seems like their only alternative in society. Our acts against oppression become integral with self, motivated and empowered from within.

(ibid.: 58)

For Lorde, then, feelings are a guide to analysis and to action. While they are shaped by society and are socially constructed in that sense, Lorde insists on a deeper reality of feeling closer in touch with what it means to be human. This formulation echoes the Freirean vision of humanization as a new way of being in the world, other than that of oppressor and oppressed. Lorde terms this the power of the erotic; she speaks of the erotic as 'a measure between the beginnings of our sense of self and the chaos of our strongest feelings', a resource 'firmly rooted in the power of our unexpressed or unrecognized feeling' (ibid.: 53). Because the erotic can challenge the dominant, it has been denied as a source of power and knowledge. But for Lorde, the power of the erotic provides the basis for visionary social change.

In her exploration of feelings and of the erotic as a source of knowledge about the world, Lorde does not reject analysis and rationality. But she questions the depth of critical understanding of the forces that shape our lives that can be achieved using only the rational and abstract methods of analysis given to us by dominant ideology. In Foucault's terms, she is seeking a perspective from which to interrogate dominant regimes of truth; central to her argument is the claim that an analysis framed solely in the terms of accepted discourse cannot get to the root of structures of power. That is what her well-known phrase 'The master's tools will never dismantle the master's house' implies. As she argues:

Rationality is not unnecessary. It serves the chaos of knowledge. It serves feeling. It serves to get from this place to that place. But if you don't honor those places, then the road is meaningless. Too often, that's what happens with the worship of rationality and that circular, academic analytic thinking. But ultimately, I don't see feel/think as a dichotomy. I see them as a choice of ways and combinations.

(ibid.: 100)

Lorde's discussion of feeling and the erotic as a source of power and knowledge is based on the assumption that human beings have the capacity to feel and know that can engage in self-critique; people are not completely shaped by dominant discourse. The oppressor may be within us, but Lorde insists that we also have the capacity to challenge our own ways of feeling and knowing. When tied to a recognition of positionality, this validation of feeling can be used to develop powerful sources of politically focused feminist education. For Lorde and Fisher this kind of knowing through an exploration of feeling and experience requires collective inquiry and constant re-evaluation. It is a contingent and positioned claim to truth.

If the argument for feeling as a source of oppositional knowledge is both powerful and yet fraught with contradictions, so too is the use of experience as the basis for feminist political action. Looking to experience as the source of knowledge and the focus of feminist learning is perhaps the most fundamental tenet of feminist pedagogy. This is similar to the Freirean call to 'read the world' to seek the generative themes that codify power relationships and social structures. The sharing of women's experiences was the touchstone of early consciousness-raising groups and continues to be a fundamental method of feminist pedagogy. This is a materialist conception of experience, that women need to examine what they have experienced and lived in concrete ways, in their own bodies. In an early essay Adrienne Rich pointed to this materiality of experience: 'To think like a woman in a man's world means . . . remembering that every mind resides in a body; remaining accountable to the feminine bodies in which we live; constantly testing given hypotheses against lived experience' (1979: 243). As became clear quite early in the women's movement, claims about experience as a source of women's knowledge rested on certain assumptions about women's common lives. Women were conceived of as a unitary and relatively undifferentiated group. Sarachild, for example, speaks of devising 'new theories which . . . reflect the actual experience and feelings and necessities of women' (1975: 148). That unstated assumption of a kind of universal experience of 'being a woman' was exploded by the critiques of postmodernist feminisms and by the growing assertion of lesbians and women of color that the universal category 'woman' in fact meant 'white heterosexual middle-class woman', even for white heterosexual socialist feminists or women veterans of the civil rights movement who were committed to class or race struggles. Both experience and feeling thus have been called into question as the source of an unproblematic knowledge of the world that will lead to praxis. As Diana Fuss comments: '"female experience" is never as unified, as knowable, as universal, and as stable as we presume it to be' (1989: 114).

THE QUESTION OF DIFFERENCE

Challenges to a unitary concept of women's experience by both women of color and postmodern critics has not meant the abandonment of experience as a source of knowledge for feminist teachers. Of course experience, like feeling, is itself socially constructed, in the sense that we can only understand it and speak about it in ideas and terms that are part of an existing ideology and language. But in a stance similar to that of Lorde in her use of the erotic, feminist teachers have looked to the experiences of embodied women as a source of knowledge that can illuminate the social processes and ideology that shape us. As Fuss suggests: 'Such a position permits the introduction of narratives of lived experience into the classroom while at the same time challenging us to examine collectively the central role social and historical practices play in shaping and producing these narratives' (1989: 118). One example of this approach is found in the work of Frigga Haug and the group of German feminists of which she is a part (Haug 1987). Haug and this group use what they call collective memory work to explore their feelings about their own bodies in order to uncover the social construction of their own selves:

> Our collective empirical work set itself the high-flown task of identifying the ways in which individuals construct themselves into existing structures, and are thereby themselves formed; the way in which they reconstruct social structures; the points at which change is possible, the points where our chains chafe most, the point where accommodations have been made.

(ibid.: 41)

Basic to their approach is a belief in reflection and a rejection of a view of people as 'fixed, given, unchangeable'. By working collectively on 'memory work', a sharing and comparison of their own lives, Haug and her group hope to uncover the workings of hegemonic ideology in their own subjectivities.

Another example of such collective work can be found in the Jamaican women's theatre group Sistern. Founded in 1977, Sistern is a collaborative theatre group made up of working-class Jamaican women who create and write plays based upon a collaborative exploration of their own experiences. The life histories of the women of Sistern have been collected in *Lionheart Girl: Life Stories of Jamaican Women* (Sistern with Ford-Smith 1986). In the compilation of this book, the Sistern collective used the same process of the collective sharing and analysis of experience that is the basis for their theatre work. As the director of the company, Honor Ford-Smith, writes:

> We began meeting collectively at first. Starting with our childhood, we made drawings of images based on such themes as where we had grown up, symbols of oppression, our lives, our relationship with men, our experience with race and the kind of work we had done.

(ibid.: 15)

For both Haug and her group and the Sistern collective, as for the early consciousness-raising groups and for the Freirean culture circles, the collective sharing of experience is the source of knowledge of the forces that shaped and continue to shape them. But their recognition of the shifting meaning of experience as it is explored through memory insists on the profoundly social and political nature of who we are.

Both women of color writing from a perspective of cultural feminism and postmodernist feminist theorists converge in their critique of the concept of a universal 'women's experience'. While the idea of a unitary and universal category 'woman' has been challenged by women of color for its racist assumptions, it has also been challenged by recent analyses of feminist theorists influenced by postmodernism, who point to the social construction of subjectivity and who emphasize the 'unstable' nature of the self. Postmodernist feminist critics such as Chris Weedon have argued that socially given identities such as 'woman' are 'precarious, contradictory, and in process, constantly being reconstituted in discourse each time we speak' (1987: 15). This kind of analysis considers the ways in which 'the subject' is not an object; that is, is not fixed in a static social structure, but is constantly being created, is actively creating the self, struggling for new ways of being in the world through new forms of discourse or new forms of social relationships. It calls for a recognition of the positionality of each person in any discussion of what can be known from experience. This calling into question of the permanence of subjectivities is what Flax refers to as the 'unstable self' (1987). If we view individual selves as being constructed and negotiated, then we can begin to consider what exactly those forces are in which individuals shape themselves and by which they are shaped. The category of 'woman' is itself challenged as it is seen more and more as a part of a symbolic system of ideology. Donna Haraway calls all such claims of identity into question:

> With the hard-won recognition of their social and historical constitution, gender, race, and class cannot provide the basis for belief in 'essential' unity: There is nothing about being 'female' that naturally binds women. There is not even such a state as 'being' female, itself a highly complex category constructed in contested sexual discourses and other social practices. Gender, race, or class consciousness is an achievement forced on us by the terrible historical experience of the contradictory social realities of patriarchy, colonialism, and capitalism.
>
> (1985: 72)

These analyses support the challenges to assumptions of an essential and universal nature of women and women's experience that have come from lesbian critics and women of color.[17]

Both women of color and lesbian critics have pointed to the complexity of socially given identities. Black women and other women of color raise challenges to the assumption that the sharing of experience will create solidarity and a theoretical understanding based upon a common women's standpoint. Lesbian feminists, both white and of color, point to the destructive nature of homophobia and what Adrienne Rich has called compulsory heterosexuality. As is true of white heterosexual feminist educators, these theorists base their analysis upon their own experiences, but those experiences reveal the workings not only of sexism, but of racism, homophobia and class oppression as well. This complex perspective underlies the Combahee River Collective Statement, a position paper written by a group of African-American feminists in Boston in the 1970s. This statement makes clear what a grounded theory of experience means for women whose value is denied by the dominant society in numerous ways. The Combahee River Collective argue that 'the most profound and potentially most radical politics come directly out of our own identity, as opposed to working to end someone else's oppression' (1983: 275). For African-American women, an investigation of the shaping of their own identities reveals the ways in which sexism and racism are interlocking forms of oppression:

> As children we realized that we were different from boys and that we were treated differently. For example, we were told in the same breath to be quiet

both for the sake of being 'ladylike' and to make us less objectionable in the eyes of white people. As we grew older we became aware of the threat of physical and sexual abuse from men. However, we had no way of conceptualizing what was so apparent to us, what we *knew* was really happening.

(ibid.: 274)

When African-American teachers like Michelle Russell or Barbara Omolade describe their feminist pedagogy, they ground that pedagogy in an investigation of experience in material terms. As Michelle Russell describes her teaching of an introductory black studies class for women at Wayne County Community College: 'We have an hour together . . . The first topic of conversation – among themselves and with me – is what they went through just to make it in the door, on time. That, in itself, becomes a lesson' (1983: 155). As Barbara Omolade points out in her discussion of her teaching at Medgar Evars College in New York, a college whose students are largely African-American women:

No one can teach students to 'see', but an instructor is responsible for providing the coherent ordering of information and content. The classroom process is one of information-sharing in which students learn to generalize their particular life experiences within a community of fellow intellectuals.

(1987: 39)

Thus the pedagogy of Russell and Omolade is grounded in experience as a source of knowledge in a particularly materialistic way; and the knowledge generated reveals the overlapping forms of oppression lived by women of color in this society.

The investigation of the experiences of women of color, lesbian women, women whose very being challenges existing racial, sexual, heterosexual, and class dominance, leads to a knowledge of the world that both acknowledges differences and points to the need for an 'integrated analysis and practice based upon the fact that the major systems of oppression are interlocking' (Combahee River Collective 1983: 272). The turning to experience thus reveals not a universal and common women's essence but deep divisions in what different women have experienced, what kind of knowledge they discover when they examine their own experience. The recognition of the differences among women raises serious challenges to feminist pedagogy – calling into question the authority of the teacher/theorist, raising feelings of guilt and shame, revealing tensions among students as well as between teacher and students. In classes of African-American women taught by African-American teachers, the sharing of experience can lead to the same sense of commonality and sharing that was true of early consciousness-raising groups. But in settings in which students come from differing positions of privilege or oppression, the sharing of experience raises conflicts rather than builds solidarity. In these circumstances, the collective exploration of experience leads not to a common knowledge and solidarity based on sameness, but to the tensions of an articulation of difference. It raises again the problems left unaddressed by Freirean pedagogy – the overlapping and multiple forms of oppression revealed in 'reading the world' of experience.

CONCLUSION

Both Freirean and feminist pedagogies are based on political commitment and identification with subordinate and oppressed groups; both seek justice and empowerment. Freire sets out these goals of liberation and social and political transformation as universal claims, without exploring his own privileged position or existing conflicts among oppressed groups themselves. Writing from within a tradition of Western modernism, this theory rests on a belief of transcendent and universal truth. But feminist theory, influenced by postmodernist thought and by the writings of women of color, challenges the underlying assumptions of these universal claims. Feminist theorists in particular argue that it is essential to recognize, as Mitchell (1984) comments, that we cannot 'live as human subjects without in some sense taking on a history'. The recognition of our own histories means the necessity of articulating our own subjectivities and our own interests as we try to interpret and critique the social world. This stance rejects the universalizing tendency of much male mainstream thought and insists on recognizing the power and privilege of who we are. As Martin and Mohanty comment:

> The claim to a lack of identity or positionality is itself based on privilege, on the refusal to accept responsibility for one's implication in actual historical or social relations, or a denial that positionalities exist or that they matter, the denial of one's own personal history and the claim to a total separation from it.
> (1986: 208)

Fundamental to recent feminist theory is a questioning of the concept of a coherent subject moving through history with a single essential identity. Instead, feminist theorists are developing a concept of the constant creation and negotiation of selves within structures of ideology and material constraints.[18] This line of theoretical analysis calls into question assumptions of the common interests of the oppressed, whether conceived of as women or as peasants; it challenges the use of such universal terms as 'oppression' and 'liberation' without the user locating these claims in a concrete historical or social context. The challenges of recent feminist theory and in particular the writings of feminists of color point to the need to articulate and claim a particular historical and social identity, to locate ourselves, and to build coalitions from a recognition of the partial knowledges of our own constructed identities. Recognizing the standpoint of subjects as shaped by their experience of class, race, gender, or other socially defined identities has powerful implications for pedagogy, in that it emphasises the need to make conscious the subject positions of not only students, but teachers as well. These lines of theoretical analysis have implications for the ways in which we can understand pedagogy as contested, a site of discourse among subjects, teachers and students, whose identities are, as Chris Weedon (1987) puts it, contradictory and in process.

The theoretical formulation of the 'unstable self', the complexity of subjectivities, what Giroux (1988: 93) calls 'multi-layered subjects', and the need to position ourselves in relation to our own histories raise important issues for liberatory pedagogies. If all people's identities are recognized in their full historical and social complexity as subject positions that are in process, based on knowledges that are partial and that reflect deep and conflicting differences, how can we theorize what a liberatory pedagogy actively struggling against different forms of oppression might look like? How can we build upon the rich and complex analysis of feminist theory and pedagogy to work toward a Freirean vision of social justice and liberation?

In the complexity of issues raised by feminist pedagogy we can begin to acknowledge the reality of tensions that result from different histories, privilege, oppression, and power as they are lived by teachers and students in classrooms. To recognize these tensions and differences does not mean abandonment of the goals of social justice and empowerment; but it does make clear the need to recognize contingent and situated claims and to acknowledge our own histories and selves in process. One significant area of feminist work has been grounded in the collective analysis of experience and emotion, exemplified by the work of Haug and her group in Germany or by the Jamaican women's theatre group, Sistern. In many respects these projects look back to consciousness raising, but with a more developed theory of ideology and an acute consciousness of difference. As Fisher argues, a collective inquiry 'requires the slow unfolding of layers of experience, both the contradictory experiences of a given woman and the conflicting experiences of different women' (1987: 49). Another approach bases itself on what Bernice Reagon (1987) calls the need for coalition building, a recognition and validation of difference. This is similar to what Minnie Bruce Pratt is seeking in her discussion of trying to come to terms with her identity as a privileged southern white woman (1984). Martin and Mohanty speak of this as a sense of 'home', a recognition of the difficulties of coming to terms with privilege or oppression and the benefits of being an oppressor or the rage of being oppressed (1986). This is a validation of both difference and conflict, but an attempt to build coalitions around common goals, not a denial of differences (Smith 1983).

It is clear that this kind of pedagogy and exploration of experiences in a society in which privilege and oppression are lived is risky and filled with pain. It suggests a more complex realization of the Freirean vision of a collective conscientization and struggle against oppression. But it shares Freire's call for a utopian and visionary pedagogy. As Michelle Russell writes:

> In all other areas of life, we can talk about struggle, organization, sabotage, survival, even tactical and strategic victory. However, only in dreams are liberation and judgment at the center of vision. That is where we do all the things in imagination that our awareness demands but our situation does not yet permit.

(1983: 167)

NOTES

1 For comparisons of Freirean and feminist pedagogy see also Maher (1985, 1987).
2 Freire's method of codifications and his use of generative themes have been discussed frequently. Perhaps the best introduction to these concrete methods can be found in Freire (1973).
3 See de Beauvoir (1953) for a more striking use of the male referent.
4 When definitions of feminist pedagogy are attempted, they sometimes tend toward generalization and such a broad inclusiveness as to be of dubious usefulness. For example, Carolyn Shrewsbury characterizes feminist pedagogy as follows:

> It does not automatically preclude any technique or approach. It does indicate the relationship that specific techniques have to educational goals. It is not limited to any specific subject matter but it does include a reflexive element that increases the feminist scholarship component involved in the teaching/learning of any subject matter. It has close ties with other liberatory pedagogies, but it cannot be subsumed under other pedagogical approaches. It is transformative, helping us revision the educational enterprise. But it can also be phased into a traditional teaching approach or another alternative pedagogical approach.
>
> (Shrewsbury 1987: 12)

Certain descriptions of feminist pedagogy show the influence of group dynamics and interactionist approaches (e.g. Schniedewind, n.d.). Methods used by feminist teachers include cooperation, shared leadership, and democratic process. Feminist teachers describe such techniques as keeping journals, incorporating personal responses to readings and the classroom dynamics of a course, the use of role playing and theatre games, the use of self-revelation on the part of the teacher, building leadership skills among students by requiring them to teach parts of a course, and contracting for grades. For accounts of classroom practice, see the articles in *Women's Studies Quarterly* (1987), Culley and Portuges (1985a), Bunch and Pollack (1983), Hull, Bell Scott and Smith (1982), and numerous articles in *Women's Studies Newsletter* and *Radical Teacher*.
5 A discussion of the relationship of the early women's liberation movement to the civil rights movement and the new left can be found in Evans (1980). On the basis of extensive interviews as well as pamphlets and private documents, Evans shows the origins of both political goals and methods in the earlier, male-dominated movement, particularly the model of black student organizers and the black church in the south of the US.
6 While mid-nineteenth-century suffragists developed their ideas of human equality and justice through the abolitionist movement, by the late nineteenth century white suffragists often demonstrated racist attitudes and employed racist strategies in their campaigns for suffrage. This offers another instructive parallel to the white feminist movement of the 1960s. Here, once again, feminist claims emerged out of an anti-racist struggle for civil rights, but later too often took up the universalizing stance that the experience and issues of white women represented the lives of all women. See hooks (1981, 1984) for powerful discussions of these issues.
7 Redstockings included a number of women who were influential in the women's movement, including Shulamith Firestone, author of *The Dialectic of Sex*, and Carol Hanisch, who wrote the essay 'The personal is political'. Rosalyn Baxandall, Ellen Willis, and Robin Morgan were among a number of other significant feminist writers and activists who participated.
8 See Fisher (1984) for an extended discussion of the impact of the methods and goals of the civil rights movement on consciousness raising and the early women's liberation movement.
9 See, for example, McAfee and Wood (1970) for an early socialist feminist analysis of the need to connect the women's movement with the class struggle.
10 See Howe (1984) for a collection of essays documenting this period.

11 Boxer (1988: 70) estimates there were over 300 programs and 30,000 courses in women's studies given in 1982.
12 The literature of feminist challenges to specific disciplines is by now immense. For general discussions of the impact of the new scholarship on women see DuBois *et al.* (1985) and Farnhum (1987).
13 See Jagger (1983) for an excellent discussion of these perspectives.
14 See Davis (1983) for a thoughtful discussion of the contradictory pressures on the feminist teacher both to nurture and to challenge women students.
15 See Fisher (1982) for a thoughtful discussion of the difficulties of retaining an activist stance for feminists in the academy.
16 See Hochschild (1983) for a discussion of the social construction of emotions in contemporary society. Hochschild argues that emotion is a 'biologically given sense . . . and a means by which we can know about our relation to the world' (219). At the same time she investigates the ways in which the emotions themselves are manipulated and constructed.
17 As representative see Butler (1985), Hull *et al.* (1982), Joseph and Lewis (1981), Moraga and Anzaldua (1981), Omolade (1987), Russell (1983), Spellman (1985).
18 See, for example, Flax (1987), Harding (1986), Smith (1987), Haraway (1985), Hartsock (1983), O'Brien (1981), Diamond and Quinby (1988), Alcoff (1988), *Feminist Studies* (1988).

REFERENCES

Alcoff, L. (1988) 'Cultural feminism versus poststructuralism: the identity crisis in feminist theory', *Signs* 13, 3, 405–37.
de Beauvoir, S. (1953) *The Second Sex*, New York: Knopf.
Berlak, A. (1989) 'Teaching for outrage and empathy in the liberal arts', *Educational Foundations* 3, 2, 69–94.
Du Bois, E., Kelly, G., Kennedy, E., Korsmeyer, C. and Robinson, L. (eds) (1985) *Feminist Scholarship Kindling in the Groves of Academe*, Urbana and Chicago: University of Illinois Press.
Boxer, M. (1988) 'For and about women: the theory and practice of women's studies in the United States' in E. Minnich, J. O'Barr and R. Rosenfeld, eds, *Reconstructing the Academy: Women's Education and Women's Studies*, Chicago and London: University of Chicago Press.
Britzman, D. (1990) 'Decentering discourses in teacher education: or, the unleashing of unpopular things'. Paper delivered at the meetings of the American Educational Research Association, Boston, April.
—— (forthcoming) 'The terrible problem of knowing thyself: towards a poststructuralist account of teacher identity', *Journal of Curriculum Theorizing*.
Bunch, C. (1983) 'Not by degrees: feminist theory and education' in C. Bunch and S. Pollack, eds, *Learning Our Way*, Trumansburg, NY: The Crossing Press.
Bunch, C. and Pollack, S. (eds) (1983) *Learning Our Way*, Trumansburg, NY: The Crossing Press.
Butler, J. (1985) 'Toward a pedagogy of everywoman's studies' in M. Culley and C. Portuges, eds, *Gendered Subjects*, Boston and London: Routledge and Kegan Paul.
Cherryholmes, C. (1988) *Power and Criticism: Poststructural Investigations in Education*, New York: Teachers College Press.
Combahee River Collective (1983) 'Combahee River Collective Statement' in B. Smith, ed., *Home Girls*, New York: Kitchen Table, Women of Color Press.
Culley, M. and Portuges, C. (1985a) 'Introduction' in M. Culley and C. Portuges, eds, *Gendered Subjects*, Boston and London: Routledge and Kegan Paul.

—— (1985b) 'The politics of nurturance' in M. Culley and C. Portuges, eds, *Gendered Subjects*, Boston and London: Routledge and Kegan Paul.

—— (1985c) 'Anger and authority in the introductory women's studies classroom' in M. Culley and C. Portuges, eds, *Gendered Subjects*, Boston and London: Routledge and Kegan Paul.

Davis, B.H. (1983) 'Teaching the feminist minority' in C. Bunch and S. Pollack, eds, *Learning Our Way*, Trumansburg, NY: The Crossing Press.

Diamond, I. and Quinby, L. (eds) (1988) *Feminism and Foucault*, Boston: Northeastern University Press.

Ellsworth, E. (1989) 'Why doesn't this feel empowering?', *Harvard Educational Review* 59, 297–324.

Evans, S. (1980) *Personal Politics*, New York: Vintage Press.

Farnhum, C. (ed.) (1987) *The Impact of Feminist Research in the Academy*, Bloomington: University of Indiana Press.

Feminist Studies (1988) Special issue on feminism and deconstruction, 14, 1.

Fisher, B. (1980) 'What is feminist pedagogy?', *Radical Teacher* 18, 22.

—— (1982) 'Professing feminism: feminist academics and the women's movement', *Psychology of Women Quarterly* 7, 1, 55–69.

—— (1984) 'Guilt and shame in the women's movement: the radical ideal of political action and its meaning for feminist intellectuals', *Feminist Studies* 10, 2, 185–212.

—— (1987) 'The heart has its reasons: feeling, thinking, and community building in feminist education', *Women's Studies Quarterly* 15, 3 and 4, 40–58.

Flax, J. (1987) 'Postmodernism and gender relations in feminist theory', *Signs* 12, 4, 621–43.

Freire, P. (1971) *Pedagogy of the Oppressed*, New York: Herder and Herder.

—— (1973) *Education for Critical Consciousness*, New York: Seabury Press.

—— (1985) 'The adult literacy process as cultural action for freedom' in P. Freire, *The Politics of Education*, Westport, CT: Bergin and Garvey.

Freire, P. and Shor, I. (1987) *A Pedagogy for Liberation*, London: Macmillan.

Friedman, S. (1985) 'Authority in the feminist classroom: a contradiction in terms?' in M. Culley and C. Portuges, eds, *Gendered Subjects*, Boston and London: Routledge and Kegan Paul.

Fuss, D. (1989) *Essentially Speaking*, New York: Routledge.

Giroux, H. (1988) *Schooling and the Struggle for Public Life*, Minneapolis: University of Minnesota Press.

—— (ed.) (1991) *Postmodernism, Feminism and Cultural Politics*, Albany, NY: State University of New York Press.

Giroux, H. and Simon, R. (eds) (1989) *Popular Culture, Schooling and Everyday Life*, South Hadley, MA: Bergin and Garvey.

Gordon, L. (1975) 'A socialist view of women's studies: a reply to the editorial', *Signs* 1, 2, 555–62.

Haraway, D. (1985) 'A manifesto for cyborgs', *Socialist Review* 80, 60–85.

Harding, S. (1986) *The Science Question in Feminism*, Ithaca, NY: University of Cornell Press.

Hartsock, N. (1983) *Money, Sex and Power*, New York: Longman.

Haug, F. (1987) *Female Sexualization*, London: Verso.

Hochschild, A. (1983) *The Managed Heart*, Berkeley: University of California Press.

hooks, b. (1981) *Ain't I a Woman?*, Boston: South End Press.

—— (1984) *Feminist Theory from Margin to Center*, Boston: South End Press.

—— (1989) 'on self-recovery' in b. hooks, *talking back: thinking feminist, thinking black*, Boston: South End Press.

Howe, F. (1984) *Myths of Coeducation*, Bloomington: University of Indiana Press.

Hull, G. Bell Scott, P. and Smith, B. (eds) (1982) *But Some of Us Are Brave*, Old Westbury, NY: The Feminist Press.

Jagger, A. (1983) *Feminist Politics and Human Nature*, Brighton: Harvester Press.

Joseph, G. and Lewis, J. (1981) *Common Differences: Conflicts in Black and White Perspectives*, Garden City, NY: Anchor Books.

de Lauretis, T. (1984) *Alice Doesn't*, Bloomington: University of Indiana Press.

Lorde, A. (1984) *Sister Outsider*, Trumansburg, NY: The Crossing Press.

Maher, F. (1985) 'Classroom pedagogy and the new scholarship on women' in M. Culley and C. Portuges, eds, *Gendered Subjects*, Boston and London: Routledge and Kegan Paul.

—— (1987) 'Toward a richer theory of feminist pedagogy: a comparison of "liberation" and "gender" models for teaching and learning', *Journal of Education* 169, 3, 91–100.

Martin, B. and Mohanty, C. (1986) 'Feminist politics: what's home got to do with it?' in T. de Lauretis, ed., *Feminist Studies/Critical Studies*, Bloomington: University of Indiana Press.

McAfee, K. and Wood, M. (1970) 'Bread and roses' in L. Tanner, ed., *Voices from Women's Liberation*, New York: New American Library.

McCarthy, C. (1988) 'Rethinking liberal and radical perspectives on racial inequality in schooling: making the case for nonsynchrony', *Harvard Educational Reviews* 58, 3, 265–80.

McLaren, P. (1986) 'Postmodernity and the death of politics: a Brazilian reprieve', *Educational Theory* 36, 4, 389–401. A revised edition appears as Chapter 11 below.

Mitchell, J. (1984) *Women: The Longest Revolution*, New York: Pantheon Books.

Moraga, C. and Anzaldua, G. (eds) (1981) *This Bridge Called My Back*, Watertown, MA: Persephone Press.

O'Brien, M. (1981) *The Politics of Reproduction*, Boston and London: Routledge and Kegan Paul.

Omolade, B. (1987) 'A black feminist pedagogy', *Women's Studies Quarterly* 15, 3 and 4, 32–40.

Peslikis, I. (1970) 'Resistances to consciousness' in R. Morgan, ed., *Sisterhood is Powerful*, New York: Vintage Books.

Pratt, M. Bruce (1984) 'Identity: skin blood heart' in E. Bulkin, M.B. Pratt and B. Smith, eds, *Yours in Struggle*, Brooklyn, NY: Long Hand Press.

Reagon, B. (1987) 'Coalition politics: turning the century' in B. Smith, ed., *Home Girls*, New York: Kitchen Table-Women of Color Press.

Rich, A. (1979) 'Taking women students seriously' in A. Rich, *On Lies, Secrets and Silences*, New York: Norton.

Russell, M. (1983) 'Black eyed blues connection' in C. Bunch and S. Pollack, eds, *Learning Our Way*, Trumansburg, NY: The Crossing Press.

Sarachild, K. (1975) 'Consciousness-raising: a radical weapon' in Redstockings, *Feminist Revolution*, New York: Random House.

Schniedewind, N. (1987) 'Teaching feminist process', *Women's Studies Quarterly* 15, 3 and 4, 15–31.

—— (n.d.) 'Feminist values: guidelines for teaching methodology in women's studies', *Radical Teacher* 18, 25–8.

Shrewsbury, C. (1987), 'What is feminist pedagogy?', *Women's Studies Quarterly* 15, 3 and 4, 6–14.

Sistern with Ford-Smith, H. (1986) *Lionheart Girl: Life Stories of Jamaican Women*, London: The Women's Press.

Smith, B. (ed.) (1983) *Home Girls*, New York; Kitchen Table-Women of Color Press.

Smith, D. (1987) *The Everyday World as Problematic*, Boston: Northeastern University Press.

Spellman, E. (1985) 'Combatting the marginalization of black women in the classroom' in M. Culley and C. Portuges, eds, *Gendered Subjects*, Boston and London: Routledge and Kegan Paul.

Spivak, G.C. (1988) 'Can the subaltern speak?' in C. Nelson and L. Grossberg, eds, *Marxism and the Interpretation of Culture*, Urbana: University of Illinois Press.

Torton Beck, E. (1983) 'Self-disclosure and the commitment to social change', *Women's Studies International Forum* 6, 2, 159–64.

Weedon, C. (1987) *Feminist Practice and Poststructuralist Theory*, Oxford: Blackwell.

Women's Studies Quarterly (1987) Special issue of feminist pedagogy, 15, 3 and 4.

Chapter 2

Critical thought and moral imagination
Peace education in Freirean perspective

Marguerite and Michael Rivage-Seul

INTRODUCTION

The 1980s have brought to prominence the concept of critical thinking long familiar to students of Paulo Freire. Conferences and journals have picked up the theme, and textbooks replete with teacher supplements aimed at turning class-rooms into exciting 'communities of inquiry' have emerged.

This might seem promising to those committed to education for critical consciousness. The emphasis in new critical thought on using dialogue to lead students to think and analyze indicates a rejection of 'banking' education. It also suggests movement toward Friere's ideal of treating students as responsible human beings who can address their world as thinking subjects rather than as manipulable objects.

Furthermore, there are signs that North American educators newly interested in critical thought are beginning to recognize and own the inescapably political purposes of education and, specifically, of critical thinking. Some are even di-recting their programs toward peace education, particularly to advance democracy in the Third World.

This was evident recently when a dialogue emerged between one of the best North American strains of the new critical thought movement and Freire's circle of theoretician-practitioners in São Paulo, Brazil. The North American partner was Philosophy for Children (P4C), an approach which employs fictional models of an ideal community where characters are presented as relating to one another with openness, cooperation, care and sensitivity.[1]

Like Freire's own work, P4C represents sound pedagogical theory and offers a well-thought-out methodology. It attempts to teach creative, dialogically-based thinking at the earliest academic levels by engaging children from pre-school on in the process of grappling with the most difficult concepts of the Western philosophical tradition. Secondly, P4C accords a central place in its pedagogy to 'moral imagination', a concept linked intimately to Freire's seminal idea of *conscientização* (Lipman *et al.* 1980: 166–71). Most importantly, extending this North American program to Freire's own Third World context offers a rare opportunity to assess what turn out to be crucial differences between the 'new wave' of US critical education and Freire's own pedagogy of the oppressed. In a Third World setting the limitations of P4C's typically North American approach to critical thought become apparent in ways which often pass unnoticed in 'developed world' contexts. Thus P4C offers a case study well suited to evoking the challenge Paulo Freire offers critical educators in general and critical peace educators in particular.

Recently P4C went beyond initial dialogue with Third World critical thinkers and implemented a peace education project in strife-torn Guatemala. This provides a concrete illustration of Philosophy for Children's usefulness as a case study demonstrating the growing edge of applied North American critical thought. The program had the express purpose of promoting democratization in Guatemala. In this context P4C, like its Freirean counterpart, attempted to fuse critical thinking and peace education in its broadest sense. And in Freirean spirit the project's details situated discussion of critical thinking in time and place. Yet close examination of these details illustrates how stressing moral imagination without emphasising Freire's *conscientização* in its full sense results in critical thinking unwittingly serving the interests of political repression rather than democracy.[2]

To show this we will outline briefly this P4C peace education project, indicating the risks involved in its limited understanding and use of moral imagination. Freire's own education for democracy through critical consciousness will then be contrasted with the P4C approach. This process of comparison and contrast will suggest how Freire's work challenges and potentially enriches North American conceptions of critical thinking for democracy as represented in Philosophy for Children.

PHILOSOPHY FOR CHILDREN IN GUATEMALA

The Guatemalan P4C program of critical thinking was implemented in July 1987 and reported in November by A. Gray Thompson and Eugenio Echeverria (1987). They claimed the time for promoting democracy in Guatemala was ripe. Commitment to democratic values and processes had been demonstrated by the December 1985 election, which brought civilian president Vinicio Cerezo to power after thirty years of military dictatorship. Cerezo and Minister of Education Eduardo Meyer Maldonaldo identified the elementary school as an indispensable site for developing the democratization process – being the sole experience of formal education shared by most Guatemalans (ibid.: 44).

The P4C methodology in Guatemala was framed by pre- and post-test administration of the New Jersey Test of Reasoning Skill (NJTRS). Children drawn from three lower-class and two middle-class elementary schools then read and discussed *Harry Stottlemeier's Discovery* (Lipman 1974), a basic P4C discussion text. Evaluation of the pilot program centered on the Democratization Observation Test (DOT), developed by North American professors and P4C's Matthew Lipman. The DOT was intended to identify teacher and student behaviors which illustrated fifteen 'democratization themes':

1 acceptance of consequences for speech and other behavior;
2 respect for others' property, for honesty and truth;
3 tolerance of dissenting opinion;
4 respect for majority opinion;
5 recognition of situations where voting is irrelevant;
6 readiness to revise opinions in the light of further evidence;
7 avoidance of behavior threatening to others;
8 participation in discussing controversial issues;
9 use of logical argument for persuasive purposes;
10 treatment of others with courtesy and fairness;
11 contributions to forming a community of inquiry through listening and dialogue;
12 respect for cultural pluralism without necessarily adopting ethical relativism;
13 respect for the rule of law and for individual rights;
14 participation in discussion of contemporary events;
15 use and reinforcement of correct speech and behavior relative to the previous themes.

Thompson and Echeverria claim the pilot project enjoyed promising success. Teachers and students applauded discussion replacing traditionally dominant rote learning. Addressing students by name rather than number gave welcome relief from the impersonal formality of customary teacher–student relationships (ibid.: 47). The post-test yielded higher NJTRS scores.

Finally, evidence of students' increased democratic awareness appeared in observations of 'democratic behavior' based on DOT measures, indicating that students were polite, calling one another and their teachers by name, and entering discussion freely – looking within themselves and to each other for answers, rather than to teachers. They supported their statements with evidence, but felt free to give wrong or dissenting answers without revealing guilt feelings or having such feelings induced by responses from teachers or peers. Students sought consensus for opinions expressed in class, but accepted being outvoted without resentment or necessarily abandoning their minority opinions. They discussed democracy and the obligations of responsible citizenship and entered into dialogue about controversial issues such as superstition, newspaper advertisements, the meaning of idiomatic expressions and the racial composition of Guatemalan society – often sharing these classroom-generated discussions at home with their parents (ibid.: 48–50).

Thompson and Echeverria were confidently hopeful that the pilot's success would bring sponsorship of a three-year experiment in Guatemala, following favorable evaluation by the National Endowment for Democracy located in the US, by Guatemala's Association for Research and the Social Sciences, and by a sample of Guatemalan teachers (ibid.: 51).

CRITICAL THINKING AND MORAL IMAGINATION

The program clearly has much to recommend it when compared to conventional Guatemalan pedagogy. It also reflects many of the characteristics Freire assigns to the process of critical thought, beginning with the central place accorded student empowerment and democratic processes within and outside the classroom. It rejects 'banking' education, endorses dialogue as the uniquely privileged vehicle for teaching–learning and for sharpening critical skills, and insists on articulate analysis of democratic 'themes'. Finally, both approaches emphasize the centrality of 'moral imagination', responding to widespread invocation of the imaginative faculty by leading peace educators (Rivage-Seul 1987: 153). Even so, we will argue that the conception of 'moral imagination' embodied in P4C's approach shows a lack of incisive consciousness which ingenuously lends critical thinking to the service of anti-democratic interests.

This deficiency is noteworthy since the imaginative faculty is specifically singled out by the P4C movement itself as 'of the utmost importance' to its process of critical thought (Lipman *et al.* 1980: 166–71). Accordingly, P4C understands the exercise of imagination in terms of planning for the future and analyzing part–whole relationships involving connections of means and ends. The morally imaginative process is defined as:

> (1) thinking creatively; (2) envisaging the various ways in which an existing unsatisfactory situation might be transformed; (3) anticipating the goals which a moral individual or moral community might seek; (4) considering alternative ways to reach each goal; (5) selecting the preferred ways; and (6) planning implementation of the objectives.
>
> (ibid.: 172–3)

These descriptive definitions might aptly be summarized by the phrase 'anticipatory moral imagination', since they are mostly future-oriented and basically anticipate and evaluate outcomes of alternative possible actions. Significantly, however, this orientation toward the future proceeds from a present frame of reference which goes largely uncriticized, at least in any etiological sense. In the present case, this would encourage uncritical acceptance of a baseline of democratic commitment in Guatemala and that democracy can arise out of existing economic, social and political arrangements. Indeed, the very opening of Thompson and Echeverria's report indicates such an acceptance:

> Guatemala committed itself to democratic values and processes in its election of December, 1985 ... [It] created a new constitution with provision for democratic presidential elections monitored and declared 'democratic' by a score of other nations ... The elected government must ward off coups for the time being while democracy takes root. It is this 'time being' that is critical. The life-sustaining blood of democracy must begin flowing through the veins of the elementary school children of Guatemala rather than in its streets. Only when the majority population of Guatemala can freely take advantage of the

promises made in the name of 'democracy' will democratization have a chance of being realized.

(Thompson and Echeverria 1987: 44)

This mirrors not only a typically North American understanding of democratic commitment but also the Guatemalan government's official position, which is contested by significant segments of the population. It identifies democratic commitment with central government's drafting a constitution and holding elections certified as 'democratic' by other nations. We are told this democratic process is threatened by the military, whose coups must be warded off 'while democracy takes root'. Less clearly, it may also be threatened by those whose blood has been poured out in the streets of Guatemala's cities in clashes, presumably, with the military. In this precarious situation the hope for realising the promise of democracy lies with elementary schools, which must induct children into the ways of democracy by:

- stimulating them to think;
- improving their cognitive skills so that they may reason together;
- developing their ability to think reasonably and responsibly when confronted with moral problems whether personal, social, or political;
- challenging them to think about significant concepts from the philosophical tradition.

(ibid.: 45)

Here the project approaches the problem of democratization as being primarily cognitive. The founding belief seems to be that teaching children to think reasonably, responsibly and philosophically can eventually empower the Guatemalan majority to take advantage of democracy's promises. The implication is that democracy is not being realized because of deficiencies in reasoning on the part of Guatemalan adults. Hopes for democracy's full implementation are thus pinned on elementary schoolchildren, who, despite the fact that most attend school for no more than a few years, are to bring reason to Guatemala's political processes in a generation or so.

The implied devaluation of Guatemalans' understanding and rationality concerning democratic processes ignores the existence of a highly developed critique of what presents itself as democracy in Latin America generally and Guatemala in particular (see below). This is worrying from a critical standpoint.

In the Thompson and Echeverria study children are encouraged to discuss democracy and the responsibility of citizens within a democratic society. They are directed to examine the questions 'Who is a citizen?' and 'Who must be responsible?' (ibid.: 50). In all of this the larger context framing the inquiry passes unexamined. The term 'democracy' is apparently treated unproblematically, as if its practical meaning were self-evident and no struggle existed in Guatemala between government and the armed opposition over the theoretical and practical definition of democracy.

Similarly, students in the P4C course discuss the truth of an Esso advertisement announcing that Guatemalans have the future today. In pedagogically sound fashion their teachers ask them to list the characteristics of the future and those of today (ibid.). Subsequent discussion, however, apparently ignores the historical setting of this dialogue. No evident attention is paid to the past and to examining the process by which the country came to its today, or to the connections between that process and Guatemala's problems of insurgency and counter-insurgency. It appears P4C students are not prompted to discuss the reasons for Esso's investment in Guatemala, or the significance of the presence in the country of over 400 US corporate branches, subsidiaries and affiliates, together constituting the largest US investment in all of Central America (Goudvis and Richter 1987: 2). Finally, it appears that students participating in the P4C project fail to examine critically the apparent and related contradiction between Guatemala's rich natural resources, including oil, and the widespread grinding poverty of its great majority.

Freire and moral imagination

This sort of historically positivistic understanding of moral imagination contrasts significantly with Freire's related concept of *conscientização* which he translates as 'critical perception of reality' or as 'critical understanding'. Freire's notion supplies two dimensions not prominent in P4C's understanding of morally imaginative education for critical consciousness. First, the Freirean approach works to historify situations in which students find themselves immersed. Secondly, it provides a critical stance not found in the pedagogy of those whose perspective is determined by the viewpoint of an elite hierarchy.

The first important difference between Freire's approach to exercising moral imagination and that of Philosophy for Children is that while P4C posits a *present* from which extrapolations are made, *conscientização* is comprehensively *historical*. For Freire, critical perception of reality objectifies those situations in which students find themselves immersed and which they perceive as given and 'normal', revealing them as *historical*. In this Freire counters what he sees as the essentially conservative function of all mainstream schooling, whereby education is concerned with reforming individuals so that their political, social, and economic contextual system functions well. In less 'penetrating' versions of critical thought, improving the world means making the status quo work. Freire says of such education that 'the important thing is accommodation to this "normalized" today' (1972: 8). Where emphasis remains on behavioral and attitudinal changes of the kind sought in the Guatemalan P4C program, Freire detects manipulation by oppressive forces:

> The interests of the oppressors lie in 'changing the consciousness of the oppressed, not the situation which oppresses them' . . . for the more the oppress-ed can be led to adapt to that situation, the more easily they can be dominated . . . The solution . . . is not to 'integrate' them into the structure of oppression,

but to transform that structure so that they can become 'beings for themselves'. [This] of course, would undermine the oppressors' purposes . . .

(Freire 1972: 63)

The educational goal of transforming oppressive structures is not primarily concerned with abstract reasoning skills as such. Rather, it is contingent upon objectifying for criticism this 'normalized today', the very context of thought.

This essentially historical objectification is what Costa Rican Franz Hinkelammert refers to as the 'categorical limits of perception', which are simply assumed as given in most analyses (1984: 161). In his own work on the imaginative faculty Hinkelammert tacitly sheds light on the distinction between Freire's and P4C's uses of moral imagination. He differentiates between merely 'conceptual' imagination and what he terms its 'transcendental form'. 'Conceptual imagination' corresponds to P4C's usage, since it refers to the limits of the possible conceived within categories established by particular socio-political systems (ibid.: 161). This subordinates the welfare of individual human beings to institutions which are simply taken for granted as universal, essential and unalterable. As Freire puts it, an institution of this type is 'mythified', in that it is seen as 'a fixed entity, as something to which humans,[3] as mere spectators, must adapt' (1972: 135–6).

Meanwhile, Hinkelammert's transcendental imagination captures the heart of Freire's *conscientização*. For in its transcendental form imagination places critical human subjectivity rather than institutional preservation at the center of the possible. In Freire's terms it is the drive to humanization, and is comprehensively historical because the process treats human beings as subjects who relativize or historicize their institutional reality, not as objects relegated simply to fulfilling ahistorical institutional requirements. At baseline, moral imagination envisions what is humanly possible in terms of providing the food, shelter and clothing necessary to keep human subjects alive. From this perspective basic material necessities provide a floor whose absence renders the trappings of formal democracy not only meaningless but counter-productive.[4]

Hinkelammert argues that pursuit of social goals or the preservation of institutions which thwart the maintenance of life by other members of the community in question are 'humanly impossible', hence beyond the bounds of practical consideration (1984: 162). Freire similarly denounces such pursuits as 'dehumanising'. Given this, sacrificing human life to maintain as sacrosanct institutions of formal democracy, the free enterprise system, or the reigning distribution of land would represent a failure of moral imagination.[5]

The pedagogical upshot of Freire's use of moral imagination comes in his distinction between two layers of knowing or two levels of critical thought. The first is exemplified in the P4C program, addressing itself to a respectful dialogue between participants in the learning process, teachers and students alike. The second reflects a deeper knowing, involving what Freire calls 'structural perception', or an understanding of the social system which violently keeps people from experiencing its benefits (Freire 1985: 48). It is this level that is absent from most North American critical thought programs, such as P4C. In this connection Freire explains:

> an act of knowing implies the existence of two interrelated contexts. One is the context of authentic dialogue between learners and educators as equally knowing subjects. This is what schools should be – the theoretical context of dialogue. The second is the real, concrete context of facts, the social reality in which human beings exist.
>
> (ibid.: 51)

For Freire, reaching the first level of criticism without cutting through to the second is not merely insufficient. It is positively dangerous. It is insufficient because it ends in what Freire sees as a kind of impotent 'Socratic intellectualism', which equates clarification of concepts with the essence of knowing. While laudably characterized by dialogue, such pedagogy ignores the historicity of what is known. In the Socratic view true knowledge is independent of history: a simple recollection of what was known before birth (ibid.: 55).

For Freire, Socratic epistemology of this type is cripplingly dangerous. It alienates would-be analysts, inducing them needlessly to adjust to the mythified structures responsible for their alienation in the first place. As if by default these structures come to be understood as natural and eternal, incapable of the structural change necessary for authentic human liberation. 'There is no other road to humanization . . . than authentic transformation of the dehumanising structure' (ibid.: 49).

Moral imagination and Third World critical theory

Critical thinking which accepts ahistorically the parameters of thought as defined by guardians of the reigning social structure deprives itself of a second element which distinguishes Freire's notion of moral imagination from that inherent in approaches to critical thought like Philosophy for Children. It excludes the 'pedagogy of the oppressed' in the sense of what the exploited have to teach others about how the world works.

This denies critical thought an 'Archimedean point' external to the reigning social-economic system, from which that context might be criticized thoroughly. For Freire that point is located in the experience of those who are simultaneously exploited by the systems in question and excluded from its benefits. The oppressed have much to gain and little to lose by indicating how political and other arrangements do them definite harm rather than the good claimed by the sovereign center. Consequently they have much to teach enthralled beneficiaries of the system who are typically incapable of seeing its vitiating characteristics.

The Argentinian Enrique Dussel corroborates and explains more fully Freire's point about the critical privilege of the marginalized. He says that for marginal persons to enact their critique it is not necessary for them to be aware of their abuse, much less to analyze it in a manner acceptable to academics. It is not even required that the oppressed speak. Impersonal statistics such as those revealing high structural unemployment among the poor in political economies where the technological drive is toward ever more efficient 'labor-saving' devices imply criticism that is harsh enough (Dussel 1977: 54). In Guatemala 45 per cent of the workforce is unemployed or underemployed, and 71 per cent of the total population and 84 per cent of Amerindians are illiterate. Meanwhile 2 per cent of the population controls two-thirds of the nation's land, and four of every five peasant families in the country live at or near the destitution level (Bermudez 1986: xv).

In a more personal way, says Dussel, the poor's silent presence, the very appearance of their rude faces, is enough to undermine the entire system (op. cit: 49). The pre-verbal and more formal utterances of the poor indict the system even more radically. These include the inconsolable cries of famished infants and the prolonged, agonized 'Agh!' of their parents undergoing torture at the hands of representatives of property owners. But most devastatingly, especially in a world whose principal agricultural problem is a global food surplus, they embrace the words 'I am hungry; I have the right to eat' (ibid.: 48).

In the case of Guatemala, silenced voices of the type cited by Dussel are readily at hand. They contradict starkly the analysis on which the P4C project is built, suggesting that despite good intentions a program like Philosophy for Children in Guatemala is counter-productive in the ways we have indicated.

Fernando Bermudez, a Roman Catholic missionary in Guatemala among the Pocomchi Amerindians, and in Mexico among Guatemalan refugees, offers the following description of Guatemala's recent move toward democracy as seen by the people he serves:

> The military is not endangered by civilians coming to power, as it already fields a whole counterinsurgency program that guarantees its retention of all real power ... There is no real point in having a civilian government because all actual power is in the hands of the military. The new civilian government will be no more than a democratic facade, a mask for the military to hide behind as it continues to repress and murder the people as it has been doing for thirty years ... Thus civilian government installed in 1986 is part of the Guatemalan military's facade for the world, part of its counterinsurgency plan, and part of the overall Central American strategy of the United States. Who will benefit from the installation of the new government? Only the ruling oligarchy. The people will go on suffering hunger, misery, repression, and death.
>
> (Bermudez 1986: 52–3)

According to Bermudez and others, genocidal abuses continue under the Cerezo government, conferring on Guatemala in the process the dubious distinction of being 'still the worst violator of human rights in the Western Hemisphere' (Simon 1988: 6). A New York Times article from February 1988 quoted a Western diplomat as saying in reference to Guatemala's ongoing post-election violence: 'If there is another country in the world where human life is so cheap, I don't know what country it would be.'

Despite the claims of Guatemala's critical thinkers that such words describe the reality of the vast majority of the country's population, there is no room for such articulations in approaches to critical thought like that of the Guatemalan P4C program. Much less are such voices, silences and pre-verbal utterances embraced as offering a perspective for thought at its most critical level. This exclusion of the pedagogy offered by the oppressed is a further manifestation of the way US critical thought adopts as uniquely valid the very analysis of political power which Freire turns upside down: an analysis which routinely omits documentable accounts recording the significant memories of the great majority who lack political power, and neglects specific experiences which 'scientific' bodies of knowledge exclude as irrelevant and falling outside their purview. 'Science' deems such information merely popular in character, and/or local, regional, particular, unsystematized and incapable of theoretical organization. It does not count because it issues from the unschooled or from such marginal groups as psychiatric patients, the sick, the delinquent, peasants, the illiterate, and the like (Foucault 1980: 82). In most cases it centers on the various struggles of those who do not count against those who possess public power (ibid.: 83).

PAULO FREIRE'S EDUCATION FOR CRITICAL CONSCIOUSNESS

Paulo Freire's exercise of moral imagination in the sense of *conscientização* focuses precisely on the experience of those whose facts are discounted in critical thinking programs grounded in a standpoint unconsciously assumed on the Capitol steps, on the verandas of the elite, or on the parade grounds of the military barracks. This is evident throughout his writing and in his various programs implemented in Brazil, Chile, Guinea-Bissau, Nicaragua, Grenada, and elsewhere. While Freire's approach emphasizes in common with P4C the values of team preparation of teaching materials, critical thinking, dialogue, and the eventual 'withering away' of the teacher's office in favour of student direction, it nonetheless contrasts in important ways with that of Philosophy for Children on some of these very dimensions.

Consider, for example, how markedly Freire's approach to the kinds of text to be used in pedagogy for critical thinking differs from P4C's, surface similarities notwithstanding.

Freire and P4C each emphasize a team approach to preparing student in-class experience and stress the importance of text selection. In preparing materials and the Democratic Observation Test, P4C in Guatemala used the services of Marquette University scholars from several disciplines, along with Matthew Lipman, director of the Institute for the Advancement of Philosophy for Children. US experts were also employed indirectly in the program's assessment via the New Jersey Test of Reasoning Skills. *Harry Stottlemeier's Discovery* (Lipman 1974), which P4C uses with children in the US, was used in the Guatemalan project on the grounds that it challenges children 'to think about significant concepts in the philosophical tradition'. P4C evidently construes this tradition as transcending particularities of time and place (Thompson and Echeverria 1987: 45).

Freire criticizes the use of such texts in the Third World. They represent the extension of imperialism by continuing to explain the world in terms of the colonizer. 'A new thinking expressed in the colonizer's language goes nowhere' (Freire 1985: 187). In presenting the experience of well-nourished children living in metropolitan nations such texts convey to the malnourished an ideology of dependence and accommodation – especially when readings are divorced from critical examination of social context. Critical examination should address questions like: 'How do the children in the P4C book get to enjoy the type of life led by North Americans of that social class?' and 'Why are North Americans typically well fed while Guatemalans are not?'. Ignoring such questions and simply transplanting texts from one cultural situation to another displays a false universalism which perpetuates a political illiteracy. For Freire

> the universality of a knowledge stripped of its historical-sociological conditioning, the role of philosophy in explaining the world as merely an instrument for our acceptance of the world, education as pure exposition of facts that transfer abstract values purported to be the inheritance of a pure knowledge – all of these are beliefs proclaimed by the naive consciousness of the political illiterate.
>
> (1985: 104)

Given this, dialogue cannot transcend 'exposition of facts' when discussion fails to interrogate thoroughly the social realities underpinning what is discussed. It reduces to 'Socratic intellectualism' (ibid.: 55).

Freire's own approach insists that texts must find their roots in the daily experience of local students, not in experience shaped directly by the developed world. The scholars who make up his planning team must do extensive research into local experience and 'texts' must be as laconic as possible. In fact, he urges that students themselves play the pivotal role in by supplying their own 'vocabulary universe'. Freire contrasts the earlier approach with his own:

> The educator can organize a program only through investigating this vocabulary universe; the world defined by the given words. The program in this form comes from the learners and is later returned to them, not as a dissertation, but as a problem or the posing of a problem. Conversely, through the other kind of practice we discussed earlier, when the educator develops his primer, at least from a sociocultural point of view, he arbitrarily selects his generative words from books in his library, a process generally considered valid throughout the world.
>
> (1985: 12)

Hence Freire prescribes extensive codification of student experience, most often in the form of an illustration or photograph posing a central problem drawn from the daily lives of the discussants themselves. 'Central' implies a problem perceived by learners as immediate and insurmountable in the context of their efforts to survive. Such problems comprise 'limit situations' (1972: 92). They appear insurmountable because they are linked to larger social conditions which are invariably mythified by those who benefit from existing arrangements and want them maintained *in toto*. By analyzing such codifications critically students are able to perceive not only the false mythification but also the relation of their immediate problem to a larger thematic structure. Even more importantly, they can identify action ('limit acts') which might transform their immediate situation and initiate creative responses to larger structural difficulties.

If we look to the materials and approach used in recent years by Freire's circle of literacy and post-literacy teachers in São Paulo[6] we also find marked differences from P4C's approach to critical thinking along the dimensions of *dialogue focus, social analysis* and *program evaluation*.

The São Paulo materials comprise 21 slide codifications in which a drama unfolds for participants to discuss and analyze in the light of their own experiences. Briefly, the sequence is as follows.

In the first eight slides a woman, presumably a slum dweller like the 'learners themselves', goes to a store but does not have enough money for what she wants to buy. She leaves the store distressed. She talks outside to a neighbor who directs the 'heroine' to a Freirean 'cultural circle' discussion group. Together its members discover how her problem is linked to a wider economic picture.

The next ten slides address the problematic situation as a whole. They portray the start of the food production and distribution process with the farmer plowing and sowing, using 'primitive' equipment. The 'middle man' then arrives and pays the farmer a slim wad of notes for a lot of grain. The middle man next delivers the grain to a warehouse, receiving a handsome payment. The codifications then follow the grain to the supermarket and local convenience store where it emerges as expensive products.

The final three slides show the original woman at the wholesaler's. She and her friends are seen unloading goods which they have purchased much more cheaply as a cooperative venture. This lends the sequence its title: 'Let's make a shortcut'.

In *dialogue* a group studying the slide codification might discuss such questions as: who is this woman and where is she from? Might she have come to the city from the country in search of a better life? Has she found one? Does she have a job, and if not, why? Can she address her situation? Could she, perhaps, obtain food more cheaply? How? Are prices artificially and unjustly high? Who benefits from existing arrangements, and could these be changed? In such ways fatalism and myths can be unveiled and challenged.

Plausible transformative action, however, depends upon sound analysis. *Social analysis* might proceed by asking how basic commodities based on local production get to cost so much. Can we reinvent the social process by which so much 'value' or cost is added? Will this deeper analysis provide clues to means of obtaining food that ordinary city dwellers can afford?

How is the learning program to be *evaluated*? What counts as a successful outcome of democratic learning? The final slide sequence, where the woman and her cooperative purchase more cheaply from the wholesaler, represents the

Freirean equivalent of the Democratic Observation Test. Here the practice of democracy emerges as a *praxis* – the goal and touchstone of Freirean education for critical consciousness. The aim of democratization is to enable people to intervene in daily life in ways that allow them to meet their interests on a just basis – on terms of equal dignity, actualization, and fulfilment with other people. Freire's approach focuses much more obviously on practical democracy at the local level than the Guatemalan variant of Philosophy for Children, where concern with practice is almost entirely limited to interpersonal relationships in the classroom. Rather than merely emerging from 'critical thinking for democracy' with inert knowledge of 'democratic' processes and new layers of myth and mystified 'awareness', the heroine of the São Paulo program leaves with an obvious smile. In Freire's terms she is experiencing her own sense of empowerment, which is not illusory. She has experienced actually overcoming a limit situation. Beyond that, other horizons of change are, perhaps, opening as she and her community move toward fuller and real control of their lives and circumstances. They have moved toward effective democracy.

PAULO FREIRE'S CHALLENGE TO NORTH AMERICAN APPLIED CRITICAL THINKING

Freire's approach to critical thinking announces its clearest challenge to typical North American versions of applied critical thought precisely at the point of a shared concern about democracy. His definition of democracy differs markedly from that in versions of critical thinking like P4C. The assumptions underpinning his approach to democratic education indicate where North American critical thought might achieve a deeper awareness of how to employ moral imagination within critical thinking for peace education. These include reconceptualizing democracy, understanding hegemony and the impossibility of class neutrality, and realizing the need for conscious partiality on the part of all teachers who aspire to be peace educators.

Democracy

Absence of a pedagogy of the oppressed in the Guatemalan project is evident from the outset of Thompson and Echeverria's report. They accept as uniquely authentic a US model of democracy highly suspect in a Third World context. For Latin American critics the major problem with this model is its pretense to universality, compounded by North Americans imposing *their* notion on the developing world, where it is ill suited.

'Democracy' is *not* univocal for Latin American critical thought. Different conceptions are typically advocated by rich and poor respectively in the Third World. These differences lie at the heart of political and military struggles in Guatemala and throughout the 'less developed' world. Such struggles are less between democratic and anti-democratic forces than between forces championing competing ideas of democracy. Nobel Peace Prize winner Adolfo Perez Esquivel goes to the heart of this competition when he asks:

> what kind of democracy are we talking about? A real democracy or a formal democracy where nothing changes? The only way to consolidate a democratic process is through the full respect of human rights and the right to justice for everyone equally. And this is still not the case in Guatemala.
>
> (Goudvis and Richter 1987: 17)

Esquivel isolates three ideas crucial to Third World thought about democracy, typically unnoticed by North Americans, including those concerned with analytic teaching. The first is 'formal democracy'; the second Esquivel calls 'real democracy', and Freire 'fundamental democratization' (Freire 1973: 15); the third is the essential connection between 'real democracy' and social justice.

The notion of formal democracy championed by the United States originates in a view that political power resides in what Michel Foucault calls a nation's 'sovereign center': the apparatus of government, presidents and parliaments (Foucault 1980: 100). Significant political decisions are seen as made on these sites. For example, *government* decrees that elections will be held and human rights to universal suffrage, to freedom of the press and to assemble will be respected. Following elections, the political system is declared 'democratic'. Meanwhile decades of fraudulent elections, egregious violations of elementary human rights, government-related death squads and disappearances are explained away as anomalies which central authority is powerless to surmount. In this view the economic situations of citizens have no bearing on judgment concerning the presence or absence of 'democracy', since politics and economics are understood as separate realms.

Esquivel's 'real democracy' contests this ethnocentrically North American and European understanding. His concept, grounded in the Third World, understands political power in a radically different way from its First World counterpart. It denies that power is the exclusive possession of 'the sovereign center'. Instead, structures through which the *demos* exercises decision-making capacity are located in the school, the church, the family, corporations, the means of social communication, labor unions, etc. (Coraggio 1985: 33). In these sites people exercise primary and local control of their lives. On the national level, those possessing such power are seen as more directly represented by members of their socio-economic reference group than by professional politicians from the upper classes. In this model the emphasis is not on the pluralism of two or a handful of political parties, but on that provided by 'mass organizations' with direct representation in national assemblies, even if such representation takes place under the aegis of a single party (ibid.: 49–50).

In such arrangements the presence or absence of democracy is determined by the practical effectiveness of the majority's day-to-day decision-making power, rather than universal suffrage exercised periodically in national elections involving plural parties. 'Real democracy' places ordinary citizens, not their directors, at center stage for evaluating democratic performance (ibid.: 27). The legitimacy of a central government does not depend either exclusively or fundamentally on how it came to power. Instead it is determined by the way that government defines and manages the public interest and contradictions between that and special pleadings (ibid.: 30).

This link between Esquivel's notion of real democracy and social justice is based on an understanding that politics and economics are so interwoven we can speak meaningfully only in terms of 'political economy'. This term reflects a perception that politics comprises a superstructure built on economic infrastructures of the type Freire refers to in his notion of 'structural perception'. Consequently, this approach pays particular attention to the economic welfare of a nation's least well-off (ibid.: 27). Their welfare becomes the touchstone for determining national prosperity. A government favoring the minority while neglecting or oppressing the majority or proving incapable of providing for their safety and economic well-being would be considered undemocratic.

Hegemony and neutrality

Central to this critical perspective on social justice and democracy is the notion of hegemony, which refers to the fact that those who hold economic power in a given society are also in charge of political processes. They set before society what Antonio Gramsci calls its *social project*, corresponding to the interests of the ruling class, which militate against the interests of those without hegemonic power. In Guatemala's case the property-owning minority supported by the military exercises effective veto power over political policies which protect its class project: viz., retaining the 'sacred' institution of private property and accumulation of capital by private individuals.[7] Vinicio Cerezo recognized this hegemony when, shortly after taking office, he pledged: 'My government will not plan social reforms, because the army would oppose it' (Hernon and Malone 1986: 4).

Hence critical thought aspiring to *depth* within peace education for democracy cannot ignore class struggle and bias. As Freire insists, it cannot be class-neutral; failure to acknowledge this lies at the heart of naive approaches to critical thinking. Freire observes repeatedly that whatever is taught is inevitably taught in favor of one group's interests and against those of another (see, for example, Freire 1972: 53–6; Freire 1978: 23–4, 88, 102; Collins 1977: 17, 53, 79, 89). This class bias finds its most subtle and effective presence in material social structures which end up channelling human decisions in directions that benefit dominant classes while militating against the interests of subordinate groups. For Freire any 'Democratic Observation Test' would have to address those structures and the decision-making process, asking: (1) Who benefits from the decisions and structures?; (2) Who pays the cost inherent in them?; and (3) Who decides about the configurations of the structures and the directions of the policies? (Holland and Henriot 1983: 28). Answers to such questions deepen rather than conceal important realities of class bias and hegemony.

Such realities remain opaque to 'class-neutral critical thought' of the kind evident in the Guatemalan P4C program. This program passes up definite opportunities to delve below the surface of the officially sanctioned 'normal today'. One specific example is evident in the report's 'homogenizing' of test scores from the poor and middle-class schools where the program was implemented. Results from poor schools (*Fe y Alegria*) do not appear in Thompson and Echeverria's report of NJTRS post-tests. They explain:

> All the schools in the project were administered the NJTRS Test at the beginning of the program. Because of a variety of salary considerations for the *Fe y Alegria* faculties, emergency meetings were scheduled. These meetings interrupted the pilot schedule, consequently these schools are not included in the results. However, there is no reason to believe that the results would not approximate those from the other two schools.
>
> (Thompson and Echeverria 1987: 47)

That the authors see 'no reason' to believe that test scores from 'the poorest of the poor' (ibid.: 46) would not approximate those of near-middle- and middle-class students appears to rule out the possibility that class considerations might make a difference in the results of the schooling process.

Even more revealing is the reference to cancelling classes for emergency meetings about 'a variety of salary considerations'. This appears insensitive to class struggles contextualizing the experiences of students in lower-class schools, which may well make these experiences significantly different from those of their better-off counterparts. This is notable since, according to the authors, teachers at the *Fe y Alegria* schools receive about half the pay of their colleagues in public (state) schools (ibid.: 47). This disparity raises the question of whether the 'emergency meetings', class cancellations, and failure to complete the P4C program may have been strike-related. This question, so rich in its possibilities for raising issues about the quality and purposes of education, goes unanswered since it too is 'normalized' into the class-neutral reporting of the P4C facilitators.

Conscious partiality

The questions ignored by critical thinking of the P4C variety and the structures not plumbed in the process illuminate the necessity of making explicit the inescapable political commitments held by anybody involved in morally imaginative critical thought. Freire says that, regardless of teachers' intentions, all schooling and all learning are inevitably political and committed in class terms; they cannot escape being partial toward and against the interests of others:

> The political makeup of education is independent of the educator's subjectivity ... When an educator finally understands this, she or he can never again escape the political ramifications. An educator has to question himself or herself about options that are inherently political, though often disguised as pedagogical to make them acceptable within the existing structure. Thus, making choices is

most important. Educators must ask themselves for whom and on whose behalf they are working.

(Freire 1985: 180)

The committed nature of education repeatedly affirmed by Freire runs the risk of being ignored within new strains of critical thought. Indeed, if we consider the structured silences in the P4C program we see how pretensions to uncommitted objectivity actually help the Guatemalan government establish locally and internationally its claim that it is in fact democratic. Moreover, regardless of whether one agrees or disagrees with the claim, accepting its practical validity and leaving it unquestioned represents a political option on the part of P4C in support of the Cerezo government and against the dissenting constituency represented by Bermudez and by the Guatemalan Army of the Poor. Acceptance effectively comprises an option in support of the Guatemalan ruling classes.

For Freire, this function would be further indicated by scrutiny of the program's supporters: the Guatemalan government and the ultra-conservative National Endowment for Democracy. According to Freire, support from such sources not only indicates a choice against fundamental change in a given society; practically speaking, it also nullifies the very possibility of enhancing truly critical thought. He insists 'it would be extremely naive to expect the dominant classes to develop a type of education that would enable subordinate classes to perceive social injustices critically' (Freire 1985: 102, 160).

With such realizations in mind, Freire directs critical thinkers away from pretensions to objectivity, which serves the status quo, and toward an open political option referred to by Kathleen Weiler as 'conscious partiality' (Weiler 1988: 62, 67, 70). This notion indicates that the choice for analytic teachers and students is not about the *advisability* of adopting a committed stance. Rather, the choice is between an unconscious and a conscious commitment. Conscious partiality has teachers choose to render explicit to themselves and to their students their own biases, while openly admitting that the perspectives pursued in their classes are necessarily limited and therefore partial by virtue of the institutional, curricular, and personal elements which inevitably contextualize the teaching–learning process. This, of course, alerts students to hidden agendas while defending them against subtle manipulation.

The partiality recommended here goes still further. It must also guide teachers in identifying questions posed for discussion and texts selected as resources. Clearly, both are inevitably influenced by considerations of value reflecting the socio-economic background, political convictions, and perceptual limits of the chooser. Indeed, these very matters of history, commitment, and limits commonly form the discussion focus in the educational programs of oppressed groups themselves. Arguably, those who benefit or aspire to do so from the status quo can afford to ignore such matters.

Freire exercises his own conscious partiality in favor of the poor by his choice of themes for discussion within culture circles. These choices echo criteria expressed by Dussel for determining the focus of teaching.

In the first place, the absolute criterion is: choose a theme that is real. From among the real, choose the most urgent. From among the most urgent themes, select those which have greater transcendence.[8] From among the most transcendent, choose those which refer to the people who are most numerous and most oppressed – those who stand on the brink of death from hunger and despair.

(Dussel 1977: 180)

According to Freire, such themes are not only suitable for adult literacy classes but can also profitably be raised with children: that is, at the level with which P4C is concerned. Freire writes that eventually it dawned on him that he could in fact raise the same themes with children as he used with adults. 'I asked, Why not write about the same themes I have been putting into practice when I talk with my adult students? What is underdevelopment? What is nationalism? What is democracy?' (Freire 1985: 176).

CONCLUSION

We have aimed to illustrate Freire's contribution to peace education understood as the exercise of moral imagination in the service of critical thinking. From a negative angle, our discussion shows the dangers of ignoring the socio-historical realities of learners which occurs when texts and methods from an economically developed liberal democratic context are simply transplanted in a setting that is economically underdeveloped and oppressive. Despite using dialogue, simple transferral risks what Freire calls 'assistencialism', 'cultural invasion' and 'extension' (Freire 1972: 150; Freire 1973: 115, 93–145). Freire's observations about 'extension' might well apply to the implementing of such critical thinking programs as P4C in the Third World. Acts of extension

transform people into 'things' and negate their existence as beings who transform the world . . . They further negate the formation and development of real knowledge. They negate the true action and reflection which are the objects of these actions.

(Freire 1973: 95)

This may seem excessively harsh when applied to a program of high quality like Philosophy for Children. P4C clearly is respectful of its students and aims to avoid any vestige of mechanical transfer and manipulation. Even so, there *is* something mechanically 'assistencial' in transplanting a text which ignores the socio-cultural and political contexts of those who will learn from it. There is also an element of cultural messianism in P4C's neglect of Guatemalan critical thought about democracy as well as in its attempts to achieve class-neutrality.

More positively, it might be argued that a critical thinking program like Thompson and Echeverria's is more than merely well intentioned. It did the best it could within an educational system like Guatemala's, where the government is extremely suspicious of and repressive toward 'subversive' teaching (Thompson and Echeverria 1987: 44). Indeed, it is not far from the mark to suggest that for a Guatemalan to engage in Freirean pedagogy within the atmosphere that prevails is virtually to sign his or her own death warrant. For North Americans to do so would be impossible since a Freirean project would not be funded; nor would it be sanctioned by the host government. Given such circumstances P4C acted prudently. Moreover, it *did* achieve something in terms of critical thinking, and something is better than nothing at all.

It *might* be argued that the authors of the P4C program exercised moral imagination in the sense of what Freire calls 'limit acts' or Henry Giroux and Michael Apple have called 'possibility thinking' and 'non-reformist reforms' respectively (Giroux 1983: 203; Apple 1982: 134). All three terms indicate that employing imagination need not involve a purist, all-or-nothing approach to social change, which would refuse cooperation with any reform movement short of full-blown revolution. Instead, Giroux and Apple seem to urge working for change that is possible today in the hope that small reforms might both alter unacceptable present conditions and lead to significant structural change in the future. Maybe P4C's authors recognized the practical confines of an oppressive situation and sought to exploit 'cracks' in the system by doing what is possible today within highly restrictive institutional limits, rather than leaving the field entirely open to the exploiters (Aronowitz and Giroux 1985: 106).

Caution is in order, however. There are real differences between P4C and, for example, the Freirean-inspired theory of Henry Giroux, which warns against satisfaction with mere reforms not aimed at *more fundamental* targets. Giroux insists that exploiting the 'language of possibility' entails not only exploring with students the oppressive ideological content of academic material, but also joint discovery of the unintentional subversive truths frequently contained therein. By measuring society's performance against its claims, morally imaginative education in Giroux's sense would take hold of those truths and recast them in the service of liberation and of Esquivel's 'real democracy' (Giroux 1983: 160, 202). There is no indication, however, that Guatemalan P4C efforts were informed by any such subversive intent. Thompson and Echeverria seem to accept government claims at face value and report the project in terms of enculturating students into the political reality thus construed. This has obvious *domesticating* overtones, characteristic of recent North American versions of critical thinking generally and across a range of pressing issues.[9]

Furthermore, P4C's cooperation with the Guatemalan government and the publication of its report represent something of a public relations coup for a regime anxious to enhance its image and secure foreign (especially military) aid to continue a war against its own citizens.

In the final analysis the P4C project attests to the fact that there are degrees of critical thinking, and that the differences between them are *political* as well as theoretic. Depending on the form it takes, critical thought may serve the interests of life or, alternatively, of death. Paulo Freire's notion of *conscientização* challenges educators to pursue 'deeper' critical thinking which serves the interests of life. In this service the perspective furnished by the pedagogy of the oppressed necessarily assumes a central place.

NOTES

1 See Lipman, Sharp and Oscanyan (1980). See also Lipman 1974, 1976, 1977, 1979.
2 See Rivage-Seul (1987). This investigates Freire's implied use of moral imagination as it relates to peace education in the context of the nuclear arms race.
3 Here the original translation reads, 'something to which *men*, as mere spectators, must adapt' (our italics). In this as well as other citations gender-specific references have been changed to more inclusive forms. This is in the spirit of Freire's often-expressed criticism of his own earlier, less inclusive expressions.
4 Thompson and Echeverria reveal a less-than-firm conviction about this when they timidly speculate with reference to their program's provision of a school meal each day that 'learning and basic nutrition *appear* to be related' (1987: 46, our italics).
5 Mario Falla, Vice-President of the Guatemalan Association of Landowners, provides a further example of conceptual imagination. In angry response to the demand by the Guatemalan Episcopal Conference for widespread land reform, he gave voice to an idea of the possible limited by the framework of the free enterprise system. Having criticized the bishops for writing a letter resembling a proposal from the Nicaraguan clergy, he said, 'in Guatemala, land reform happens every day within the free enterprise system; owners sell their land when it ceases to be profitable. Thus land passes from hand to hand.' Falla appears incapable of thinking of the possible outside the limits of buying and selling for profit.
6 The slide presentation referred to in the text was obtained privately from contacts in São Paulo.
7 In the US the property-owning classes similarly exercise effective hegemony. While US ideology lionizes its two-party system as the epitome of democracy, from the viewpoint of social project there is really only a single party in power: viz., property owners who belong to the party's conservative wing (Republicans) or to its liberal coalition (Democrats). Both parties hold the same social project in common – capital accumulation and protection of the inviolable right to private property. Thus in the US advocates of abolishing private property are virtually without political voice and constitute an enemy to Democrats and Republicans alike.
8 By 'transcendence' Dussel refers to the viewpoint of those who, by virtue of their exclusion from the benefits of a reigning socio-economic system, exercise more critical perceptions of its shortcomings than do those who experience existing arrangements as benign and constructive.
9 Compare Rivage-Seul (1987). She shows how typical approaches remain uncritical of the parameters of discussion typically set by 'experts' representing the very interests called in question by anti-nuclear advocates.

REFERENCES

Apple, M. (1982) *Education and Power*, Boston: Routledge and Kegan Paul.
Aronowitz, S. and Giroux, H.A. (1985) *Education Under Siege*, South Hadley, MA: Bergin and Garvey.
Bermudez, F. (1986) *Death and Resurrection in Guatemala*, Maryknoll, NY: Orbis Books.
Collins, D. (1977) *Paulo Freire: His Life, Works and Thought*, New York: Paulist Press.
Coraggio, J.L. (1985) *Nicaragua: Revolución y Democracia*, Mexico DF: Editorial Linea.
Dussel, E. (1977) *Filosofia da Liberação*, São Paulo: Edicoes Loyola.

Foucault, M. (1980) *Power/Knowledge: Selected Interviews and Other Writings*, New York: Pantheon Books.

Freire, P. (1972) *The Pedagogy of the Oppressed*, London: Sheed and Ward.

—— (1973) *Education for Critical Consciousness*, New York: Seabury Press.

—— (1978) *Pedagogy in Process*, New York: Seabury Press.

—— (1985) *The Politics of Education*, South Hadley, MA: Bergin and Garvey.

Giroux, H.A. (1983) *Theory and Resistance in Education*, South Hadley, MA: Bergin and Garvey.

Goudvis, P. and Richter, R. (1987) 'Under the gun: democracy in Guatemala'. Transcript of PBS television production, New York: Robert Richter Productions.

Hernon, D. and Malone, B. (1986) 'Guatemala: a human rights tragedy', Washington DC: Network in Solidarity with the People of Guatemala (NISGUA), October 10.

Hinkelammert, F. (1984) *Crítica a la Razón Utópica*, San José: Departamento Ecuménico de Investigaciones.

Holland, J. and Henriot, SJ, P. (1983) *Social Analysis: Linking Faith and Justice*, Maryknoll, NY: Orbis Books.

Lipman, M. (1974) *Harry Stottlemeier's Discovery*, Upper Montclair, NJ: Institute for the Advancement of Philosophy for Children.

—— (1976) *Lisa*, Upper Montclair, NJ: Institute for the Advancement of Philosophy for Children.

—— (1977) *Mark*, Upper Montclair, NJ: Institute for the Advancement of Philosophy for Children.

—— (1979) *Suki*, Upper Montclair, NJ: Institute for the Advancement of Philosophy for Children.

Lipman, M., Sharp, A.M. and Oscanyan, F.S. (1980) *Philosophy in the Classroom*, 2nd edition, Philadelphia: Temple University Press.

Miller, V. (1985) *Between Struggle and Hope: The Nicaraguan Literacy Crusade*, Boulder and London: Westview Press.

Rivage-Seul, M.K. (1987) 'Peace education: imagination and the pedagogy of the oppressed', *Harvard Educational Review* 57, 2, 153–69.

Simon, J.-M. (1988) 'Government apathy toward human rights', *Report on Guatemala*, 9, 3, 6–7.

Thompson, A.G. and Echeverria, E. (1987) 'Philosophy for Children: a vehicle for promoting democracy in Guatemala', *Analytic Teaching*, 8, 1, 44–52.

Weiler, K. (1988) *Women Teaching for Change: Gender, Class and Power*, South Hadley, MA: Bergin and Garvey.

Chapter 3

Conscientization and political literacy
A British encounter with Paulo Freire

Ian Lister

INTRODUCTION: A PERSONAL NOTE

For over two decades I have worked in the related fields of political education and educational reform. In educational reform I have been most engaged with the alternative movement, and most challenged by the insights and provocations of Ivan Illich. In political education I have been most influenced and challenged by Bernard Crick, with whom I tried to elaborate a concept of 'political literacy' (Crick and Lister 1978: 37–46), and by Paulo Freire, whose work I first met in the 1970s in the samizdat manuscripts of the radicalized Student Christian Movement (which had become more concerned about the Third World than about the next world).

From 1974 on I worked on the national Programme for Political Education, which tried to introduce political literacy into English secondary schools – that is, through a planned program in formal institutions – and, while we sought to alter the distribution of socially powerful knowledge, we knew that the question which Freire posed was: Should we not be trying to do more? (We also knew that the question which Illich posed was: Should we be trying to do it at all?) The Programme for Political Education was followed by some new movements, arguing for 'global education' and focusing on such key words as 'development', 'peace', 'human rights', 'multiculturalism' and 'environment', and my own work continued in the field of teaching and learning about human rights, an area close to the work of Paulo Freire, which is essentially concerned with humanity and humanization. More recently my work has moved to education for modern citizenship, including its wider and international dimensions – again a theme close to Freire's work for common humanity. In this chapter I will seek to relate the theory and practice of Paulo Freire to the movements for political education in Britain – that is, in sequence, to political literacy, to human rights, and to education for modern citizenship.

BERNARD CRICK AND PAULO FREIRE

As the concept of political literacy in Britain is most associated with the name of Bernard Crick, I have called this section 'Bernard Crick and Paulo Freire'. This has the advantage of first presenting real people, with flesh and blood and biographies, and then presenting the key concepts – political literacy and conscientization – which may seem abstract and complicated (even though, in essence, they may be simple).

Bernard Crick and Paulo Freire are both university professors and, whatever their particular titles, both are political philosophers and political educators. Crick's important work *In Defence of Politics* appeared in 1964. In it he defended politics against its friends – 'the non-political conservative' (who claims to 'be above politics'); 'the a-political liberal' (who wishes to enjoy all the fruits of politics without paying the price or noticing the pain); and 'the anti-political socialist' (with tendencies toward dogmatism and utopianism and a reluctance to act politically). He praised politics as 'a preoccupation of free men' (p. 140) and as 'a type of moral activity . . . inventive, flexible, enjoyable and human'. In short, for Crick politics is an *activity* and a *process*. Issues about which people disagree – contested questions – are the core of politics.

The similarities with Freire are clear here. The view of politics is one based not on government, legislation and administration, but on the centrality of issues, and the importance of such general features as power and authority, discussion and debate, decision-making and resource allocation. Like Freire, Crick argues for 'a speculative recognition of alternatives'. Both are opponents of an unthinking acceptance of the status quo. Freire's work seems to overcome 'the culture of silence' (the belief that the social order is inevitable and unchangeable) and Crick's work seems to overcome those who argue that 'politics should be kept out of all areas of life, except the House of Commons, and those who present politics as limited to central government and local government (Whitehall and City Hall)' – in short, what was presented in schools as 'The British Constitution'. (To pupils this was known as 'Brit. Con.'. It was *all* Brit., and there was quite a lot of Con.)

CONSCIENTIZATION AND POLITICAL LITERACY

Freire's theory and practice of political education are associated with the key concept of 'conscientization'. Crick's theory and practice of political education are associated with the key concept of 'political literacy'. Although there are differences – conscientization has the connotation of 'consciousness raising' and of seeing the world in a new way, while political literacy has the connotation of 'reading political situations' – both are aimed at the empowerment of learners and at helping them acquire new knowledge and develop skills. Both redefine and relocate politics so that it can no longer be the preserve of professional politicians in far-away places, who send communiqués from the metropolis to the provinces, from 'the center' to 'the periphery', from above to those below. In Britain this is to challenge the presentation of politics as a gladiatorial contest between two party leaders, fought out in Parliament and television studios (and Parliament itself has now become a television studio) and, very occasionally, general elections. For the people this left politics as a kind of ritual performance, and as a spectator sport. Both Freire and Crick, in presenting politics as an ongoing *activity* and a continuing *process*, stress the importance of ordinary people as political *actors*. Some of the differences between conscientization and political literacy, in practice, are related to the way in which they operated in different contexts – the first with adults and non-formal education, the second with young adults in schools. Non-formal education and formal education afford different possibilities and present different limit situations to political educators. There are, though, a number of common problems and common opponents.

ISSUES: THEIR IDENTIFICATION AND FORMULATION

With the Freire method, issues were identified through a kind of anthropological research process – by program workers in dialogue with the people. These issues arose from life situations, and were not derived from theorizing about the nature of know ledge. In the British Programme for Political Education, issues were identified by program workers and by teachers, but rarely by the students (Stradling and Porter 1978). Issues were identified and selected according to several criteria:

1   What were the issues in the news (television and newspapers)?
2   Which issues (including issues not 'in the news') had political dimensions – that is, related to questions concerning power and authority, debate, decision-making and resource allocation?
3   Which issues seemed to have most 'pedagogical potential' – that is, were exemplary issues, which might encourage transfer in learning?

It was thought important to include local, national and international issues in the program, and to explore the local, national and international dimensions of particular issues. The program built up an issues inventory and research workers logged issues as they appeared in classroom lessons. These logged issues included:

Local issues:
• lack of adequate public transport in a new town (known as the land of a thousand roundabouts), posing mobility problems for young adults and the retired (that is, those without private transport);
• the sea wall repeatedly being breached at the end of town inhabited by the poor, with consequent flooding;
• a strike in the steelworks in Steeltown;
• National Front (a neo-Nazi group) activities in Northtown, threatening the ethnic minority population.

National issues:
• the National Health Service, and the allocation of health resources;
• cuts in education (under-funding of the public sector);
• electoral reform (including the reform or abolition of the House of Lords);
• not 'supporting "lame ducks"' versus social subsidies for British industry.

International issues:
- the Third World and poverty and the terms of trade;
- the Cold War;
- the Arab–Israeli dispute;
- the Common Market;
- minority rights;
- terrorism.

This list is representative, but not exhaustive. Issue-based teaching and learning in school classrooms raised a number of questions which the old methods (narration, digestion, regurgitation) left unasked. How might issues best be explored? Could teachers and students sympathetically review more than one side of the question, and could they see more than *two* sides of a question? (On this last, researchers found that, generally, they could not.) Were some issues comfortable, even cosy, while others were too hot to handle? (Steeltown School teachers were happy to discuss such issues as Common Market sugar beet versus Third World sugar cane, but the strike in the steelworks, on which the town largely depended, did not get onto the program.) What should teachers do when analysis of issues led to students wanting to take action? (In recent years the dumping of non-returnable bottles on the managing director's front lawn was met with general approval, but the teacher whose students wanted to lay themselves across the railway line, along which nuclear waste was transported was – in his own words – 'riding a tiger by the tail'.)

Researchers noted the absence of *local* issues in school programs – that is, those issues which afforded most access for participation and real-life (rather than book) study. Teachers claimed that students (1) were not interested in local issues, and (2) did not know much about them. Researchers felt that teachers were probably talking about themselves, and not about the students, many of whom were very interested in, and knowledgeable about, local issues. (Students lived locally, and many teachers did not.) Some teachers used the school itself as a political model, and then copped out ('teacher closure' is what the researchers called it) when students asked sensitive questions about resource allocation. ('What happens if you disagree among yourselves?', asked the student. 'There's no problem there', replied the teacher, 'We're all very reasonable people.' She then returned to the staffroom, where the issue of whether the money available would be used to buy a history teacher or a science teacher continued to be debated heatedly.)

Of course, Paulo Freire is right when he says that teachers who ask awkward questions, and who challenge 'limit situations', get into trouble. However, what worried researchers was the realization that teachers seemed to have their own self-censoring mechanism and that they set their own 'limit situations' quite a long way back from where 'the limit situation' might have been. These dilemmas will be recognizable and familiar to Freire workers and to political literacy workers. On the one hand there is the need to explore the limits of the possible. On the other there is the danger of being closed down altogether.

ACTION AND POLITICAL SKILLS

Paulo Freire views politics and education as *activities* – that is, with an important action dimension which goes beyond theory and reflection. His pedagogy is an active process, for learners as well as for teachers. It proclaims a radically new relationship between teachers and learners, between learners and fellow learners, and between learners and knowledge. Dynamic dialogue between teachers and learners may even lead to them *creating* new knowledge.

The Programme for Political Education promoted a kind of political education which went beyond political knowledge and beyond political attitudes. Much previous work had defined political knowledge as knowing the names of major political figures (presidents, prime ministers, ministers) and the main features of the machinery of government (the constitution). It was concerned with promoting attitudes which were supportive of the political system and which would facilitate civic cohesion. The Programme for Political Education, influenced by progressive educators – Dewey as well as Freire – wanted to develop the hitherto neglected area of *political skills*. If people are to be political *actors* they need the predisposition to act and they need skills for effective performance. Working on issues requires and develops skills. How to identify an issue as a *political issue*; how to analyze an issue; how to work with others on an issue; how to identify alternative courses of action; how to mobilize support; in short, how to *act* on an issue – all these are items for a possible inventory of political skills.

In schools this meant proposing the end of the conventional classroom, dominated by teacher talking and students note-taking. (In British classrooms, as in classrooms around the world, teachers and students, in Freire's striking phrase, were 'suffering from narration sickness'.) The new pedagogy was characterized by *activity-based* teaching and learning. Methods included problem-solving exercises; collaborative projects; socio-drama and role play; games and simulations. Two simulations – Star Power (about economic and political power and inequality) and Tenement (about housing problems and social inequality) – were used by the project team in all the project schools. They were used both to encourage active learning and to explore the possibilities of assessing the practice of political skills. In these key areas researchers asked themselves a lot of questions. Some of these questions are also relevant to the Freire method.

First, although many students found the games and simulations the most memorable elements in a program, some students completely misunderstood their political meaning – for example, the student who thought that a simulation aimed to explain three forms of government (dictatorship, democracy and anarchy) was really about putting sheets of cardboard together (which, with differently ordered groups to do it, was the means, and not the meaning, of the exercise). It was difficult for observers to recognize or record students *developing* skills, although some instances of skilled performance were identified. Videos were made of the simulation sessions but researchers could not find ways of using them for evaluation purposes. (The videos ended up as stimulus material for teachers' seminars.) How far did students in the program, and how far did people in Freire programs, actually *acquire* and *develop* skills, and was the skill mastery such that it could be applied, without the program workers and without Freire, on future occasions?

AN ISSUE-BASED GROUP

Mainly because of my admiration for Freire's work I thought, at one time, that the most effective political education for young adults would be, not in school classrooms, but in issue-based groups (such as Shelter, which deals with housing issues, and Amnesty International, which deals with human rights issues). In such groups people have to organize, raise funds, and campaign. Their aim is not just to understand the world, but to change it. My hope was that people in such groups would necessarily acquire and develop political skills. My hesitation was that some issue-based groups would be too issue-specific (and thus offer a narrow form of political education). To explore the possibilities and problems of political education through membership of an issue-based group, detailed research was carried out on an issue-based group in Milltown in the north of England. The group was the Milltown branch of the Anti-Nazi League which, nationally, aims to oppose any resurgence of fascism and which, in Milltown, aimed to undermine support for the National Front and for the British Movement (another neo-Nazi organization), which were particularly strong in the locality.

The researcher, who observed the group over a two-year period, produced findings which both encourage and challenge elements of the Freire method and the work of the Programme for Political Education (Webb 1981). The underlying political skill lay

> in responding to circumstances through a limited number of abilities – social sensitivity, inferring/reasoning, creative thinking, advocacy and manipulation – and in coordinating them. Situations appeared to vary in the *degree* to which those capacities were required, not in the *kind* they demanded.
>
> (ibid.: 11)

The effective application of political skills varied within individuals themselves, according to different situations, and between individuals. 'A few consistently employed these skills to greatest effect in virtually all situations' (p. 11). In short, although there was a small group of the generally skilled (the 'versatile activists'), most of the group had an uneven command of skills and some of the group had a very low level of skills (and some of these did not improve during the period of the research).

This was not because there was no concept of pedagogy – of teaching and learning skills – within the group. On the contrary, some of the most skilled acted as 'trainers', or 'coaches', inducting new members into political activities with graded tasks, or graded tests. (Fly-posters – sticking posters in places where it was forbidden – was one of the first exercises.) Group members were also *aware* of some of their shortcomings. A member who was highly articulate in academic contexts complained of his contributions at political meetings. He felt he was not getting his ideas across. Fellow members also complained about his performance. They felt that he was treating every meeting 'like a bloody seminar'. Some members improved with practice. Others did not. In its attempt to be effective *as a group* a division of labor – allocating tasks to individuals according to their skill competencies – occurred, and took priority over helping more group members acquire and develop political skills.

One of the conclusions drawn by the researcher was to confirm Freire's and our belief that 'the abilities necessary for skilled political action are acquired and developed *through practice*' (Webb 1981: 18; my italics), but he went on to say: 'Neither possession of prerequisite abilities, nor the practice of their coordination in political contexts, is by itself sufficient for the enhancement of skill' (ibid.). In short, an issue-based group in itself is not enough. Further, programs of political education through group-action projects need to have not only a coherent pedagogy but also a system of observation and evaluation (for which 'reflection' might not be fully adequate). Otherwise quite a lot of 'liberation pedagogy' might consist of hopeful intentions and acts of faith.

ACHIEVEMENTS AND LIMITATIONS

The opponents and critics of the Programme for Political Education offered arguments which would be all too familiar to Paulo Freire. Political knowledge was too complicated for immature minds. (For those who make this argument the age of immaturity has risen with the rise of the school-leaving age.) Political education was 'a Pandora's box' and opening it would lead to unforeseen, but definitely horrible, consequences. Most people did not want to participate actively in political life anyway – that is, they had *chosen* the 'culture of silence'. Proper political education was impossible to achieve in schools, where teachers were state servants and part of the bureaucracy and the status quo, and the schools were themselves a state apparatus.

The immaturity argument was made both by patrician Tories and by a conservative Communist. And Ivan Illich, for whom schools were a metaphysical category, malign if not malevolent, made us aware of the dangers of school-based programs – particularly that they might disable rather than empower. But political education, like politics, is about the art of the possible – 'an acre in Middlesex is better than a principality in Utopia' (Francis Bacon). A lot of the opposition was circumvented, and the Programme for Political Education achieved support from the Department of Education in London, from Her Majesty's School Inspectors, from leading politicians of all parties and from government ministers. It achieved a legitimacy for the concept of 'political literacy' in educational debate and planning in a remarkably short space of time – a period of just three years. The program started in 1974, and by 1977 political literacy was being recommended by leading Inspectors in the Education Ministry. The program also demonstrated that impressive programs of political education could be offered by schools and that issue-based teaching and learning, and a broader concept of 'the political', could be promoted in practice.

The program seriously under-estimated the problems of issue-based teaching and of trying to present a broad concept of the political so that politics would be relocated and relate to people's life situations. I have already raised a number of pedagogical questions about issue-based teaching. What we had not seen before we observed programs over a period of time was that a program which was entirely based on issues could be a curriculum of social pathology, with lots of lamentation and little celebration. Rather than empower students it could run the risk of confirming them in their own sense of impotence to affect major issues, such as atomic weapons. The view of politics in the culture – it is dirty, not here and not for you – was more of a barrier than we had imagined. And we had not thought how powerful conventional knowledge categories would be in framing and restricting thought. I was impressed when teachers showed to intellectually sophisticated 18-year-olds a scene from the film *Kes* in which a working-class boy is 'interviewed' by a 'careers officer'. The scene was highly political – being about power and who determines whose life situations. (Such boys do not have *careers*. They have jobs, or they are unemployed.) The not-so-hidden curriculum of the 'interview' is the careers officer telling the boy, over and over again: 'You will go down the pit. Your father went down the pit, and your brother went down the pit. So you will go down the pit.' The teacher saw this as an example of power in action, but a student did not see it that way. He just said: 'Sir, that's sociology, not politics!'

Now Paulo Freire would be less likely to encounter such barriers in his work, as he did not operate on the basis of conventional knowledge categories. However, there is a further finding from our research, concerning the nature of knowledge, which poses questions for Paulo Freire as well as for political educators in Britain, and it is appropriate to put it high on the agenda for a critical encounter among friends. It is our feeling that, in stressing the importance of *process* (particularly the application of *skills* to *issues*) we had under-valued the importance of *knowledge content*, including contextual knowledge about institutions and the law. This weakness has been further revealed by the programs of the vanguard educators, which, in the words of Howard Mehlinger, are 'goal-rich and content-poor'.

THE NEW MOVEMENTS AND PAULO FREIRE

By 1980 the political literacy movement in Britain had run out of steam (maybe it had become too respectable), just at a time when in education the conservative restoration, encouraged by a Labour prime minister in 1976, was about to be implemented during a decade of Thatcherism. A dynamism was provided by a new generation of political and social educators, who worked under the new key words like 'peace', 'development', 'human rights', 'multiculturalism' and 'environment'. Like Paulo Freire, they were humanists and humanizers – concerned with human rights and human dignity and social justice. Like Freire they sought to help realize higher levels of humanity by the dismantling of oppressive structures and the liberation of human spirit. Like Freire they stressed the importance of learning *as a process* and of relating it to living *as a process*. Like Freire they sought to enable people to view the world in a new way. (Some, in a global education movement, used 'road to Damascus phrases' like: 'When I became global'.) I have written about these vanguard educators, at length, elsewhere (Lister 1987) and I have my fraternal and sororal differences with them. (Some of them, I feel, seek to convert rather than to educate.) Here I want to highlight three aspects of their work which might illuminate our recent past and inform our future in political education.

The first is that they have further clarified difficulties of relating young adults in formal institutions (schools) to social action. Research on their programs has shown that raising some issues (such as major violations of human rights) could have negative outcomes if the issues appeared to students as distant, inaccessible, long-term and intractable. Of one pioneering program on human rights a researcher writes:

> A general criticism was that students felt themselves bombarded with values and problems. Some actually felt guilty at their powerlessness to affect a situation like Apartheid in South Africa, and had a sense that they were being taught about it 'in order to feel guilty about it'.
>
> (Cunningham 1986: 16)

Research on a pioneering program on Third World–First World studies (development education – see Dyson 1984) revealed difficulties with some of the key concepts (such as 'interdependence', 'development', and 'structural violence') and difficulties in dealing with ethnocentric and racist world views of the students. One disappointed teacher is recorded as saying: 'The students find it boring and too hard. They come with a limited set of stereotypes and keep them. I'm disappointed that there wasn't more empathy shown for the lot of people in the Third World' (Dyson 1984: 65). I raise these problems not as argument for abandoning an enterprise which is based on major generative themes, but in order that the enterprise should be better informed and refined.

Secondly, the vanguard educators' concern for *process* was so strong that they were careless (or could not have cared less) about *content*. Partly because of the domination of traditional education by the transmission and regurgitation of 'inert knowledge', it is usual for progressive educators to attack the nature of content in the conventional school. Sometimes they do this by stereotyping and caricaturing conventional school practice. One classic example is provided by Paulo Freire (1972: 46–7); another is provided by Carl Rogers (1983: 185–94). My own view is that stereotyping and caricaturing, while seeking to make us recognize, through feeling, revealed truths, can be unreasonable and unreasoning as methods of argument. (Would we accept such means as fair commentaries on progressive practice?) It is also too easy, and too dangerous, to denigrate and degrade the importance of *content* in education. While there is a lack of evidence that process skills are being acquired and developed (the observation and the evaluation are missing), there *is* evidence of lack of content knowledge among many of the students. (Another disappointed teacher on the pioneering program of Third World–First World studies lamented: 'The students lack a concept of the scale of the problems and issues ... *They don't even know the location of the countries'* (Dyson 1984: 64))

Throughout the period from 1970, 'knowledge' surveys of school leavers, as well as case study research, has revealed widespread *ignorance* among school leavers about political concepts, processes, organizations, policies and events. Students need a basic knowledge of content items and an understanding of the key concepts related to issues, and they should have an analytical framework of key questions to apply to issues. Progressive educators cannot be careless about content, if they want education to progress. Content is so important that it needs to be preserved in a reviewed and reconstructed and clear form. In recent years the political danger of content carelessness has become all too apparent. We have seen a backlash of knowledge conservatives (who claim 'the high ground' of standards and quality and the terrain of knowledge content, and who want to keep large parts of the social world out of an insulated school. In Britain we have seen an attempted restoration of traditional knowledge forms ('history' and not 'world studies', for example) by the knowledge conservatives, some of whom argue that schools should only teach those things about which a consensus exists – which, by definition, would exclude political issues from the curriculum. Both Britain and the USA have seen back-to-basics movements. In the USA, E.D. Hirsch Jr has both asserted serious knowledge deficiencies in citizens (Hirsch 1987) and offered them the remedy in the form of *The Dictionary of Cultural Literacy: What Every American Needs to Know* (Hirsch *et al.* 1988). A comparison of Hirsch's view of cultural literacy and Freire's view of cultural literacy should make progressive educators aware of the task which now confronts us.

A third aspect of the work of the vanguard educators draws great potential from Freirean and other democratic programs of political education. Their work, and Freire's work, rests on a notion of common humanity and on a foundation of human rights and fundamental freedoms. During the past decade human rights educators have articulated programs for teaching, learning and acting about human rights. A framework of human rights – civic and political, economic and social, and cultural rights – can inform the political and social education of the future. The procedural values of the Programme for Political Education were freedom, fairness, toleration, respect for truth (evidence) and respect for reasoning. These values relate to the twin governing notions of human rights – basic rights and fundamental freedoms, and fair treatment and due process. They also run through the work of the vanguard educators and Paulo Freire.

MODERN CITIZENSHIP AND EDUCATING FOR A HUMAN FUTURE

It is now a quarter of a century since Paulo Freire went into exile from his native land and it is twenty years since his writings first appeared for English-speaking audiences. Although Freire's most obvious influence in Britain has been with adult educators in the non-formal sector – people like Tom Lovett (1975), Paula Allman (1987) and Doreen Grant (1989) – I have tried to show how the challenges of the Freire method were felt by workers in the Programme for Political Education operating in schools and how they, in their turn, raise some questions for Freire. In Britain we are now at a critical juncture in our recent history of educational reform. The government has legislated a national curriculum which could promise a better future for many school students – particularly if it were able to guarantee them access to quality knowledge in the institutions. It also exposes a number of dilemmas, or paradoxes, of the present time. A 'national' curriculum is being introduced at a time when there is uncertainty about which 'nation' it is intended for – it will not run in the elite, private schools where those who legislated it send their children – and there is some doubt about what it means 'to be British' in our post-colonial, multicultural and (almost) post-industrial society. It is not surprising that, in such a context, the government should argue for 'active citizenship' as voluntary social work by young people for old people, and to limit citizenship rights to civil and political rights – that is, to exclude *welfare* rights. There is little doubt that some would like to take the politics out of citizenship and the welfare out of politics. Thus, the debate over citizenship will be crucial for the future of education and culture in Britain.

The other, related, debate, which is equally crucial, is how contemporary Britain is presented to the young, particularly through history. It is again symptomatic of the underlying problems that no less a person than the prime minister of the day should demand that the majority of history offered in the schools should be *British* history. (In the past this has meant *English* history on the home front and the British Empire overseas.) This, again, is at a time when Europe is moving toward greater unity; when the Cold War has ended; and when major problems – such as war and peace; poverty and underdevelopment; damage to the environment – are seen as *international* problems.

Recent youth studies in Britain have revealed numbers of young people 'at the margins' of society – excluded both from the labor market and from the political process. Case study research has shown them to be alienated from politics and cynical about politicians in general, and to have strong attitudes of racism, sexism, parochialism and ethnocentricity. The research report, which summarized a number of youth research projects, concluded:

> [There was an] overall political disillusion . . . time and again the young people reported that they had little interest in and knew nothing about politics. Their responses to items about political knowledge confirmed their ignorance . . . Some regretted that they had been taught nothing about politics at school, and said that their teachers seemed to deliberately avoid political topics. When

young people mentioned that they would have liked some instruction about politics at school, they were not advocating exposure to the policies of particular parties. Rather, they were seeking information about the general operation of economics and politics.

(McGurk, 1987)

In short, they were asking for political education.

The major project on which political educators in Britain are now working is the reconstruction of citizenship. This needs to be a citizenship appropriate to modern, multicultural society in an interdependent world. It will be a citizenship of entitlement, including entitlement to those cultural resources necessary for the realization of *equal* citizenship. It will be a citizenship in which active citizens *act* – to understand the world, to reflect on it, and to effect change in it. This project, too, is informed by Freirean ideals, and it is a project that Paulo Freire will understand.

REFERENCES

Allman, P. (1987) 'Paulo Freire's education approach: a struggle for meaning' in G. Allen, ed., *Community Education*, Milton Keynes: Open University Press.

Crick, B. (1964) *In Defence of Politics*, Harmondsworth: Penguin.

Crick, B. and Lister, I. (1978) 'Political literacy' in B. Crick and A. Porter, eds, *Political Education and Political Literacy*, London: Longman.

Cunningham, J. (1986) *Human Rights in a Secondary School*, York: University of York.

Dyson, J. (1984) *Development Education for the 14–16 Age-Group*, York: University of York.

Freire, P. (1972) *Pedagogy of the Oppressed*, Harmondsworth: Penguin.

Grant, D. (1989) *Learning Relations*, London and New York: Routledge.

Hirsch, E.D. Jr (1987) *Cultural Literacy*, Boston: Houghton Mifflin.

Hirsch, E.D. Jr *et al.* (1988) *The Dictionary of Cultural Literacy*, Boston: Houghton Mifflin.

Lister, I. (1987) 'Contemporary developments in political education' in C. Harber, ed., *Political Education in Britain*, Lewes: Falmer Press.

Lovett, T. (1975) *Adult Education, Community Development, and the Working Class*, London: Ward Lock.

McGurk, H. (1987) *What Next?*, London: Economic and Social Research Council.

Rogers, C. (1983) *Freedom to Learn in the 1980s*, Columbus, OH: Merril.

Stradling, R. and Porter, A. (1978) 'Issues and political problems' in B. Crick and A. Porter, eds, *Political Education and Political Literacy*, London: Longman.

Webb, K. (1981) *Political Skills and their Development*, York: University of York.

Chapter 4

Toward liberatory mathematics
Paulo Freire's epistemology and ethnomathematics

Marilyn Frankenstein and Arthur B. Powell

Our task is not to teach students to think – they can already think; but to exchange our ways of thinking with each other and look together for better ways of approaching the decodification of an object.

(Freire 1982)

INTRODUCTION

In its connection with pedagogy, a key underlying assumption in the emerging field of ethnomathematics is that, through interacting in a myriad of daily-life activities, people already think and, more specifically, they think mathematically. To understand their ways of thinking mathematically we need to reconsider and redefine conventional notions of mathematical knowledge. We need to learn about how culture – daily practice, language, and ideology – interacts with people's views of mathematics and their ways of thinking mathematically. Learning about these views and ways of thinking are opportunities to deepen our mathematical and pedagogical knowledge. We need to reclaim the hidden and distorted histories of the contributions of all cultures to mathematics. Further, to enable students to discover that they already think mathematically and, therefore, can learn 'school' or 'academic' mathematics, we advocate connecting their mathematical understandings with a deconstructed history of mathematics and with the 'academic' mathematics they are studying.

In this chapter we start with a discussion of Paulo Freire's theories about the nature of knowledge and introduce the range of intellectual traditions that underlie the concept of ethnomathematics. We proceed to argue that his epistemology informs the theoretical basis of ethnomathematics. Then we categorize and elaborate areas central to ethnomathematics. In concluding, we indicate implications for further investigations of mathematical knowledge and its connections to cultural and political action.

A theme that emerges throughout our reflections is that the separate categories so commonly made in much academic thought need to be reconsidered. For Freire (1970, 1982) this means breaking down the dichotomy between subjectivity and objectivity, between action and reflection, between teaching and learning, and between knowledge and its applications. For Fasheh (1988) and Adams (1983), this means that thought which is labelled 'logic' and thought which is labelled 'intuition' continuously and dialectically interact with each other.[1] For Lave (1988: 154), this means understanding how 'activity-in-setting is seamlessly stretched across persons acting'. For Diop (1991), this means that the distinctions between 'Western', 'Eastern', and 'African' knowledge distort the human processes of acquiring and creating knowledge from interactions with each other and with the world. Further, we argue in this chapter that underlying all of these false dichotomies is the split between practical, everyday knowledge and abstract, theoretical knowledge. Understanding these dialectical interconnections, we believe, leads us to connect mathematics to all other 'disciplines' and to view mathematical knowledge as one aspect of humans trying to understand and act effectively in the world. We see ethnomathematics as a useful way of conceptualizing these interconnections from both theoretical and curricular perspectives.

PAULO FREIRE'S EPISTEMOLOGY

The epistemology of Paulo Freire is in direct opposition to the dominant educational paradigm of positivism. In this philosophical paradigm, here in agreement with Freire, proponents view facts or states of affairs as objective, existing totally outside of human consciousness. The problem, however, is that positivists claim that knowledge, though a product of human consciousness, is itself also neutral, value-free, and objective. Further, knowledge is completely separate from how people use it. Learning is the discovery of static facts and their subsequent description and classification (Bredo and Feinberg 1982). In contrast, critical education theorists critique the positivist paradigm by attending to what is omitted. For instance, Giroux (1981: 43–4) states that

> [q]uestions concerning the social construction of knowledge, and the con-
> stitutive interests behind the selection, organization, and evaluation of 'brute
> facts' are buried under the assumption that knowledge is objective and value
> free. Information or 'data' taken from the subjective world of intuition, insight,
> philosophy and nonscientific theoretical frameworks is not acknowledged as
> being relevant. Values, then, appear as the nemeses of 'facts', and are viewed
> at best as interesting, and at worst as irrational and subjective emotional
> responses.

Likewise, Freire insists knowledge is not static; there is no dichotomy between objectivity and subjectivity, or between reflection and action; and knowledge is not neutral.

For Freire, knowledge is continually created and re-created as people act and reflect on the world. Knowledge, therefore, is not fixed permanently in the abstract properties of objects, but is a process where gaining existing knowledge and producing new knowledge are 'two moments in the same cycle' (Freire 1982). Embedded in this notion is the recognition that knowledge requires subjects; objects to be known are necessary, but they are not sufficient.

> Knowledge . . . necessitates the curious presence of subjects confronted with the world. It requires their transforming action on reality. It demands a constant searching . . . In the learning process the only person who really learns is s/he[2] who . . . re-invents that learning.
>
> (Freire 1973: 101)

Knowledge, therefore, is a negotiated product emerging from the interaction of human consciousness and reality; it is produced as we, individually and collectively, search and try to make sense of our world.

Necessarily, then, the human act of sense-making implies the subjectivity of our descriptions of the world. However, contrary to the view that subjective statements contain no connection to objective reality and that there exist objective statements about the world, unpolluted by subjective perspectives, Freire insists that subjectivity and objectivity are not separate ways of knowing.

> To deny the importance of subjectivity in the process of transforming the world and history is . . . to admit the impossible: a world without people . . . On the other hand, the denial of objectivity in analysis or action . . . postulates people without a world . . . [and] denies action itself by denying objective reality.
>
> (Freire 1970: 35–6)

Because of the unity between subjectivity and objectivity, people cannot *completely* know particular aspects of the world – no knowledge is finished.[3] As humans change, so does the knowledge they produce. Only through praxis – reflection and action dialectically interacting to re-create our perception and description of reality – can people become subjects in control of organizing their society.

This praxis is not neutral. Knowledge does not exist apart from how and why it is used, and in whose interest. Freire asserts that even, for example, in the supposedly neutral technical knowledge of how to cultivate potatoes,

> there is something which goes beyond the agricultural aspects of cultivating potatoes . . . We have not only . . . the methods of planting, but also the question which has to do with the role of those who plant potatoes in the process of producing, for what we plant potatoes, in favor of whom. And something more. It is very important for the peasant . . . to think about the very process of work – what does working mean?
>
> (Brown 1978: 63)

In Freire's view, people produce knowledge to humanize themselves. Overcoming dehumanization involves resolving the fundamental contradiction of our epoch: domination against liberation. Ethnomathematics contributes to this struggle by theorizing a more liberatory conception of mathematics.

ETHNOMATHEMATICAL KNOWLEDGE

A new conceptual category has emerged from the discourse on the interplay among mathematics, education, culture, and politics: ethnomathematics. Naturally, it has various definitions and associated perspectives; each definition and perspective, and the term itself, has been debated and then rejected or embraced in scholarly journals and in other academic forums.[4] Among recent, written efforts to define and describe the terrain of ethnomathematics, two dominant positions are represented by the ideas of Ascher and Ascher (1986; Ascher 1991) and D'Ambrosio (1985, 1987, 1988, 1990).

Ascher and Ascher define ethnomathematics as 'the study of the mathematical ideas of nonliterate peoples' (1986: 125). While acknowledging that mathematical ideas exist in all cultures, Ascher (1991) points out that this does not imply that, across cultures, mathematical ideas are the same.

> In Western culture and among the Tshokwe of Africa, the cultural surroundings of the graph theoretical ideas are not the same, nor should we expect that they would be. The strip patterns that we see around us, those of the Incas, and those of the Maori are quite different in style, in usage, and in their cultural linkages. Shared is the creation of strip patterns and an interest in them, but not necessarily shared is the motivation for their creation, nor the world view or aesthetic that leads to the particular strip that results.
>
> (186)

> [Mathematical] ideas exist in all cultures, but which ones are emphasized, how they are expressed, and their particular contexts will vary from culture to culture.
>
> (187)

> The differences, however, are *not* the ability to think abstractly or logically. They are in the subjects of thought, the cultural premises, and what situations call forth which thought processes.
>
> (190)

These statements reveal the anthropological and mathematical roots and concerns of the Aschers' project. Their project also has ideological concerns: they intend to challenge Eurocentric historical and anthropological notions about the locus of mathematical ideas, including pernicious statements in the mathematical literature concerning the value of the mathematical ideas of non-literate, non-Western people.[5] As they point out, most statements about non-literate peoples are usually (1) in preliminary chapters in histories of mathematics or in texts on the spirit of the subject and (2) theoretically and factually flawed (1986: 125). Non-literate peoples are thought of as primitive or existing earlier along a linear evolutionary path. As such, their ideas are placed at the beginning of discussions of mathematics. In contrast, Ascher and Ascher (1975, 1981, 1986) and Ascher (1983, 1987, 1988a, 1988b, 1990, 1991) have demonstrated that certain notions of non-literate peoples are akin to and as complex as those of modern, 'Western' mathematics; they have broadened the history of mathematics by imbuing it with a multicultural, global perspective. However, circumscribing the terrain of ethnomathematics to the mathematical ideas of non-literate, non-Western peoples is, we insist, too small a circle. The radius should be longer since much lies in the complement of the circle.

To discover the complement requires a broader perspective of ethnomathematics. Insightfully, D'Ambrosio (1985), the founder and most significant theoretician of the ethnomathematics program[6] as well as a colleague of Freire, points out that belief in the universality of mathematics can limit one from considering and recognizing that different modes of thought or culture may lead to different forms of mathematics, radically different ways of counting, ordering, sorting, measuring, inferring, classifying, and modeling. That is, once we abandon notions of general universality, which often cover for Eurocentric particularities, we can acquire an anthropological awareness: different cultures can produce different mathematics and the mathematics of one culture can change over time, reflecting changes in the culture. For D'Ambrosio ethnomathematics, existing at the crossroads of the history of mathematics and cultural anthropology, overcomes the Egyptian and Greek distinction between scholarly and practical mathematics, a distinction rooted in socio-economic class differentiation (1985: 44–5). Now in the twentieth century, this distinction is manifested in the contrast between the 'academic' mathematics that is taught in schools, which allows an elite to assume management of a society's productive forces, and the 'everyday' mathematics, which allows individuals to function effectively in the world. On the other hand, ethnomathematics is

> the mathematics which is practised among identifiable cultural groups, such as national-tribal societies, labor groups, children of a certain age bracket, professional classes, and so on. Its identity depends largely on focuses of interest, on motivation, and on certain codes and jargons which do not belong to the realm of academic mathematics. We may go even further in this concept of ethnomathematics to include for example much of the mathematics which is currently practised by engineers, mainly calculus, which does not respond to the concept of rigor and formalism developed in academic courses of calculus.
>
> (D'Ambrosio 1985: 45)

Here we have a conception of ethnomathematics which embraces a broader spectrum of humanity than the previous one. Within this conception, cultural groups within Western societies also have an ethnomathematics. Moreover, D'Ambrosio (1987) argues that we ought not to minimize or ignore the influence of cultural atmosphere and motivation. As with the production of other cultural products – music, for example – mathematical ideas take shape within particular contexts and which ideas are produced is connected to contextual content.

This calls for a somewhat different way of looking into the History of Science and the epistemological foundations of scientific knowledge. It calls for an ethnological interpretation of mental processes and the recognition of different modes of thought, as well as different logics of explanation, which depend upon experiential background of the cultural group being considered. Thus we are led to disclaim the assertion that there is only one underlying logic governing all thought.

(D'Ambrosio 1987: 3)

Here, then, different cultural groups – industrial engineers, children, peasants, computer scientists, for example – have distinct ways of reasoning, of measuring, of coding, of classifying, and so on. Consequently each group has its own ethnomathematics, *including* academic mathematicians. Further, it is the informal and *ad hoc* aspects of ethnomathematics that broaden it to include more than academic mathematics. This point has been aptly elaborated by both Borba (1990) and Mtetwa (1992). For instance, stating that ethnomathematics is '[m]athematical knowledge expressed in the language code of a given socio-cultural group', Borba points out that this implies that '[e]ven the mathematics produced by professional mathematicians can be seen as a form of ethnomathematics' (40). Further, he echoes the critique of universality:

Although academic mathematics may be international in that it is currently in use in many parts of the world, it is not international in that only a small percentage of the population of the world is likely to use academic mathematics.

(40)

Hence ethnomathematics should not be misunderstood as 'vulgar' or 'second class' mathematics, but as *different* cultural expressions of mathematical ideas.

(41)

Beyond critiquing the imperialism of academic mathematics, Borba argues for a recognition of diverse expressions of mathematical ideas instead of one ethnomathematics dominating another. The genesis of ethnomathematical ideas depends on the cognitive practices of a culturally differentiated group, and those ideas maintain, evolve, or disappear according to the dynamics of the group and its relation to other cultural groups. At some stage, a professional class of mathematicians may decide to theorize an aspect of ethnomathematical knowledge; they appropriate it and later return it in a codified version. In this context, D'Ambrosio writes:

We may look for examples in mathematics of the parallel development of the scientific discipline outside the establishment and the accepted model of the profession. One such example is Dirac's delta function which, about 20 years after being in full use among physicists, was expropriated and became a mathematical object, structured by the theory of distributions.

(1985: 47)

D'Ambrosio's broader view of ethnomathematics accounts for the dialectical transformation of knowledge within and among societies. Moreover, his epistemology is consistent with Freire's in that D'Ambrosio views mathematical knowledge as dynamic and the result of human activity, not as static and ordained. Necessarily, this conception of ethnomathematics admits a critique of the historiography of mathematics (D'Ambrosio 1988). That is, there are mathematical notions of peoples that written history has hidden, frozen, or stolen. Including these ideas makes it clear that what is labeled 'Western' mathematics is more accurately called 'world mathematics' (Anderson 1990). We argue that ethnomathematics includes the mathematical ideas of peoples, manifested in written or non-written, oral or non-oral forms, many of which have been either ignored or otherwise distorted by conventional histories of mathematics. We and other mathematics educators are pushing the boundaries of both ethnomathematics and academic mathematics so that the two fields merge to encompass all of the intellectual enterprises and other actions of everyday life having to do with mathematics.[7] Fasheh goes so far as to define the underlying project of ethnomathematics as 'working hard to understand the logic of other peoples, of other ways of thinking'.[8]

RECONCEIVING MATHEMATICAL KNOWLEDGE: ETHNOMATHEMATICS AND FREIRE'S EPISTEMOLOGY

The work of Freire and other critical education theorists has important implications for ethnomathematics and its epistemological underpinnings. A key implication is that individuals and cultures are located in the act of knowing, in the act of creating mathematics. This position, naturally, counterstates prevailing methods of teaching which treat mathematics as a deductively discovered, pre-existing body of knowledge. Even more insidiously, within these methods mathematics educators present the discipline as a body of knowledge that is decidedly European, a male domain, and practised only by divinely anointed minds. Taken together, prevailing pedagogical practices have prevented and alienated many students, disproportionately people of color and women, from engaging in mathematics. As Freire has stated, '[a]ny situation in which some men [and women] prevent others from engaging in the process of inquiry is one of violence. The means used are not important; to alienate men [and women] from their own decision-making is to change them into objects' (as quoted in Gordon 1978: 251).

Gordon (ibid.) argues that the experience of learning mathematics objectifies individuals to the extent that subjectivity and personal acts of choosing and valuing are denied. He and others[9] affirm that belief, commitment, and personal experiences are part of the act of knowing. Further, he writes that

> [t]he human acts of teaching and learning are shared acts of presenting and accepting oneself and others in coming to a particular way of knowing. As acts of control, they make us submerge our awareness of our existence. As acts of and toward understanding, they make us acutely aware of our human capacity

and need for meaning and explanation of our experience. As liberating acts, they require honesty and, as honest acts, they require sensitivity to and recognition of subjectivity. To view the mathematics experience in both 'repair and transcendence' is to understand that liberation requires the creation of personal meaning which, subsidiarily, tests the taken for granted.

(252)

We agree with Gordon that to make mathematics education a liberatory act, educators need to attend to subjectivity. Moreover, we contend that an ethnomathematical, Freirean perspective recognizes and is sensitive to the impacts of various cultural conventions and inclinations – from daily activities and linguistic practice to one's social and ideological context – for doing and learning mathematics. That is, besides personal meaning, liberatory education attends to ideological, linguistic, and other cultural meanings produced in the praxis of our everyday lives. Indeed, educational acts, and no less those of mathematics education, are powerful engines to maintain and reproduce and to critique and transform personal, social, economic, and political structures and other cultural patterns.

With its attention to culture, Freire's epistemology informs a theory that accounts for how inserting ethnomathematics into mathematics education can shift education away from maintenance and reproduction toward critique and transformation. Freire insists that knowledge is not static and this notion underlies the ethnomathematical project to reconceive the nature of mathematical knowledge. He attends to the dialectical connections between objectivity and subjectivity, and between reflection and action, and this attention directs ethnomathematical educators to consider culture and context – daily practice, language and ideology – as inseparable from the praxis of mathematics learning. Further, Freire focuses on the non-neutrality of all knowledge and thus forces us to interrogate the consequences of considering mathematical knowledge as neutral, and to re-search an undistorted world history of mathematical ideas, a history that includes the contributions of all peoples to the development of mathematics.

However, just as Gordon over-attends to personal meaning, Freire over-attends to culture in his discussion of critical consciousness leading to radical change. His work is particularly vulnerable to that critique: by ignoring 'the political economy of revolution in favor of an emphasis on its cultural dimension . . . [His] talk of revolution tends to become utopian and idealized' (Mackie 1981: 106; see also Youngman 1986: 150–96). Although Freire's later writings focus more attention on the role of institutional structures in and on education (Youngman 1986) and his later comments[10] recognize the limitations of education to bring about liberatory social change, this aspect of his work remains under-theorized. However, the implications of the connections between ethnomathematical knowledge and Freire's epistemology do result in a clear critique of most current conceptions of mathematics and of related pedagogical practices.

In this section we examine those implications and argue that reconsidering what educators value as mathematical knowledge, considering the effect of culture on mathematical knowledge, and uncovering the distorted and hidden history of mathematical knowledge are the significant contributions of a Freirean, ethnomathematical perspective in reconceiving the discipline of mathematics and its pedagogical practice.[11] As we indicate in our final section, less clear are the implications of a Freirean, ethnomathematical program for societal transformation.

Reconsidering what counts as mathematical knowledge

In a French mathematics study a 7-year-old was asked the following question: 'You have 10 red pencils in your left pocket and 10 blue pencils in your right pocket. How old are you?' When he answered: '20 years old', it was not because he did not know that he was *really* 7, or because he did not understand anything about numbers. Rather it was, as Puchalska and Semadeni (1987: 15) conclude, because the unwritten 'social contract' between mathematics students and teachers stipulates that 'when you solve a mathematical problem . . . you use the numbers given in the story . . . Perhaps the most important single reason why students give illogical answers to problems with irrelevant questions or irrelevant data is that those students believe mathematics does not make any sense.'

As the situation described by Puchalska and Semadeni reveals, we can observe the split between 'everyday' mathematical knowledge and 'school' mathematics in many different contexts. Earlier, we noted that D'Ambrosio (1985) traces the historical development of this split to the social stratifications of Egyptian and Greek societies. In a contemporary context, Frankenstein (1989) finds that her working-class, adult students in the United States are often surprised to learn that the decimal point is the same as the point used to write amounts of money. Similarly, Spradbery worked with 16-year-old students in England who

> had failed consistently to master anything but the most elementary aspects of school Mathematics . . . They had received, and remained unhelped by, considerable 'remedial' teaching and, finally, they left school 'hating everyfink what goes on in maffs'. Yet in their spare time some of these same young people kept and raced pigeons . . . Weighing, measuring, timing, using map scales, buying, selling, interpreting timetables, devising schedules, calculating probabilities and averages . . . were a natural part of their stock of commonsense knowledge.
>
> (1976: 237)

Besides social and class divisions, Harris (1987a) shows that sexism also underpins the dichotomy between 'school' mathematics and one's stock of commonsense knowledge, and perverts what counts as mathematical knowledge. For example, the academy labels as mathematical a problem about preventing the lagging in a right-angled cylindrical pipe from inappropriately bunching up and stretching out, a problem presumably only males tackle, whereas the identical domestic problem of designing the heel of a sock is called 'knitting', women's work, and is not considered to have mathematical content. We, instead, classify both the engineering and domestic problems as ethnomathematics.

The mathematical knowledge embedded in the activity of adults handling money, students racing pigeons, and women knitting socks is Freirean in the sense that it is not fragmented from the knowledge of each of these activities; rather, it is created and re-created in praxis. However, the academically enforced disjuncture between 'practical' and 'abstract' mathematical knowledge contributes to students feeling that they do not understand or know any mathematics. Further, Joseph (1987) considers that this disjuncture fuels the intellectual elitism that regards mathematical discovery as following only 'from a rigorous application of a form of deductive axiomatic logic' (p. 22). Moreover, this elitism, combined with racism, considers non-intuitive, non-empirical logic a unique product of European – Greek – mathematics. This Eurocentric view dismisses Egyptian and Mesopotamian mathematics as merely the 'application of certain rules or procedures ... [not] "proofs" of results which have universal application' (ibid.: 22–3). Joseph disputes this biased definition of proof, arguing that

> the word 'proof' has different meanings, depending on its context and the state of the development of the subject ... To suggest that because existing documentary evidence does not exhibit the deductive axiomatic logical inference characteristic of much of modern mathematics, these cultures did not have a concept of proof, would be misleading. Generalizations about the area of a circle and the volume of a truncated pyramid are found in Egyptian mathematics ... As Gillings [1972: 145–6] has argued, Egyptian 'proofs' are rigorous without being symbolic, so that typical values of a variable are used and generalization to any other value is immediate.
>
> (ibid.: 23–4)

An example that shatters the notion of a dichotomy between concrete and abstract thought and demonstrates the subjective, culturally determined nature of 'abstract' categories is provided by Glick (as cited in Rose 1988: 291) in recounting the frustrations of researchers working with a group of people whom 'academic anthropologists' would label 'primitive'. The investigators had twenty objects, five each from four categories: food, clothing, tools and cooking utensils. When asked to sort the objects, most people produced ten groups of two, basing their sorting on practical connections among the objects (for example, 'the knife goes with the orange because it cuts it').

> [the people] at times volunteered 'that a wise man would do things in the way this was done'. When an exasperated experimenter asked finally, 'How would a fool do it?' he was given back groupings of the type ... initially expected – four neat piles with foods in one, tools in another.

Walkerdine (1990) cites an encounter which illuminates the creation of the categories 'concrete' and 'abstract'. She describes two observations: a mother and her sons arguing about buying drinks that they could not afford; and a father and son making a game out of calculating change – 'what if I bought . . .'. She contrasts the concrete material necessity in the conversation between the mother and sons with the imaginary constructions in the dialogue between the father and son. She asks intriguing questions about these exchanges:

> What is the effect of relative poverty and wealth on the way in which certain problems can be presented as 'abstract' versus 'concrete', or, as I would prefer to put it, problems of practical and material necessity versus problems of 'symbolic control'? And what is the relationship between the classic concrete/abstract distinction and the one between a life in which it is materially necessary to calculate for survival and a life in which calculation can become a relatively theoretical exercise? Might calculation as a theoretical exercise have become the basis of a form of reasoning among imperial powers which depended for the accumulation of their capital on the exploitation of the newly discovered colonies? Do theoretical concepts come with wealth and what, if so, does this mean for economic and psychological theories of development and underdevelopment?
>
> (ibid.: 52)

She goes on to argue that to describe the interaction between the father and son as 'abstracted' from everyday practices is misleading because the imaginary calculation 'exists as a discursive relation in a new set of practices, namely those of school mathematics, with its own modes of regulation and subjection' (ibid.: 54). Rather than dichotomizing concrete versus abstract, Walkerdine speaks for viewing the different conversations as shifting from 'one discursive practice to another'.

Considering interactions between culture and mathematical knowledge

In his educational practice, Freire initiates the process by first considering who creates culture. This is done to clarify the point that all people, whether literate or illiterate, are cultural actors. Towards this end he emphasizes an anthropological concept of culture. In the following quotation he indicates signposts of a definition of culture:

> the distinction between the world of nature and the world of culture; the active role of men [and women] *in* and *with* their reality; the role of mediation which nature plays in relationships and communications among men [and women]; culture as the addition made by men [and women] to a world they did not make; culture as the result of men's [and women's] labor, of their efforts to create and re-create; the transcendental meaning of human relationships; the humanist dimension of culture; culture as systematic acquisition of human experience (but as creative assimilation, not as information-storing); the democratization

of culture; the learning of reading and writing as the key to the world of written communication. In short, the role of man [and woman] as Subject[s] in the world and with the world.

(1973: 46)

The salient points for our discussion are that cultural products are the creation of people and that transformations of nature are made by all people. Mathematics is a cultural product and, therefore, is created by humans in the interconnected midst of culture. The interactions are dialectical: people's daily practice, language, and ideology affect and are affected by their mathematical knowledge. Bishop (1990), and other mathematics educators, reviewing anthropological studies and investigating mathematical activities in different cultures, view mathematics as a 'pan-cultural phenomenon . . . a symbolic technology, developed through engaging in various [integrated] environmental activities' which can be classified as

counting: the use of a systematic way to compare and order discrete objects . . . locating: exploring one's spatial environment, and conceptualising and symbolising that environment, with models, maps, drawings, and other devices . . . measuring: quantifying qualities like length and weight, for the purposes of comparing and ordering objects . . . designing: creating a shape or design for an object or for any part of one's spatial environment . . . playing: devising, and engaging in, games and pastimes with more or less formalized rules that all players must abide by . . . explaining: finding ways to represent the relationships between phenomena.

(ibid: 59–60)

Further, Gattegno (1970, 1988) argues that mental functionings, or structures, needed to learn to speak a language are akin to those used in doing mathematics. The implication he draws is that anyone who succeeds in learning a language has already mathematized his or her linguistic domain and, therefore, is capable of mathematizing other domains. He posits not only that mathematics is a birthright but also that mathematical structures are developed through a specific cultural activity: learning to speak a language.

Observers of less universal cultural contexts also narrate how people acquire 'unschooled' knowledge of mathematics. Considerable research studies document that unschooled individuals, in their daily practice, develop accurate strategies for performing mental arithmetic. For example, studying Brazilian children who worked in their parents' markets, Carraher, Carraher and Schliemann (1985: 21) conclude that 'performance on mathematical problems embedded in real-life contexts was superior to that on school-type word problems and context-free computational problems involving the same numbers and operations'. Through interviews with the youngsters, these investigators learned that in the marketplace the children reasoned by mental calculations, whereas in the formal test they usually relied on paper and pencil, school-taught algorithms.

Mistakes often occur as a result of confusing the algorithms. Moreover, there is no evidence, once the numbers are written down, that the children try to relate the obtained results to the problem at hand in order to assess the adequacy of their answers ... The results [of this study] support the thesis ... that thinking sustained by daily human sense can be – in the same subject – at a higher level than thinking out of context.

(ibid: 27)[12]

Using these studies, and ethnographic data of adults in the United States engaged in supermarket and weight-watching activities, Lave (1988: 154) argues against considering mathematical knowledge and context separately. Rather, she theorizes that 'activity-in-setting [is] seamlessly stretched across persons-acting' and that the context often shapes the mathematical activity, becoming the calculating device, rather than merely the place in which the mathematical calculations are applied. Scribner (1984) found that this occurs when dairy workers invent their own units (full and partial cases) to solve problems of product assembly on the job. In another example, Lave (1988: 154) describes how a shopper who found, in a bin, a surprisingly high-priced package of cheese investigated for error by searching through the bin for a similar-sized package, checking to see whether there was a price discrepancy. If, instead, the problem were solved as a textbook problem rather than as a calculation shaped by the setting, the shopper would have divided weight into price and compared that quotient with the price per pound printed on the label. Lave uses the phrase 'dissolving problems', in both its senses, for discussing what happens in practice. Mathematics problems 'disappear into solution with ongoing activity rather than "being solved". Such transformations pose a challenge to scholastic assumptions concerning the bounded character of math problem solving as an end in itself' (ibid.: 120).

Lave then theorizes about the societal reasons why so many shoppers attend to arithmetic. School mathematics, she contends, is filled with shopping applications, so that money becomes a value-free, 'natural' term, just a form of neutral school arithmetic. When adults go shopping their choices are first made qualitatively. That is, an item may be the best buy mathematically but is rejected because the package is too big to fit on their pantry shelf. However, they fall back on arithmetic calculations when there are no other criteria for choice. This provides a basis for believing that their decision is rational and objective. Thus, as Lave argues, 'price arithmetic contributes more to constructing the incorrigibility of "rationality" than to the instrumental elaboration of preference structures' (ibid.: 158).[13,14]

Even other supposedly more value-free mathematical concepts are shaped by specific philosophical and ideological orientations. For example, Martin (1988) cites Forman, who analyzed how the intense antagonism to 'rationality' which existed in the German Weimar Republic after World War I resulted in a particular interpretation of a mathematical construction.

Forman suggests that this pressure led the quantum physicists to search for ... a mathematical formalism which could be interpreted as non-causal. In crude terms, the acausal Copenhagen interpretation and its associated mathematical framework was adopted because they looked good publicly ... In the decades since the establishment of the orthodox or Copenhagen interpretation, a number of alternative interpretations have been put forth. Some of these use the same mathematical formulations, but interpret their physical significance differently, while others use different mathematical formulations to achieve the same or different results ... [So] the interpretation of the equations of quantum theory as supporting indeterminism was not *required* by the equations themselves. Furthermore, it seems possible that many of the achievements of the theory might have been accomplished using a somewhat different mathematical formulation which could well have been *difficult* to interpret indeterministically.

(210–11)

On other occasions philosophy and ideology have prompted variant interpretations of fundamental mathematical concepts and techniques. For instance, the dialectics and historical materialism of Karl Marx, along with his project to elaborate the principles of political economy, between 1873 and 1881, led him to study, criticize, and develop an alternative theoretical foundation for the differential calculus (Marx 1983). His critique of prevailing methods for deriving the derivative of a function was twofold: (1) the derivative of a function was always present before the actual differentiation occurred and (2) none of the methods accounted for the dialectical nature of motion and change to which a function is subjected in the process of differentiation (Powell 1986: 120). Out of touch with professional mathematicians and unaware of Cauchy's work on the calculus and limits, Marx overcame his critique of the theoretical foundations of the calculus by developing both a conceptual formulation and a technique for differentiation that captured symbolically the vexing problematic that was the impulse behind the method of Newton and Leibniz: motion and change. Indeed, his discoveries, stimulated and informed by his philosophical and ideological framework, represented rediscoveries and, in some instances, anticipated future conceptual and philosophical developments (Gerdes 1985; Powell 1986).

Though it was grounded in a praxis – the conceptual, mathematical description of dynamics – Marx attempted to underpin the calculus with a cultural construct – dialectics – which was part of the philosophical and ideological perspective of an identifiable cultural group. Mathematical knowledge seems unconnected to cultural context since, in isolation and at historical moments distant from their genesis, particular mathematical ideas, such as the derivative, may appear detached from a specific cultural interpretation or application. Ideas, however, do not exist independently of social context. Moreover, as some critical theorists and realist philosophers remind us, our categories, concepts, and other ideas are essentially dependent on objective reality or nature. In a critique of anti-realist epistemology, Johnson (1991) rightly argues that

all these (social) things are materialized in, and dependent on, that which is essentially mind-independent, namely: the natural world. The very human activity of 'cutting up' the world into [for example] hammers and chairs presupposes a world of naturally existing things (like trees and iron ore) capable of being fashioned into tools. In other words, the essential independence goes one way: *nature is essentially independent of mind, but mind (and all its products) is not essentially independent of nature.*

(25)

The social and intellectual relations of individuals to nature or the world, and to such mind-dependent cultural objects as productive forces, influence products of the mind that are labeled mathematical ideas. Further, though there are recognized philosophical variants to the foundations of mathematics, the seemingly non-ideological character of mathematics is reinforced by a history which has labeled alternative conceptions as 'non-mathematical' (Bloor 1976, as cited in Martin 1988: 210).

Uncovering distorted and hidden history of mathematical knowledge

Freire (1970, 1973) insists that in our struggle toward human liberation the 'culture of silence' represents a major obstacle to be overcome. Through its mechanisms the oppressed participate in their own domination by internalizing the views of oppressors and by not speaking or otherwise acting against those oppressive views. A significant reason why oppressed people, such as many women and people of color, are 'mathematically silent' is because of the wide-spread myths presented in Western 'his-stories' of mathematics. The prevailing Eurocentric, and male-centric, myth, expressed in the writings of many Western mathematicians such as Kline (1953), is that

[mathematics] finally secured a firm grip on life in the highly congenial soil of Greece and waxed strongly for a short period . . . With the decline of Greek civilization, the plant remained dormant for a thousand years . . . [until it] was transported to Europe and once more embedded in fertile soil.

(9–10)

This and other myths permeate the history of mathematics so deeply that even the images of mathematicians presented in textbooks, such as of Euclid who lived and studied in Alexandria, are 'false portraits . . . which portray them as fair Greeks not even sunburned by the Egyptian sun'. There are no actual pictures of Euclid, and there is no evidence to suggest that he was not a black Egyptian (Lumpkin 1983: 104–5). Joseph (1987: 18) discusses the cosmopolitan, racially diverse nature of Alexandrian society, 'a meeting place for ideas and different traditions . . . [involving] continuing cross-fertilization between different mathematical traditions, notably the algebraic and empirical traditions of Babylonia and Egypt interacting with the geometric and anti-empirical traditions of classical Greece'. African, Egyptian, Alexandrian society created the environment in which some of its citizens (and probably their students) – for example, Euclid, Archimedes, Apollonius, Diophantus, Ptolemy, Heron, Theon, and his daughter Hypatia – contributed to the development of mathematics.

We gain further insight into why such myths were created and perpetuated, which deny a community and culture its history, when we examine how racism and sexism have impacted on academic research. For example, European scholars arbitrarily, yet purposefully, changed the date of the origination of the Egyptian calendar from BC 4241 to BC 2773, claiming that 'such precise mathematical and astronomical work cannot be seriously ascribed to a people slowly emerging from neolithic conditions' (Struik 1967: 24–5, cited Lumpkin 1983: 100).[15] For another example, the name of a key researcher in the theory of the elasticity of metals – the research that made possible such remarkable engineering feats as the Eiffel Tower – was not listed among the 72 scientists whose names are inscribed on that structure. They are all men, and the contribution of Sophie Germain remains unrecognized (Mozans, cited in Osen 1974: 42). This is just a small piece of a much larger historical picture that obliterated knowledge that, despite sexism, women did contribute to the mathematical sciences.

We gain additional insight into the complexity of the Eurocentric myth when we note that while Euclid is adamantly described as 'Greek', Ptolemy (*circa* 150 AD), whose work dominated astronomy until replaced by Copernicus's theory around 1543, is often described as 'Egyptian'. Ptolemy's more 'practical', applied work could be contrasted with Euclid's more 'theoretical' contributions (Lumpkin 1983: 105). As we have discussed, Harris (1987a) shows how this distinction continues to denigrate women's knowledge. Diop (1991) and Bernal (1987) discuss a number of cases in which European scholars used this practical–theoretical hierarchy to deny the sophisticated mathematical knowledge of the ancient Egyptians. Their discussion provides examples of the interaction and intersection of racism and sexism with intellectual elitism, which, in part, is fueled by the different values attributed to practical and theoretical work respectively. Such hierarchical distinctions are antithetical to the epistemological position of Freire. For the dichotomy in work and value assigned to theory is what Anderson (1990) theorizes as a key factor in the alienation that results from capitalist modes of production, which 'distances people from their creative source and their creativity . . . and allows capital to extract more surplus value from human labor and gain more control over our minds and socio-political activities' (352). Instead, if we understand the creation and development of mathematics as inextricably linked to the material development of society, we can undistort and uncover its hidden history.

In ancient agricultural societies the need for recording numerical information that demarcated the times to plant gave rise to the development of calendars such as that found on the Ishango bone, approximately 25,000 years old, discovered at a fishing site on Lake Edwards in Zaire (Marshack 1991). And, since African women, for the most part, were the first farmers, they were most probably the first people involved in the struggle to observe and understand nature, and, therefore, to contribute to the development of mathematics (Anderson 1990: 354). Then, as societies evolved, the more complex mathematical calculations that were needed to keep track of trade and commerce gave rise to the development of price-value notation by Babylonians (*circa* BC 2000) (Joseph 1987: 27). And this continues to the present day when, for example, military needs and funding drive the development of artificial intelligence (Weizenbaum 1985).

CONCLUSION: IMPLICATIONS FOR FURTHER ETHNOMATHEMATICAL RESEARCH

As the field of ethnomathematics develops, we will need to continue reinterpreting conclusions others have drawn about various people's mathematical knowledge, and continue uncovering and disseminating the distorted/hidden history of mathematical knowledge. This research will expand and deepen the knowledge we create and re-create about our world; it will also lead us to re-examine how we generate knowledge. So, for example, we suggest co-investigation between students and teachers into discovering each other's ethnomathematical knowledge. This will improve our teaching, as we discuss below, and will also point the way to new research methodologies. Finally, in support of Freire's theory that the purpose of knowledge is for people to resolve the fundamental contradiction of our epoch between domination and liberation, we need to explore the connections between the cultural action involved in teaching and learning ethnomathematics and the economic and political action needed to create a liberatory society.

As ethnomathematical knowledge forces us to reconsider what counts as mathematical knowledge, it also forces us to reconsider all our knowledge of the world. Henderson (1990: 5) argues that although 'formal, symbolic expressions are often excellent ways of capturing certain aspects of our experience', the erroneous view that 'formal' mathematics is the ultimate, *real* mathematics 'limits the understandings which we construct of our human experience . . . [and] damages the human spirit'. Pinxten, van Dooren, and Harvey (1983: 174) argue that mathematics education of Navajos should start from a fully developed knowledge of their spatial system (a dynamic system which is in direct contrast to the static concepts of academic mathematics), not solely because this is the only way to avoid the socio-cultural and psychological alienation of Navajos, but also because '[a]s long as science cannot pretend to have valid answers to all basic questions . . . it is foolish to exterminate all other, so-called primitive, prescientific, or otherwise foreign approaches to world questions'. Adams (1983: 43) reminds us that in Eastern societies, such as India and Africa, 'There are no distinct separations between science and religion, philosophy and psychology, history and mythology. All of these are viewed as one reality and are closely interwoven into the fabric of daily life.'[16] He argues that Western science would deepen its knowledge of the world by reconsidering the value of emotional, intuitive and spiritual knowledge. He quotes Einstein, who claimed 'there is no inductive method which could lead to the fundamental concepts of physics . . . there is no logical path to these laws; only intuition, resting on a sympathetic understanding of experience, can reach them' (ibid.: 41). We feel much more research needs to be done to uncover how the logics of all peoples can interact with each other to help us all understand and act more effectively in the world.

One place for mathematics teachers to start this research is with our students' ethnomathematics. These explorations suggest the importance of developing methodologies that probe effectively and ethically our students' mathematical knowledge. When discussing the theory of her work with the Landless People's Movement in Brazil, Knijnik defines an ethnomathematical approach as

> the research of the conceptions, traditions, and mathematical practices of a specific social group and the pedagogical work involved in making the group realize that they do have knowledge; they can codify and interpret their knowledge; they are capable of acquiring erudite knowledge; [and] they are capable of establishing comparison between these two different types of knowledge in order to choose the most suitable one when they have real problems to solve.
>
> (1992: 4)

Powell (Powell and López 1989; Powell and Ramnauth 1992) uses a participatory research model, combined with journal and other writing activities, to prompt students to reflect on both the cognitive and affective components of learning mathematics and to engage them in analyzing critically methodological dimensions of teaching and learning. According to López

> [I] became interested in the study due to my poor math skills. I felt that if I took a more active role in the learning of mathematics I might be able to do better in the course. Throughout the semester I kept a journal detailing my observations of the class, course, and my learning of mathematics . . . We met after classes and whenever our schedules allowed us to discuss what I felt that I had gained as a result of writing in a mathematics course. I was then asked to comment on the writing experience and the journals that I had kept, to see exactly how it was that I had gained a better understanding of the mathematics I was learning. I found many instances where certain ideas or concepts became clearer to me as a result of writing about them.
>
> (Powell and López 1989: 172)

Extending the idea that writing is effective in learning mathematics and that teacher and student jointly can study this process, Powell, Jeffries and Selby (1989) have inserted into the discussion the need to attend to the more general, human process of empowerment. Their concern is for the empowerment of all actors in various settings of mathematics education. Not only did students and instructors study students' journals, but students critiqued the instructors' pedagogical approach. In analyzing the project, students went on to define research activities in pedagogy to be participatory and to have the potential to be empowering when they give authority to the voices of students. For students generally feel, and are often considered to be, without power in many instructional settings. To give authority to the voices of students and to incorporate their perspectives into the transformation of mathematics pedagogy, instructors must begin by listening to students and finding in-depth ways to incorporate students' perspectives into educational research.

On the other hand, we need to avoid what Youngman (1986: 179) calls Freire's tendency toward an 'uncritical faith in "the people" [which] makes him ambivalent about saying outright that educators can have a theoretical understanding *superior* to that of the learners and which is, in fact, the indispensable condition of the development of critical consciousness'. While we listen to students' themes, we organize them using our critical and theoretical frameworks, and we re-present them as problems challenging students' previous perceptions. We also suggest themes that may not occur to our students, themes we judge are important to shattering the commonly held myths about the structure of society and knowledge that interfere with the development of critical consciousness.

We need to do more research to find ways of helping our students learn about their ethnomathematical knowledge, contributing to our theoretical knowledge, without denying inequality of knowledge, but as much as possible 'based on co-operative and democratic principles of equal power' (Youngman 1986: 179). And we need to attend to Freire's concept of praxis – the inseparability of action and reflection – to break down the dichotomies between teaching and learning, between formulating research questions and finding answers. As Lave concludes about the Adult Math Project study of supermarket mathematics, 'description and analysis have been part of the project as a whole in all its phases, rather than uniquely divided between methods (or disciplines)' (1988: 121).[17]

But the underlying question throughout all this work is how the cultural action involved in teaching and learning ethnomathematics can play a role in the economic and political action needed to create a liberatory society. Carby (1990: 85) highlights this issue in her remarks on the changes in the literary canon at the universities, where African-American women have become subjects on the syllabus, but the material conditions of most African-Americans are still ignored. She challenges us to think through the issues of real power: 'Are the politics of difference effective in making visible women of color while rendering invisible the politics of exploitation?'. Moreover, as Lange and Lange (1984: 14) found, although mathematics education can be empowering in a more general way, it is not necessarily the best approach in working with people on specific empowerment issues. The piece-rate workers they were organizing in the textile industry in the southern United States were struggling with a pay system made intentionally obscure, and the Langes felt it was more empowering to create a slide-rule distributed by the union that did the pay calculations for the workers, making the mathematics problem disappear, so that the workers could 'focus on the social and economic relations underlying the way they are treated and paid'.

On the other hand, the general empowerment through ethnomathematical knowledge is, we feel, a very important part of the struggle to overcome a colonized mentality. Samora Machel argues that colonialism is the greatest destroyer of culture that humanity has ever known. African society and its culture were crushed, and when they survived they were co-opted so that they could be more easily emptied of their content. This was done in two distinct ways. One was the utilization of institutions in order to support colonial exploitation . . . The other was the 'folklorising' of culture, its reduction to more or less picturesque habits and customs, to impose in their place the values of colonialism.

(1978: 400)

As we have discussed above, the connections between educational action and liberatory social change are the most undeveloped aspects of Freire's theories. Our practice confirms that ethnomathematical knowledge increases students' self-confidence and opens up areas of critical insight in their understanding of the nature of knowledge. But there is no confirmation that this knowledge results in action against oppression and domination. In the current historical context of an advanced capitalist society, it may be that the most critical collective change that a pedagogy of the oppressed can bring about is a subtle shift in ideological climate that will encourage action for a just socialist economic and political restructuring. This is not insignificant. Nteta (1987: 55) argues that 'revolutionary self-consciousness [is] an objective force within the process of liberation'. He shows how the aim of Steve Biko's theories and the Black Consciousness Movement in South Africa was 'to demystify power relations so that blacks would come to view their status as neither natural, inevitable nor part of the eternal social order . . . [creating] conditions that have irreversibly transfigured South Africa's political landscape' (60–1). We argue that as we understand more clearly the limits of our educational practice we will increase the radical possibilities of our educational action for liberatory change. Thus, we feel the most important area for ethnomathematical research to pursue is the dialectics between knowledge and action for change.[18] Fasheh points the way to the direction of investigation by hypothesizing that

teaching math through cultural relevance and personal experiences helps the learners know more about reality, culture, society and themselves. That will, in turn, help them become more aware, more critical, more appreciative, and more self-confident. It will help them build new perspectives and syntheses, and seek new alternatives, and, hopefully, will help them transform some existing structures and relations.

(1982: 8)

NOTES

1 Further, D'Ambrosio (1987) challenges the static notion that 'there is only one underlying logic governing all thought', and Diop (1991: 363) illustrates how the interactions between 'logic' and 'experience' change our definition of 'logic' over time.

2 One of Freire's first comments at the Boston College course he taught (1982) concerned

his debt to the many American women who wrote to him praising *Pedagogy of the Oppressed* but criticizing his sexist language. He has changed his language; we, therefore, change his quotes in this respect.

3 In the words of McLaren (1990: 117) '[e]mancipatory knowledge is never fully realized, but is continually struggled for'.

4 One such forum is the newsletter of the International Study Group on Ethnomathematics (ISGEm). To subscribe or receive further information, contact Gloria Gilmer, 9155 North 70th Street, Milwaukee, WI 53223, USA.

5 Joseph's work (1987 and, especially, 1991) represents further recent significant challenges to Eurocentric historiography.

6 Since the mid-1970s D'Ambrosio, a Brazilian mathematician and philosopher of mathematics education, has presented his ethnomathematics program in English and Portuguese in a variety of forums. For his most elaborate discussion, see D'Ambrosio (1990).

7 For example, see Ascher (1983), Crowe (1971, 1975), Gattegno (1988), Gerdes (1986, 1988a, 1988b), Harris (1987b), Ginsburg (1986), Joseph (1991), Zaslavsky (1973, 1990, 1991).

8 Fasheh's remark was made during a panel presentation, 'Mathematics education in the global village: what can we expect from ethnomathematics?', at the Sixth International Congress on Mathematics Education, in Budapest, Hungary, July 1988.

9 See, for example, Belenky *et al.* (1986: 214–29), Fasheh (1982), and Buerk (1985). Weissglass (1990: 352) also argues that the emotional aspects of knowing and acting must be attended to in order to bring about educational change and that '[t]he educational community's failure to help teachers, administrators, and parents work through their feelings about education and change is a major obstacle to achieving fundamental educational reform'.

10 For instance, 'in meetings like this we cannot change the world, but we can discover and we may become committed' (1982).

11 See Powell and Frankenstein (in press) for a discussion and examples of the curricular applications of ethnomathematics.

12 We do not interpret this work as suggesting that these youngsters *cannot* do school mathematics. Carraher *et al.* (1985: 28) conclude only that the school mathematics curriculum should *start* from the mathematical knowledge that the children already have. Further, Ginsburg (1982: 207–8) reflects on this issue cross-culturally:

> although culture clearly influences certain aspects of cognitive style (i.e., linguistic style), other cognitive systems seem to develop in a uniform and robust fashion, despite variation in environment or culture. Children in different social classes, both black and white, develop similar cognitive abilities, including basic aspects of mathematical thought.

In the same study he also concludes that 'upon entrance to school virtually all children possess many intellectual strengths on which education can build ... Elementary education should therefore be organized in such a way as to build upon children's already existing cognitive strengths.' He further argues (1982: 208–9) that the reason why poor children do not do 'well' in school 'may include motivational factors linked to expectations of limited economic opportunities, inadequate educational practices, and bias on the part of teachers ... [therefore] reform efforts must not be limited to the psychological remediation of the poor child. They must also focus on teaching practices, teachers, and the economic system.'

13 Borba (1991), in a manuscript on the politics intrinsic to 'academic' mathematics, argues that the use of mathematics in everyday life not only makes our choices seem more 'rational', but serves to end the discussion. Once we use mathematics to

justify a decision, no one can question that decision – after all, it is now 'scientifically proved'.

14 Frankenstein (1987) also contends that the shopping applications of school arithmetic curricula contribute to the appearance of 'naturalness' in the way our social and economic structures are organized. Her adult students find it ludicrous to imagine a restructured society where food is free, for example, and where eating is a civil right and not a paid-for commodity.

15 Lumpkin goes on to report that new discoveries caused Struik to reconsider. In a personal communication to her, he states that '[a]s to mathematics, the Stonehenge discussions have made it necessary to rethink our ideas of what neolithic people knew. Gillings (1972) has shown the ancient Egyptians could work with their fractions in a most sophisticated way.'

16 In this essay Adams provides an incredible example of the exaggerated distortion of the knowledge of African peoples. To explain how the Dogon of Mali acquired their extensive astronomical knowledge some Western scientists went as far as hypothesizing that alien ships landed from outer space to tell the Dogon about the stars (1983: 36–37).

17 Lave's work on the inseparability of cognition and context and an ethnomathematical perspective on the meaning of 'logical thought' forces us to re-evaluate A.R. Luria's (1976) conclusions about reasoning and problem solving. His political project was progressive, stemming from a desire to show that, with schooling, peasants were intellectually equal to people in the other classes in Russian society. But his interpretations were limited by his static view of what 'abstract' reasoning is. His cognitive psychological experiments in mathematics problem solving with unschooled people in remote Russian villages led him to theorize that these people could not abstract 'the conditions of the problems from extraneous practical experience . . . and [derive] the appropriate answer from a system of reasoning determined by the logic of the problem rather than graphic practical experience' (120). Luria felt that 'the significance of schooling lies not just in the acquisition of new knowledge, but in the creation of new motives and formal modes of discursive verbal and logical thinking divorced from immediate practical experience' (133). But if, as Lave recognizes, cognition occurs always inextricably, seamlessly intertwined in practice, then possibly Luria's experimental findings were the result of a cultural dissonance (affective, linguistic, ideological and so on) between the experimenters and the experimented upon. And if, as a Freirean ethnomathematical view theorizes, we cannot and do not want to dichotomize the abstract and the practical, then we can conclude that the school's attempts to do this are attempts to *obscure* knowledge in the interest of the status quo. We hope some people more versed in cognitive psychology than we are will pursue these questions. Also, we think such a re-evaluation of Luria would be an important case study in how even the most progressive, critical projects occur in a historical context which limits their work. As Freire's epistemology says, *no* knowledge is static, all knowledge must be critically interrogated, re-examined, and re-created.

18 To this end, John Volmink and the authors have organized a Criticalmathematics Educators Group. Contact the authors for a copy of our newsletter.

REFERENCES

Adams III, H.H. (1983) 'African observers of the universe: the Sirius question' in I.V. Sertima, ed., *Blacks in Science: Ancient and Modern*, New Brunswick, NJ: Transaction.

Anderson, S.E. (1990) 'Worldmath curriculum: fighting eurocentrism in mathematics', *Journal of Negro Education* 59, 3, 348–59.

Ascher, M. (1983) 'The logical-numerical system of Inca quipus', *Annals of the History of Computing* 5, 3, 268–78.

—— (1987) 'Mu Torere: an analysis of a Maori game', *Mathematics Magazine* 60, 2, 90–100.

—— (1988a) 'Graphs in cultures (II): a study in ethnomathematics', *Archives for History of Exact Sciences* 39, 1, 75–95.

—— (1988b) 'Graphs in cultures: a study in ethnomathematics', *Historia Mathematica* 15, 3, 201–27.

—— (1990) 'A river-crossing problem in cross-cultural perspective', *Mathematics Magazine* 63, 1, 26–9.

—— (1991) *Ethnomathematics: A Multicultural View of Mathematical Ideas*, Belmont, CA: Brooks/Cole.

Ascher, M. and Ascher, R. (1975) 'The quipu as a visible language', *Visible Language* 9, 4, 329–56.

—— (1981) *Code of the Quipu: A Study in Media, Mathematics, and Culture*, Ann Arbor, MI: University of Michigan Press.

—— (1986) 'Ethnomathematics', *History of Science* 24, 125–44.

Beckwith, J. (1983) 'Gender and math performance: does biology have implications for educational policy?' *Journal of Education* 165, 159–73.

Belenky, M.F., Clinchy, B.M., Goldberger, N.R. and Tarule, J.M. (1986) *Women's Ways of Knowing: The Development of Self, Voice, and Mind*, New York: Basic Books.

Bernal, M. (1987) *Black Athena: The Afro-Asiatic Roots of Classical Civilization*, London: Free Association.

Bishop, A.J. (1990) 'Western mathematics: the secret weapon of cultural imperialism', *Race and Class* 32, 2, 51–65.

Borba, M.C. (1990) 'Ethnomathematics and education', *For the Learning of Mathematics* 10, 1, 39–43.

—— (1991) 'Intrinsic political aspects of mathematics in education'. Paper presented at the Annual Meeting of the Mathematical Association of America, San Francisco, CA: January.

Bredo, E. and Feinberg, W. (eds) (1982) *Knowledge and Values in Social and Educational Research*, Philadelphia, PA: Temple University Press.

Brown, C. (1978) *Literacy in 30 Hours: Paulo Freire's Process in Northeast Brazil*, Chicago: Alternative Schools Network.

Buerk, D. (1985) 'The voices of women making meaning in mathematics', *Journal of Education* 167, 3, 59–70.

Carby, H.V. (1990) 'The politics of difference', *Ms Magazine*, September/October, 84–5.

Carraher, T.N., Carraher, D.W. and Schliemann, A.D. (1985) 'Mathematics in the streets and in schools', *British Journal of Developmental Psychology* 3, 21–9.

Crowe, D.W. (1971) 'The geometry of African art I: Bakuba art', *Journal of Geometry* 1, 169–82.

—— (1975) 'The geometry of African art II: a catalog of Benin patterns', *Historia Mathematica* 2, 253–71.

D'Ambrosio, U. (1985) 'Ethnomathematics and its place in the history and pedagogy of mathematics', *For the Learning of Mathematics* 5, 1, 44–8.

—— (1987) 'Reflections on ethnomathematics', *International Study Group on Ethnomathematics Newsletter* 3, 1, 3–5.

—— (1988) 'Ethnomathematics: a research program in the history of ideas and in cognition', *International Study Group on Ethnomathematics Newsletter* 4, 1, 5–8.

—— (1990) *Etnomatemática: Arte ou Técnica de Explicar e Conhecer*, São Paulo: Editora Atica.

Diop, C.A. (1991) *Civilization or Barbarism: An Authentic Anthropology*, Brooklyn, NY: Lawrence Hill.

Fasheh, M. (1982) 'Mathematics, culture, and authority', *For the Learning of Mathematics* 3, 2, 2–8.

—— (1988) 'Mathematics in a social context: math within education as a praxis versus within education as hegemony' in C. Keitel, P. Damerow, A. Bishop, and P. Gerdes, eds, *Mathematics, Education, and Society*, Paris: UNESCO.

Frankenstein, M. (1987) 'Critical mathematics education: an application of Paulo Freire's epistemology', in I. Shor, ed., *Freire for the Classroom*, Portsmouth, NH: Boynton/Cook.

—— (1989) *Relearning Mathematics: A Different Third R – Radical Maths*, London: Free Association.

Freire, P. (1970) *Pedagogy of the Oppressed*, New York: Seabury.

—— (1973) *Education for Critical Consciousness*, New York: Seabury.

—— (1982) 'Education for critical consciousness'. Boston College course notes taken by M. Frankenstein.

Gattegno, C. (1970) *What We Owe Children: The Subordination of Teaching to Learning*, New York: Avon.

—— (1988) *The Science of Education: Part 2B: The Awareness of Mathematization*, New York: Educational Solutions.

Gerdes, P. (1985) *Marx Demystifies Calculus* (B. Lumpkin, trans.), Minneapolis: Marxist Educational Press.

—— (1986) 'How to recognize hidden geometrical thinking: a contribution to the development of anthropological mathematics', *For the Learning of Mathematics* 6, 2, 10–12, 17.

—— (1988a) 'On culture, geometrical thinking and mathematics education', *Educational Studies in Mathematics* 19, 137–62.

—— (1988b) 'On the possible uses of traditional Angolan sand drawings in the mathematics classroom', *Educational Studies in Mathematics* 19, 3–22.

Gillings, R.J. (1972) *Mathematics in the Time of the Pharoahs*, Cambridge, MA: MIT Press (Dover reprint, 1982).

Ginsburg, H.P. (1982) 'The development of addition in the context of culture, social class and race' in T.P. Carpenter, J.M. Moser and T.A. Romberg, eds, *Addition and Subtraction: A Cognitive Perspective*, Hillsdale, NJ: Lawrence Erlbaum.

—— (1986) 'The myth of the deprived child: new thoughts on poor children' in U. Neisser, ed., *The School Achievement of Minority Children: New Perspectives*, Hillsdale, NJ: Lawrence Erlbaum.

Giroux, H. (1981) *Ideology, Culture and the Process of Schooling*, Philadelphia: Temple University Press.

Gordon, M. (1978) 'Conflict and liberation: personal aspects of the mathematics experience', *Curriculum Inquiry* 8, 3, 251–71.

Harris, M. (1987a) 'An example of traditional women's work as a mathematics resource', *For the Learning of Mathematics* 7, 3, 26–8.

—— (1987b) *Maths in Work*, London: Macmillan.

Henderson, D.W. (1990) 'The masquerade of formal mathematics and how it damages the human spirit' in R. Noss, A. Brown, P. Drake, P. Dowling, M. Harris, C. Hoyles, and S. Mellin-Olsen, eds, *Proceedings of the First International Conference: Political Dimensions of Mathematics Education: Action and Critique*, Institute of Education: University of London.

Johnson, D.K. (1991) 'A pragmatic realist foundation for critical thinking', *Inquiry: Critical Thinking across the Disciplines* 7, 3, 23–7.

Joseph, G.C. (1987) 'Foundations of eurocentrism in mathematics', *Race and Class* 28, 3, 13–28.

—— (1991) *The Crest of the Peacock: The Non-European Roots of Mathematics*, London: I.B. Tauris.

Kline, M. (1953) *Mathematics in Western Culture*, New York: Oxford University Press.

Knijnik, G. (1992) 'An ethnomathematical approach in mathematical education – a matter of political power'. Unpublished manuscript.

Lange, B. and Lange, J. (1984) 'Organizing piece-rate workers in the textile industry', *Science for the People* May/June, 12–16.

Lave, J. (1988) *Cognition in Practice*, Cambridge: Cambridge University Press.

Lumpkin, B. (1983) 'Africa in the mainstream of mathematics history' in I.V. Sertima, ed, *Blacks in Science: Ancient and Modern*, New Brunswick, NJ: Transaction.

Luria, A.R. (1976) *Cognitive Development: Its Cultural and Social Foundations*, Cambridge, MA: Harvard University Press.

Machel, S. (1978) 'Knowledge and science should be for the total liberation of man', *Race and Class* 19, 4, 399–404.

Mackie, R. (1981) 'Contributions to the thought of Paulo Freire' in R. Mackie, ed., *Literacy and Revolution: The Pedagogy of Paulo Freire*, New York: Continuum.

Martin, B. (1988) 'Mathematics and social interests', *Search* 19, 4, 209–14.

Marshack, A. (1991) *The Roots of Civilization*, revised edition, Mount Kisco, NY: Moyer Bell.

Marx, K. (1983) *Mathematical Manuscripts of Karl Marx* (New Park, trans.), London: New Park.

McLaren, P. (1990) 'Review of *Freire for the Classroom: A Sourcebook for Liberatory Teaching*', *Journal of Urban and Cultural Studies* 1, 1, 113–25.

Mtetwa, D. (1992) '"Mathematics" and ethnomathematics: Zimbabwean students' view', *International Study Group on Ethnomathematics Newsletter* 7, 1, 1–3.

Nteta, C. (1987) 'Revolutionary self-consciousness as an objective force within the process of liberation: Biko and Gramsci', *Radical America* 21, 5, 55–61.

Osen, L.M. (1974) *Women in Mathematics*, Cambridge, MA: MIT Press.

Pinxten, R., van Dooren, I., and Harvey, F. (1983) *The Anthropology of Space*, Philadelphia: University of Pennsylvania.

Powell, A.B. (1986) 'Marx and mathematics in Mozambique', *Science and Nature* 7/8, 119–23.

Powell, A.B. and Frankenstein, M. (in press) 'Ethnomathematics: challenging eurocentrism in mathematics' in S. Federici, ed., *Enduring Eurocentrism*, London: Free Association.

Powell, A.B., Jeffries, D.A., and Selby, A.E. (1989) 'An empowering participatory research model for humanistic mathematics pedagogy', *Humanistic Mathematics Network Newsletter* 4, 29–38.

Powell, A.B., and López, J.A. (1989) 'Writing as a vehicle to learn mathematics: a case study' in P. Connolly and T. Vilardi, eds, *The Role of Writing in Learning Mathematics and Science*, New York: Teachers College.

Powell, A.B. and Ramnauth, M. (1992) 'Beyond questions and answers: prompting reflections and deepening understandings of mathematics using multiple-entry logs', *For the Learning of Mathematics* 12, 2, 12–18.

Puchalska, E., and Semadeni, Z. (1987) 'Children's reaction to verbal arithmetic problems with missing, surplus or contradictory data', *For the Learning of Mathematics* 7, 3, 9–16.

Rose, M. (1988) 'Narrowing the mind and page: remedial writers and cognitive reductionism', *College Composition and Communication* 39, 3, 267–302.

Scribner, S. (1984) 'Studying working intelligence' in B. Rogoff and J. Lave, eds, *Everyday Cognition: Its Development in Social Context*, Cambridge, MA: Harvard University Press.

Spradbery, J. (1976) 'Conservative pupils? Pupil resistance to curriculum innovation in mathematics' in G. Whitty and M. Young, eds, *Explorations in the Politics of School Knowledge*, Driffield: Nafferton.

Walkerdine, V. (1990) 'Difference, cognition and mathematics education', *For the Learning of Mathematics* 10, 3, 51–6.

Weissglass, J. (1990) 'Constructivist listening for empowerment and change', *The Educational Forum* 54, 4, 351–70.

Weizenbaum, J. (1985) 'Computers in uniform: a good fit?', *Science for the People* 17, 1 and 2, 26–9.

Youngman, F. (1986) *Adult Education and Socialist Pedagogy*, London: Croom Helm.

Zaslavsky, C. (1973) *Africa Counts: Number and Patterns in African Culture*, Boston: Prindle, Weber and Schmidt.

—— (1990) 'Symmetry in American folk art', *Arithmetic Teacher* 38, 1, 6–12.

—— (1991) 'Multicultural mathematics education for the middle grades', *Arithmetic Teacher* 38, 6, 8–13.

Chapter 5

Twenty years after *Pedagogy of the Oppressed*
Paulo Freire in conversation with Carlos Alberto Torres

Carlos Alberto Torres and Paulo Freire

INTRODUCTION: PAULO FREIRE – A MYTH IN HIS OWN LIFETIME?

Brazilian educator and philosopher Paulo Freire has been described by the renowned Swiss educator Pierre Furter as 'a myth in his own lifetime' (1985: 301). He has become an outstanding figure in the academic world through his unique combination of theory with practical experience in the field of adult education. It is widely known that Freire became famous in the early sixties for his powerful method of literacy training (Freire 1965, Gadotti 1989, Brandao 1979, Torres 1980, Brown 1987), but his writing went far beyond explicating mere techniques for literacy training to become a landmark for critical pedagogy all over the world.

His personal involvement with important literacy campaigns and innovative experiences in adult education in the Third World (Brazil prior to 1964, Chile, Nicaragua, Guinea-Bissau, Grenada, São Tome, Cabo Verde, Principe and Tanzania) have brought unique insights into highly complex matters. His writing has impacted on women's and workers' education in Europe, even as a source of contradiction, and his new analyses of the role of liberating pedagogy in industrially advanced societies (conveyed in his recent books with Ira Shor and Donaldo Macedo) currently provide an important focus for debate and ongoing pedagogical thinking. It is no exaggeration to say that, as John Dewey was the dominant figure in pedagogy in the first half of the century, Paulo Freire has been the catalyst, if not the prime *animateur*, for pedagogical innovation and change in the second half.

Freire has received numerous honorary doctorates, awards, and prizes for his work, including the 1987 UNESCO Peace Prize. In 1985 he and his late wife, Elza, received the Prize for Christian Educators in the United States. The importance of his work is witnessed in the fact that his major works (especially *Pedagogy of the Oppressed, Education for Critical Consciousness*, and *Pedagogy in Process: Letters from Guinea-Bissau*) have been translated into diverse languages including English, German, Italian, Spanish, Korean, Japanese, and French. *Pedagogy of the Oppressed* has run to more than thirty-five reprints in Spanish, nineteen in Portuguese, and twelve in English.

The 'Freirean approach' has been implemented in social studies and curriculum studies within adult education, as well as in such wide-ranging areas as the teaching of mathematics and physics, educational planning, feminist studies, Romance languages, educational psychology, and critical approaches to reading and writing. During the last two decades Paulo Freire's work has been the subject of dozens of doctoral and masters dissertations. The burgeoning bibliographies on his work now amount to thousands of references, from those which report implementation of some aspect of his proposals to those which report critical argument against them.

Freire's 1987 book with Donaldo Macedo calls for a view of literacy as *cultural politics*. That is, literacy training should not merely provide reading, writing and numeracy, but should be considered 'a set of practices that functions to either empower or disempower people. Literacy [for Freire and Macedo] is analyzed according to whether it serves to reproduce existing social formations or serves as a set of cultural practices that promotes democratic and emancipatory change' (Freire and Macedo 1987: viii). Literacy as cultural politics is also related in Freire's work to emancipatory theory and critical theory of society. Hence, emancipatory literacy 'becomes a vehicle by which the oppressed are equipped with the necessary tools to reappropriate their history, culture, and language practices' (ibid.: 159).

In short, Paulo Freire is currently one of the most vibrant educators and political philosophers of education. The long-term impact of his pedagogical thinking will doubtless evolve well into the next century.

PAULO FREIRE AS SECRETARY OF EDUCATION FOR THE MUNICIPALITY OF SÃO PAULO, BRAZIL

The interview that follows offers a fresh view of Freire's perspective on politics and education less than a year after taking over as Secretary of Education in the municipality of São Paulo. The interview was conducted in fall 1989, and an earlier version was published in the journal *Aurora*.[1]

Paulo Freire is one of the founding members of the *Partido dos Trabalhadores* (Workers' Party) of Brazil, a democratic socialist party that was founded in 1980 after a series of metallurgical workers' strikes in the state of São Paulo, and that quickly gained national prominence (Anonymous 1989, Gadotti and Pereira 1989). The party's president and charismatic leader, Luis Inácio Lula da Silva, currently a Federal Representative in the Brazilian Congress, was in 1989 runner-up in the election for the Brazilian presidency, losing by a narrow margin to Fernando Collor de Melo.

The Workers' Party won the municipal elections of November 15, 1988, in São Paulo. The new mayor, Luiza Erundina de Sousa (de Sousa 1991), a noted social worker who represented the interests of diverse social movements in São Paulo, appointed Freire as Secretary of Education.

The city of São Paulo, with 12 million people, is one of Latin America's largest municipalities and the financial center of Brazil. It poses serious educational challenges (CEDI 1990, Cunha 1992: esp. 22–101, 197–227). Paulo Freire presided over 660 schools with 720,000 students K–8 (Kindergarten to grade 8), and 40,000 employees – the latter comprising 30 per cent of all employees of the São Paulo municipality.

Freire instituted drastic changes in municipal education, including a comprehensive curriculum reform, new models of school management through the implementation of school councils – comprising teachers, principals, parents and government officials – and a movement for literacy training, MOVA-São Paulo, built on participative planning and delivery with support from non-governmental organizations and social movements (Torres 1990, 1991).

Freire eventually resigned on May 27, 1991, to resume his academic activities, lecturing and writing. His former Chief of Cabinet, 37-year-old Mario Sergio Cortella, a professor of philosophy and theology at the Pontifical Catholic University of São Paulo and a doctoral student under Freire's supervision at the same university, was appointed as the new Secretary of Education. He continued the overall policy outlined by Freire and the Workers' Party. New municipal elections took place in November 1992 and the PT lost the election. The new administration was inaugurated in January 1993. Thus the fate of changes prompted by Freire's administration are yet to face the test of time.

POLITICS AND EDUCATION: PAULO FREIRE IN CONVERSATION WITH CARLOS ALBERTO TORRES

CT: Twenty years ago you wrote and published your influential book *Pedagogy of the Oppressed*, based on your educational experiences in Brazil and Chile. This book, as you know, has had a profound impact on contemporary pedagogy and has been translated into several languages and reprinted many times. Many would argue that this book has become a classic in contemporary pedagogy. Why did you decide to write this educational book? What is the history behind *Pedagogy of the Oppressed*, as seen in perspective twenty years later?

PF: I think the first thing I ought to say is that I write about what I do. In other words, my books are as if they were theoretical reports of my practice. In the case of *Pedagogy of the Oppressed*, I started to write it exactly at the beginning of 1968 – after the second or third year of my exile. What happened? When I left Brazil and went into exile I passed my time firstly learning to live with a borrowed reality, which was the reality of exile. Secondly, I struggled with my original context which was the context of Brazil, and which I saw myself forced to abandon. From afar I began to take stock of Brazil and therefore to take stock of and analyze my earlier practice, discovering in it things that the new context of borrowed reality was making me discover. So there was a moment, naturally, when I began to arrive at a more radical understanding of my own work. With this supported by the experience of Chile, made in quasi-comparison with the earlier experience of Brazil, I felt the need to put to paper another moment of my pedagogic and political experience. *Pedagogy of the Oppressed* appeared as a practical, theoretical necessity in my professional career.

CT: How did that title occur to you?

PF: That is also interesting. My books earn a title even before they are written. *Pedagogy of the Oppressed*, which I think is one of my best titles, came to mind during the process of my experience in Chile, and it recalled many of my earlier experiences of Brazil.

Secondly, the title came as a need to underscore the existence of another pedagogy, which does not have a subtitle, and is the pedagogy of the oppressor. I intended, with the title *Pedagogy of the Oppressed*, to distinguish this type of pedagogy from another which, even though it existed, had concealed itself under other titles, other names. I was concerned also to call to attention the role of the *subject*, as opposed to that of the pure actor,[2] for the working classes in the process of their own liberation. Hence the title 'Pedagogy of the Oppressed People' which, in a general way, is also expressed in the singular. Fundamentally, my preoccupation was with a pedagogy of oppressed people, in the plural. But it ended up in the singular as *Pedagogy of the Oppressed*.[3]

CT: I would like now to take you from Latin America to the United States and Canada. You have recently published two influential books in the United States in collaboration respectively with Ira Shor and Donaldo Macedo. You know the United States and Canada very well from your frequent lecturing, teaching, and visiting in both countries. How do you think the political philosophy underlying *Pedagogy of the Oppressed* could be applied in teacher training in these two industrial societies?

PF: I will try to express this in simple terms and begin from an understanding of what teaching is, and thus education and training of both educators and students. For me, the process of forming educators necessarily implies the act of teaching, which should be developed by the teacher, and the act of learning, which should be developed by an apprentice.

It is necessary to clarify what teaching is and what learning is. For me, teaching is the form or the act of knowing, which the professor or educator exercises; it takes as its witness the student. This act of knowing is given to the student as testimony, so that the student will not merely act as a learner. In other words, teaching is the form that the teacher or educator possesses to bear witness to the student about what knowing is, so that the student will also know instead of simply learning. For that reason, here the process of learning implies the learning of the object that ought to be learned. This preoccupation has nothing to do exclusively with the teaching of literacy skills. This preoccupation establishes the act of teaching and the act of learning as fundamental moments in the general process of knowledge, a process of which the educator on the one hand and the educatee on the other are a part. And this process implies a subjective stance. It is impossible that a person, not being the subject of his or her own curiosity, can truly grasp the object of his or her knowledge. So, this requirement of the knowledge process is realized not only by grasping the object of knowledge; it is the words, the reading, and the writing. The same occurs when the object of knowledge is sociology, biology, and physics or whatever. Now, when you ask me, 'Paulo, how do you see your proposal at the First World level and not only at the level of literacy training?', I reply that it is a question of the theory of knowledge that I established in pedagogical form in the *Pedagogy of the Oppressed*. Therefore, it also has to do with a democratic option. If an educator in Canada or the United States, who is neither authoritarian nor traditional, understands that his or her job of teaching demands the critical task of knowing on the part of his or her educatees, then there is no way not to apply this also in Canada or the United States. Canadians and Americans, since they are part of the First World, have not ceased to involve themselves daily in the process of knowledge.

CT: Is it possible to develop the pedagogy of the oppressed with a rational pedagogy which is at the same time radical in the political context of a hegemonic power like the United States?

PF: That is a very important question. Educational practice is part of the super-structure of any society. In the end, and for that very reason, in spite of its incredible importance in the socio-historical processes of the transformation of societies, educational practice nevertheless is not in itself the key to trans-formation – even though it is fundamental. Dialectically, education is not the key to transformation, although transformation is in itself educational.

The question you raise, Carlos, seems to me also to be founded necessarily on a further problem, namely the problem of political option and decision. In the first place, with respect to a democratic pedagogy, there is no reason why the pedagogy cannot be applied just because we are dealing with the First World. Secondly, it is necessary to deepen the democratic angle of this pedagogy I am defending. Deepening and widening the horizon of democratic practice will necessarily involve the political and ideological options of the social groups carrying this pedagogy out. So, obviously, a power elite will not enjoy putting in place and practicing a pedagogical form or expression that adds to the social contradictions which reveal the power of the elite classes. It would be naive to think that a power elite would reveal itself for what it is through a pedagogical process that in the end would work against the elite itself.

CT: Your pedagogical and political work has been directed toward, and elaborated in tension with, the purview of the popular classes, the marginals, the working class, the peasants in Latin America, the oppressed people elsewhere. It is my impression that in the last decades, with the increasing dependent development of capitalist social formations, the more interdependent relationship between nations in the world system, and the growing levels of poverty, exploitation and domination of the underclasses in many Third World countries (and in industrialized societies as well), the existential situation of the popular classes has been worsening rather than improving. Changes in material conditions of life should have an impact on changes in consciousness. Looking at the role of education promoting 'conscientization', the term that became associated with your work, what is similar and what is different today in Brazil and Latin America more generally, by comparison with your experiences twenty years ago?

PF: Some of the fundamental problems my generation had to confront twenty-five years ago continue to be the same. Let me name two or three of the problems my generation confronted and that my grandchildren's generation now confronts.

Brazilian illiteracy, on account of which I ended up expelled from my country, continues to be a growing problem even in today's Brazil. The number of school-age children who do not reach the schools is another absurdity that continues to accompany the political and social life of Brazil. Today we have eight million Brazilian children prevented from being in school. The number of children who are pushed out of school, a phenomenon known to the official pedagogy as 'scholastic evasion' or academic drop-out, continues to be a problem for today's educators just as it was a problem for the educators of thirty or forty years ago.

In my generation we had the issue of domination by foreign capital, which we spoke of as the consignment of profits to foreign lands. Today we still experience the power of the multinationals. The lack of decorum, the lack of shame in Brazilian political and public life, which was a problem of my generation, is an immense problem today. Economic inflation ends up spoiling our ethics and so lays waste to the entire depth of society. These problems remain. The answer, however, is not the same now. It cannot be the same. I am not going to repeat today the literacy training I practiced twenty-five years ago.

We are now launching in São Paulo something called *MOVA-São Paulo*, a movement of literacy and post-literacy training. Within greater São Paulo today, we have to confront 1.5 million illiterate people, and within the city itself, 1 million. And we have to make a contribution or give testimony to the fact that with public power, if one has political will, something can be done.

CT: The challenges in your job as Secretary of Education are many, considering the size of São Paulo, and its seemingly insurmountable problems of abandoned children living in the streets, growing poverty and urban violence, fiscal constraints, particularly due to Brazil's growing external debt, and the peculiarities of post-dictatorship Brazilian politics and electoral struggle. The following question is related to the previous one: namely, what are the limits and possibilities of implementing a pedagogy of the oppressed that will be effective in achieving its goals, in the context of a municipality such as São Paulo?

PF: Today, I am Secretary of Education for the city of São Paulo, with much more clarity, with much more political and pedagogical understanding, I hope, than when I was thirty or thirty-five years old. I see things more clearly now and I feel more radical, although never sectarian, in the face of my country's reality. I have a more lucid vision of what we must do to change schooling from the public schooling we have now, into a school that is happy, into a school that is rigorous, into a school that works democratically. A school in which teachers and students know together and in which the teacher teaches, but while teaching does not domesticate the student who, upon learning, will end up also teaching the teacher.

If you were to ask me, 'Are you attempting to put into practice the concepts you described in your book?', of course I am, but in a manner in keeping with the times. It is one thing to write down concepts in books, but it is another to embody those concepts in praxis. Those things are showing themselves to be very challenging, but they continue to give me a sense of joy and satisfaction. It is not perchance that I am struggling to make at least a minimum contribution in the radical line of the pedagogy of liberation.

CT: There is a kind of wind of optimism from the south that inspires me. I certainly find you younger every day, since every day you are more optimistic, and it is good to know that you are making headway in putting your pedagogy into practice with so much enthusiasm. Let me pose now a final question about the relationship between the political compromise of a socialist intellectual party member and the possibilities and the limits of education in the context of Brazil today – that is, the possibilities and limits of promoting an education for social transformation in the context of modern Brazil. What is your sense of the situation at present?

PF: Now, I am going to tell you something you will understand as a man who thinks dialectically and doesn't merely talk of dialectics. You must know intellectuals who talk about dialectics very well but do not think dialectically.

Today I live the enormous joy of perceiving with every passing day that the strength of education resides precisely in its limitations. The efficiency of education resides in the impossibility of doing everything. The limits of education would bring a naive man or woman to desperation. A dialectical man or woman discovers in the limits of education the raison d'être for his or her efficiency. It is in this way that I feel that today I am an efficient Secretary of Education because I am limited.

NOTES

1   This is an updated and complete version of the interview of October 2, 1989, published in abridged form in 1990 in *Aurora* 13, 3. The interview was translated from Spanish by Paul Belanger.

2 *Interviewer's note:* 'The role of the subject' refers to the workers taking their destiny into their own hands, while the notion of 'pure actor' merely refers to someone who might be acting a role in a play, but who at any rate has no control over his or her discourse or actions.

3 *Translator's note:* The English translation loses some of the Spanish meaning here. Freire juxtaposes the expression *los oprimidos* with *el oprimido* which English renders as 'the oppressed' in both instances.

REFERENCES

Anonymous (1989) 'PT. Um projecto para o Brasil'. Seminar held in São Paulo, April 15–16. São Paulo: Editora Brasilience.

Brandao, C.R. (1979) 'Eva via a luta: algunas anotação sobre a Pedagogia do Oprimido e a Educação do Colonizador', *Educacao e Sociedade* 3, 15–23.

Brown, C. (1987) 'Literacy in 30 hours: Paulo Freire's process in Northeast Brazil' in I. Shor, ed., *Freire for the Classroom: A Sourcebook for Liberatory Teachers*, Portsmouth, NH: Boynton/Cook.

CEDI (Centro Ecumenico de Documentacao e Informacao) (1990) 'Educação no Brasil, 1987–1988', *Aconteceu*, vol. 19, São Paulo: CEDI.

Cunha, L.A. (1992) *Educação, Estado e Democracia no Brasil*, São Paulo: Niteroi, and Brasilia: Cortez Editora/Editora da Universadade Federal Fluminense/FLACSO.

Freire, P. (1965) 'Alfabetización de adultos y conscientización', *Mensaje* 14, 142, 494–501.

—— (1991) *A Educação na Cidade* (M. Gadotti and C.A. Torres, preface), São Paulo: Cortez Editora.

Freire, P. and Macedo, D. (1987) *Literacy: Reading the Word and the World*, South Hadley, MA: Bergin and Garvey.

Furter, P. (1985) 'Profile of educators: Paulo Freire'. *Prospects* 15, 2, 301–10.

Gadotti, M. (1989) *Convite á Leitura de Paulo Freire*, São Paulo: Scipione.

Gadotti, M. and Pereira, O. (1989) *Pra que PT: Origem, Projeto e Consolidação do Partido dos Trabalhadores*, São Paulo: Cortez Editora.

Shor, I. and Freire, P. (1987) *A Pedagogy for Liberation. Dialogues on Transforming Education*, South Hadley, MA: Bergin and Garvey.

de Sousa, L.E. (1991) *Exercicio da Paixão Politica*, São Paulo: Cortez Editora.

Torres, C.A. (1980) *Paulo Freire: Educación y Conscientización*, Salamanca: Ediciones Sigueme.

—— (1990) 'Paulo Freire on adult education: an interview and panel discussion' in A. Konrad, ed., *Everyone's Challenge: Proceedings of the Literacy Conference*, Edmonton, Alberta: University of Alberta. (Also available as *Learning the World: Paulo Freire in Conversation with Dr Carlos Alberto Torres*, Edmonton, Alberta, Access Network [Canadian Public Television], October, videotape.)

—— (1991) 'Democratic socialism, social movements, and educational policy in Brazil: the work of Paulo Freire as Secretary of Education in the municipality of São Paulo'. Paper presented at the Fifteenth World Congress of Political Science, Buenos Aires, July 21–5.

Chapter 6

Conscientization and social movements in Canada
The relevance of Paulo Freire's ideas in contemporary politics

Peter Findlay

INTRODUCTION

This chapter will explore two broad themes. The first is the significance of contemporary 'social movements' for social and political change in a relatively developed North American country, Canada. The second is the general relevance of the ideas of the renowned Brazilian education theorist and practitioner Paulo Freire to these social and political change strategies in one pocket of the highly developed North American economy and society. The final purpose is to assess the intersignificance of these two themes: do the new social movements – peace, environment, ecology, women's rights, social justice, rights of the disabled and of prisoners, and so on – have potential for progressive social transformation as some claim; and are the ideas advanced by Paulo Freire, which were primarily or originally focused on other social, cultural and economic contexts, germane to whatever potential these social movements may have?

Freire's ideas, as is well known, have mostly been applied in less economically developed contexts in South America and Africa, or in literacy work in more developed economies. As well, there have been efforts to explore and incorporate some of the principles and precepts that he adduced and elaborated, following on in the tradition of the Movement for Basic Education in Brazil, into education and social development training programs in North America. As would be expected, given the central importance of 'liberation theology' in the South American development of these principles and precepts, some of the spreading of Freire's concepts and approaches to pedagogy came through the institution of the churches, particularly the Catholic church. More generally, however, his ideas and writings have had a widespread and substantial impact on approaches to education and learning in parts of North America, especially the notions of cultural specificity, androgogy, and rejection of the 'banking concept' in teaching and learning. And the great central process of teaching and learning covered under the key term '*conscientização*', its English counterpart 'conscientization', and its popular cousin 'consciousness raising' have been widely embraced in North American progressive education and social development circles.

What has been less embraced is the implicit and explicit Marxist analytic which is fundamental in Freire's conception. In his work there is no question that unmasking and demystifying the realities of class struggle is a crucial, if not *the* crucial, consideration. The main route to social transformation in conscientization is considered to be through learning, expressed both in terms of the proscriptions about the learning process and in the focus on 'generative themes'. These themes are to be uncovered through 'codifications' whereby, for example, middle-class people who lead the learning process must work with the learners in a mutual interaction which avoids 'cultural invasion' or ingrained class oppression. More importantly, this learning process can succeed only through sustained, profound emphasis on achieving critical consciousness which will permit and ensure the unmasking of oppressive structures, particularly those based on class relationships. It is in this dimension of Freire's work – its emphasis on material conditions and the nature of production with the attendant class-based oppression – that provides its transformative content. And it is this dimension that leads to a consideration of social movements.

Social movements are presented by some as a new form of political action, arising in response to dramatically changing material conditions and historical political realities. The great bipolar struggle between capital and wage labor and between their social representations, bourgeoisie and proletariat, is no longer seen to capture the complex nature of contemporary industrial societies. For Carl Boggs, who has provided an important international analysis of the phenomenon, 'the new movements embody a range of diverse and popular forms of revolt over issues that seem endemic to the phase of mature industrial development: economic stagnation, ecological disequilibrium, militarism and nuclear politics, bureaucracy' (Boggs 1986: x). These new circumstances and the subjective responses to them on the part of many people are seen to have fundamentally altered political action and to require new theoretical explication. A 'post-Marxist' paradigm is seen to be needed to situate and comprehend the new social movements.

However accurate this statement may be internationally and epochally, it is clear that particular national and even local conditions must be analyzed for their historical, cultural, demographic, and political-economic specificities. Vincente Navarro (1988), for example, argues convincingly that 'it is far too premature to add our voices to the growing Gorzian chorus singing farewell to class and the working class' (p. 435). Writing about the United States, he points out that it is faulty to separate the categories of class and social movements, since 'classes are always inside the social movements'. Likewise, he points out that class struggle is never clearly defined, but rather is an 'objective reality', which, though it may take various forms and focuses, is always there. Moreover, he reviews strong evidence that American workers perceive themselves as members of a dominated class and understand class not as status description but as power relations. Challenging the analysis of the 1984 presidential campaign of Reverend Jesse Jackson, presented in the influential book *The Rainbow Challenge*, Navarro states 'class is everywhere and class conflicts determine how racism and sexism appear and are reproduced' (p. 435)

It is not the purpose here to clarify, let alone resolve, whether or not social class and class struggle remain the central theoretical categories in North America, nor whether the working class continues to be the crucial agent for social change. That project requires sustained cross-cultural and case-by-case empirical analyses. Some of this work is being done in analyses of various 'welfare states' (e.g., Rosenblum 1980; Milner 1989) and in analyses of social movements such as, for example, 'youth movements' (e.g., Braungart 1984), the farm labor movement (e.g., Majka and Majka 1984) or the worker ownership movement (e.g., Rothschild-Whitt 1984). As indicated, the intent here is to review various aspects or manifestations of newer political currents in Canada which can be characterized as social movements to see whether or not the precepts of conscientization are germane to their development.

SOCIAL MOVEMENTS IN CANADA

The starting point must be a summary review of the particular historical conditions that characterize Canada as an economic, political, cultural and social entity. In a broad sweep, it is a geographically immense land-base for a relatively small human population (nearly 10 million square kilometres populated by some 26 million people, or 2.5 persons per square kilometre), with an economy shaped by an historical alliance on natural resources exploitation or 'staples' trade. This ecological and economic history has taken place within an explicit colonial context, originally that of France, more lastingly Britain, and ultimately replaced to a great extent by the United States economically and culturally, if less formally in terms of political institutions and affiliation.

In recent years a more formal integration with the United States has been pursued as an explicit policy by the predominant political interests in the country, through a bilateral trade agreement aimed at eliminating tariff and other barriers to the freer movement of capital, goods and services, and labor between the two national economies. This of course has been congruent with developments in other trading blocs within the developed world, but has here the special and profound characteristic of being an association with the most powerful and dedicated capitalist free market country in the world – economically, politically and ideologically. While clearly a part of the economic and political processes of 'globalization', the relationship of Canada to the United States is also fundamentally distinct in many respects, a fact which is especially significant for this discussion of social movements in that one of the most vigorous of them has arisen in resistance to and struggle against the trade agreement.[1]

Two further large-scale factors must be noted here. The first is the historical and continuing significance of Canada's bicultural, bilingual, and binational make-up, a feature that shapes any consideration of class relations and social movements in this context. There are in fact two distinct societies in Canada with, correspondingly, two particular configurations in class relations and social movements. Although this chapter cannot deal with the immense complexity this entails, it is important to bear in mind that there are two realities involved which in some respects have each their own institutions, features and dynamics, while in other respects interact and intertwine in intensely vigorous and complex ways.[2]

The second factor, arising from and related to the binational character of the country, is the confederal form of government that prevails. In contrast to more unitary or centralized states (whether institutionally so or ideologically), Canada has had a clear and basic separation of jurisdiction and political power between the central or 'federal' government and the provincial level – comprised of ten provinces, each quite varied from all of the others in terms of their history, economic base, political perspectives and collective aspirations. The provinces range from the smaller islands of Newfoundland and Prince Edward Island (the latter, for example, having a population of only some 200,000 people), through the industrialized and urbanized provinces of Ontario and Quebec, where live over 16 million of the total population of 26 million, to the three western prairie provinces of the great plains, which together have some 2 million, and on to the 'Pacific rim' province of British Columbia, where a further 1.5 million people live 'ultra Montagne'. On top of this, figuratively and literally, are two territorial governments having some but different jurisdiction over the vast but sparsely settled Canadian north. And as noted above, one of these 'provinces' is perceived by most who live in it and many who live elsewhere to be the 'homeland' to those of French ancestry and language.[3]

The point here is not to belabor, let alone explain, the complexity of governance in Canada; most if not all the countries and regions of the world have their own constitutional complexities and certainly their own rich histories. But each of the factors adumbrated above – geographic location and scale, economic bases, colonial history, binational character, and governmental complexity – has significance for this consideration of social movements and the consequent relevance of conscientization and cultural struggle in Canada. And taken together in their dynamic interaction, they make the task of unravelling class relations, cultural resistance, and social movements in particular quite difficult and necessarily somewhat tenuous.

To begin, however, there have been two synthetic descriptive and analytic treatments of social movements specifically in Canada. The first covers the broad coalition which arose in opposition to the free trade initiative that had emerged as the central economic policy of the Canadian government in the last decade, a coalition among traditional class resistance organizations, anchored by the trade union movement and the farmer and cooperative movements on the one hand, and the newer 'popular' and communitarian groups, including those with more universal affiliation and concern, such as the women's movement, the peace movement and the environmental movement, on the other. The second collection of essays is a more general survey of the experiences of attempts to transform society being made by various organizations within some of the newer movements, which are seen as part of the large project to transcend or transform a reliance on working-class politics and trade unions, or on traditional (and out-dated) socialist or sectarian theories and parties as the agencies of change, and particularly as inspired by a feminist-socialist perspective.

There is some degree of overlap between the two social phenomena being described, as they exist in the 'real' world of Canadian political life and social change, but they are also somewhat separate both in the everyday world and in the two main depictions of them which are relied on here. The first of these is material on the reactions of various groups in opposition to the findings or conclusions of a major official government study of Canadian economic prospects and policies, and their continued coalition in opposition to free trade, with the principal accounts being provided in *The Other MacDonald Report* (Drache and Cameron 1985) and *The Free Trade Papers* (Drache and Cameron 1988). The other main survey of attempts to find new and differently based oppositional strategies is provided in *Social Movements and Social Change: The Politics and Practice of Organizing* (Cunningham *et al.* 1988), which offers twelve case studies of attempts to address issues of gender, race, disability and so on. These will be reviewed in turn, before consideration of the relevance of conscientization to them.

The Pro-Canada Network

In 1984 the government of Canada announced it would be seeking the negotiation and signing of a new trade agreement with the United States of America. This was one of the more stunning reversals of a previously espoused position on a matter of grand policy in Canadian history. Despite the magnitude, which in fact was undeniably an absolutely breathtaking turnabout to a policy which had previously been eschewed totally by the prime minister, it was endorsed by the electorate in a subsequent election which returned the same party to power. This, however, was not accomplished without resistance; a lively, widespread, vigorous (and often furious) opposition coalition immediately developed, which carried the governing party almost to the wall on the issue, and which continues its efforts even though the policy is now legislation and the Agreement is in effect. More importantly, this oppositional coalition brought together groups and associations which had not previously worked together or even seen commonality of interest – in effect a new kind of social movement.

This movement was identified and described by Drache and Cameron as 'what we call "the popular sector": churches, trade unions, women's groups, social agencies, and organizations representing Native People, farmers and the disadvantaged' (1985: ix). They argue that, taken together and also seen as following other coalitions previously formed in Canada to contest regressive labor and social policies in the Province of British Columbia, or missile testing in the Canadian north, or restrictions to reproductive choice for women among others, 'the groups active in these coalitions are Canada's counter-institutions, and they draw on a counter-discourse of political economy' (ibid.: ix). Drache and Cameron clearly perceive and present the response of these groups to the economic agenda which was then to be worked out by the government's official inquiry as being significant both politically and theoretically: 'This fundamental regrouping of forces represents an alternative to the rigidities of Canada's two-and-a-half party system and the simple two-class model of society' (ibid.: ix). Correct or not as an assertion about practical political realignment or more abstract characterization of Canadian society, there is no doubt this movement had and put forward an alternative vision of Canada's future.

The content of that vision is not surprising and can be summarized quickly. It includes organizing the economy to meet human need rather than capital accumulation, modifying 'market forces' through government intervention in economic and social policies, assuring meaningful employment and humanizing technology. Drache and Cameron see this as 'a rethinking of the relationship between ethics, the economy, culture and society by going beyond the bounds of conventional political discourse' (ibid.: xxxvii). Interesting as it is to examine this putative vision of a transformed Canada, especially in the context of Canadian social thought, the purpose of this essay is otherwise – to assess the relevance of Freirean ideas about achieving social and political transformation. To do this, the subsequent history of this movement, however short it has been on an historical scale, needs to be examined.

The coalition of popular groups originated with presentations made by them separately to the government's formally appointed Royal Commission of inquiry into the problems and prospects of the Canadian economy. This occurred in a world context of economic restructuring which presented new and difficult challenges to Canadian political leaders. In 1982 a 'conservative' party was elected, paralleling events in the United States and Great Britain. However, in keeping with the Canadian tradition of accepting state intervention over laissez-faire market individualism, the attack on state services was not nearly as virulent as in the other countries. Attempts were made to reduce the number of public servants, privatizing or contracting out public services, cutting back income security provisions, and deregulating business. These were relatively mild, although they have continued and have been slowly notched up since the government's re-election to a second term. The major policy initiative, in fact, was less conservative or neo-conservative than it was neo-liberal. It was the dramatic push to negotiate and sign a freer trade agreement with the United States, ostensibly to enhance Canada's competitive position in the world economy and increase the success of the Canadian economy. It was in reaction against this policy choice that the coalition presaged in the common vision expressed by the popular groups took shape.

The leading proponent of the trade agreement was the Business Council on National Issues (BCNI), an organization made up of the chief executive officers of the 150 leading business corporations in Canada. It has been described perceptively by David Langille, who has studied its origins, purposes and practices as being 'a forum for multinational capital' (Langille 1987: 45). According to his account, the BCNI was formed and acted because 'neither the state executive nor the bureaucratic apparatus appeared capable of adequately representing the interests of monopoly capital, or of organizing the compromise that would maintain the latter's hegemony' (ibid.: 46). Therefore, the leaders of large multinational businesses in Canada established their own well-financed, potent organization to ensure that their interests were met through negotiating their way into an integrated North American economy. To date they have had considerable success: the Trade Agreement is now a *fait accompli* and the economic consequences are unfolding.

However, the oppositional groups have continued their efforts, and have had some structural and conjunctural factors on their side, as Langille points out. These include the fact that the anarchy of the market and the resulting competition among firms inhibits discipline within the corporate sector; the fact that to remain competitive internationally, corporations in Canada may still require some state support; and the possibility that corporations will 'seek more lucrative military contracts' (Langille 1987: 78) and will continue to rely on the state to provide the infrastructure to do this and to continue the export of resources. Most notably for this chapter, Langille suggests a final reason why the multinational corporate agenda may be deterred or deflected: the people whose lives are being affected may object, given the Canadian tradition of acceptance of and reliance on public services and state intervention to improve the quality of life and economic functioning (ibid.: 77).

As noted above, objections have continued. The loose coalition of individuals and groups which had formed to combat the trade initiative continued to develop as the Pro-Canada Network, with participation in the national organization from ten provincial coalitions and some thirty national organizations. It operates as 'an umbrella group ... that includes labor, farmers', women's, anti-poverty, aboriginal, environmental, peace, church, cultural and senior citizens' groups' and its purpose is 'to continue the struggle to ensure that the future of Canada is shaped by and for people, not profits'.[4] It endeavors to accomplish this at the national level through research and communication on public issues identified by the participating organizations. The focus on issues has moved from the Free Trade Agreement solely to include taxation, the national budget, and social and economic planning generally.

The Pro-Canada Network is committed to the principles of decentralized participation, conscientization, cultural struggle and praxis. The strategies it pursues, the organizational form and practices it adheres to, and the issues it addresses are all self-consciously chosen and worked out democratically. Its stated analysis is that 'the trade deal is the centrepiece of a larger social and economic strategy which involves restructuring Canada along continentalist and market-oriented lines', and its intent is to uncover, document and demystify this strategy by gathering information from its participating organizations, working collectively to make sense of that information, and disseminating the critical assessments thus arrived at.

There are, of course, other oppositional groups and forces at work. The traditional political parties, liberal and social democratic, continue their usual practices and policies; and as well there are some regional protest pre-party formations arising from local discontents with certain national policies. There is also a Council of Canadians, initiated in 1985 by several prominent Canadian nationalists as an individual membership organization intending to educate, advocate and lobby against what they perceive as the erosion of Canadian sovereignty. In addition, many of the national organizations and the provincial coalitions comprising the Pro-Canada Network carry out their own activities in opposition to the dominant policies of the party in power. The Network, however, is the only one of these that is explicitly a cross-class alliance carrying forward cultural struggle along Freirean lines. The efficacy of this approach will be considered shortly, after some other social movements in Canada have been reviewed.

Post-socialist 'social movements'

As elsewhere in the world, there have developed in Canada since the 1960s a number of social movements which, in the words of the editors of a volume of essays reviewing some of them, 'have challenged the classical socialist definition of politics' (Cunningham *et al.* 1988: 9). As the authors note, there have been many social movements before; the new feature here was the effort being made not only to challenge the legitimacy of liberal democratic governments and policies, but also to transcend the traditional social democratic, socialist and Communist parties.

A number of factors were involved. The cultural protest and political ferment of the 1960s appeared to be exhausted. Attempts at revitalizing parties of the left were resisted, and sectarian vanguard formations proved unable to accommodate the challenge to their doctrinal adherences coming from the theoretical and practical perspectives being advanced by those who espoused more egalitarian principles, feminist demands for gender equality, or national liberation. Attempts at developing a genuine socialist party which could act effectively in the political arena as the expression of the working class through knitting together various single-issue or radical groups in coalition with labor were not successful. In order to understand the consequences of these factors, the editors of the volume in question assembled a dozen case studies of particular social movements.

These included studies of the development of a continuing organization to forge alliances in the women's movement among those who espoused feminist liberation principles primarily and those women who were also resisting oppression based on race and class; an attempt to maintain a labor–ecological coalition; an alliance between labor and popular groups in Quebec; the problems encountered by the disabled within movements; the day-care, pro-choice, sexual orientation, and visible minority movements; the peace movement; and the parents' movement to gain purchase on control over education. Finally, the volume contains studies of an anarchist collective's efforts to develop a culture of resistance and an assessment of 'self-help' groups. These studies were intended to 'explore the potential of movements to transform the existing relations of power' (ibid.: 17). As is clear from the problematics they addressed, the intent was not to accomplish the revolutionary transformation of the system of economic production or its resultant social relations in the whole. Rather, they derived their purpose and energies from focusing on particular issues which cut across various social groupings, or which attracted allegiance from those sharing a particular characteristic or perspective. They were also, in the main, successful in achieving some aspects of their purposes and in maintaining themselves as functioning groups. At the same time, as would be expected, they encountered difficulties and problems.

These included the intractability of the state, both political and bureaucratic. As the editors point out, the organizations reported here remain committed in principle to social transformation, but 'have accepted the reality that the state plays a specific role in limiting transformation' (ibid.: 17). Consequently, their attempts at developing alliances and coalitions into social movements around the issues perceived to be of common concern recognized the need to address the state as a major target of influence or, better, of institutional change. This itself can be seen to be a source of tension within social movements, insofar as there are often natural disagreements over how the state apparatuses should be approached.

Decisions about which or what mix of strategies and tactics are to be selected can be exceptionally troublesome to make when they are being made within organizations which are attempting to amalgamate groups whose interests arise from different bases. Whether or not to challenge and confront, accommodate and cooperate, use or refuse support, or mix and combine some or all of these are vexing choices in social movements comprising diverse groups. And where the groups arise in relation to fundamental characteristics such as gender, race, and class, or sexual orientation and differential abilities, tensions and conflicts about which paths to pursue can go far beyond vexation.

These difficulties are exacerbated for two further reasons. The participating groups often have their own operating traditions or styles, which can increase organizational conflicts. A classic illustration of this is the difference between trade unions, committed to democratic representative structures with formalized decision-making procedures within hierarchic forms, and women's groups, community groups, or other movement groups equally committed to participatory direct democracy rather than representative structures, consensual decision-making, and non-hierarchical organizational forms (Simard 1988: 74–80; Canadian Centre for Policy Alternatives 1984). More importantly, the issues being addressed are often embedded in deeply held convictions.

This point is clearly made in the case studies reported. The damage to people's lives experienced through the present class structure, and the oppressions experienced through the racism, sexism, and heterosexism perpetuated within that structure, are clearly identified in several of the accounts, most notably in the history of an ongoing action of the women's movement in Toronto, Canada's largest city. As the authors recount, the March 8th Coalition has developed as a 'unique and vibrant coalition of feminists – which includes activists from immigrant groups, the reproductive rights movement, lesbian groups, rape crisis centres, women of color groups, and many other organizations' (Cunningham *et al.* 1988: 20). The deeply personal dimension of these categories is made clear in the analysis of difficulties encountered by the Coalition as it pursued its activities; as the authors conclude:

> The most important lessons learned in the challenge of dealing with class, race and sexuality has been the importance of recognizing the existing antagonisms and contradictions and of integrating an anti-racist, anti-heterosexist class-analysis into every area of our work, if we are to break down the barriers and build the necessary unity to overcome the . . . system that maintains our oppression.
>
> (Ibid: 46)

This clearly is a formidable task, given the intense convictions and emotions involved.

Likewise, other studies in the collection recount the experiences of movements attempting to deal with profoundly personal issues such as repro- ductive choice, gay political actions in relation to police repression, child-care and parental rights in the face of the education and welfare bureaucracies, and peace. Movement mobilization on each of these, as with all social change efforts, must deal with internal conflicts and antagonisms rooted in deeply held convictions and feelings, at the same time as they endeavor to confront an historically entrenched economic and social system.

Notwithstanding the immense challenge presented by the hegemonic system and class, these case studies illustrate that effective work is possible. The editors make no claim that they are representative of the myriad social movements and social organizations in Canada which have been formed to work for greater social justice and progressive social change, although they do point out it is surprising 'that they do in fact cover so many of the issues addressed by social movements today: issues of gender, race, sexual regulation, the disabled, peace, education, the labor movement' (ibid.: 17). And taken together they clarify many of the prospects and problems inherent in this approach to social change, and permit examination of the processes needed to make it more effective.

SOCIAL MOVEMENTS, SOCIAL CHANGE AND CONSCIENTIZATION

The particular angle on the processes needed which is being examined here is, of course, taken from ideas and insights advanced by Paulo Freire. Freire's ideas about conscientization are relevant to the Canadian social movements illustrated above along two dimensions, which can be labeled 'internal' and 'external'. As described, the social movements, in their efforts to address cross-class, cross-gender, and cross-race issues and to deal with issues that are often if not always intensely personal, encounter internal tensions, conflicts and antagonisms which are often strenuous, occasionally vicious, and almost always debilitating. Hence their internal processes are often problematic. At the same time, social movements represent collective interpretations and decisions about the external social milieu, both the hegemonic structures that are to be challenged and the resources and capacities of the potential forces of resistance, struggle and change. Freire's ideas are germane on both dimensions.

On the internal side, his pedagogical precepts are aimed directly at uncovering, unmasking, and laying bare the sources of oppression and social antagonisms, a necessary first task to be pursued within social movements which aim to achieve progressive effectiveness and which, as noted above, are inevitably unstable amalgamations of differentiated groups. A first and continuing task for all social movements is the struggle to achieve and maintain common understandings of the problems they intend to address, and thereafter to work toward continually renewed consensus on strategies, tactics and procedures through which they will go on. In this effort, Freire's insights about learning processes as well as some of his ideas about techniques and practices can be exceedingly fruitful. On the external side, his focus on the ideological hegemony of the dominant class – now achieved through cultural institutions as much as by force – points very clearly to targets and strategies for change which social movements must comprehend, develop and pursue. The complexity, scale and sophistication of post-industrial multinational economies and societies is extraordinarily distant in many respects from the peasant-based societies in which Freire developed his approach to social transformation, but the broad principles of uncovering and demystifying the root structures of domination still pertain *mutatis mutandis*.

Most importantly, these two dimensions must be pursued together and simultaneously if one of Freire's most insistent insights is to be incorporated. As stated by Giroux,

> domination for Freire is not to be found in either the subjective realm or the objective conditions of oppression, limited either to the realm of consciousness or the realm of material exploitation. Instead, domination is rooted in a subjective–objective dialectic.
>
> (Giroux 1981: 27)

For social movements this means working through an understanding and resolution of internal organizational tensions and recurring interorganizational conflicts at the same time as they try to comprehend and combat the material conditions and cultural hegemony of the dominant society.

This is neither simple nor painless, as the experiences reviewed above attest. The seemingly seamless cultural hegemony being confronted, buttressed as it is by powerful economic forces and equally potent political ideologies, makes the project of sustaining the 'subjective–objective' dialectic daunting and frustrating if not entirely impossible. On the subjective side, the pressures against raising fundamental challenges to ways of seeing, feeling, acting and being are immense. A consequent danger is the degeneration of efforts to achieve 'critical consciousness' into personal growth techniques or even purported therapeutic models, robbed of their intended transformative intent.

On the objective side, another dilemma pertains. In eschewing conventional party and electoral politics, or the development of a broad, all-embracing socialist movement, or the primacy of the working class as the primary agency of reform, the new social movements are turning to new ways of challenging the hegemonic definitions of reality which remain powerfully entrenched in Canada at least. In terms of the two key elements in effective social transformation – support among popular (or very powerful and ruthless) 'constituencies' and the existence of adequate or effective 'agencies' – Canadian social movements have yet to achieve the scale or coherence required in such a vast, complex, and culturally vulnerable country. It is far from clear whether or not they can be successful in effecting large-scale social change, nor is it clear how it is intended that larger-scale change should be achieved.

On this level, the limitations of Freire's ideas in their application to Canadian social movements need further examination. An earlier study of the relevance of conscientization to Canada identified several limitations to the concepts employed. Most importantly, it argued that 'the central relation of Freire's philosophy, that between consciousness and social context, is shown to be flawed by the lack of a systematic approach to analysis of political economy' (Martin 1975: 12). Written by a Canadian educator in 1975, in a world, continental, and national context very different from the Canada of today, this study concluded with the 'lesson . . . that the raising of popular political consciousness is not a sufficient condition for revolutionary change' (ibid.: 115).

At the same time, the author's further conclusion pointed the way to the nascent strategies now being pursued by social movements in Canada. Acknowledging the 'ethical imperative' underpinning Freire's conceptions, Martin asserted that those who concur 'must seek a basis of cooperation with others engaged in analysis of organic and conjunctural trends in the society, and pose to "the oppressed" the need for popular organizations as a precondition for popular change' (ibid.: 116).

What this basis might be for the various social movements reviewed above remains problematic. Their fundamental cross-class character, and in fact the continuing uncertain nature of the evolving class structure in Canada, remains a perplexing reality in such a large and variegated country. It is unclear whether longer-range structural shifts are in the direction of a further development of a larger 'professional middle class' on the one hand, or on the other hand a shrinkage of the 'disappearing middle' with a consequent repolarized society. Faced with this conjunctural confusion, and particularly in face of the surface success of neo-conservative political parties at both the national and provincial levels, the strategy of seeking progressive accomplishments through more narrowly focused social movements may be the only available approach, if not the most effective one in the long run.

Clearly, the social movements can and do challenge the ideological hegemony repeatedly and in significant ways.[5] But just as clearly in Canada at least, their separate efforts have yet to form coalitional combinations which present a 'counter-hegemonic' political force. Rather, the preponderant situation is that many of the separate movements remain at cross-purposes, if not often mutually suspicious and occasionally antagonistic when presented with opportunities for common action.[6] Most importantly, there has not yet been sufficient dissemination of analyses which unravel the changing political economy, the evolving balance of class forces, and the ongoing nature and role of the state in maintaining the current relations of power. In Gramsci's powerful image, the new social movements remain absorbed in the 'war of position' rather than yet being able to engage in the 'war of manoeuvre'.[7]

Nevertheless, the importance of 'consciousness' was a central element in Gramsci's conception of this war of position, which brings us back to the importance of Freire's ideas. There is no question that his analytic confronts the class-based nature of domination, and in particular the dilemmas of working through a totalized comprehension of oppression. His methods and insights regarding the learning process provide powerfully useful guidance and direction for those who wish to continue the project of building a counter-hegemony. At the same time, some of those insights make clear that much more concrete work must be done.

Freire continually emphasized the importance of attaining critical consciousness through engaging the immediate concrete reality. While the problems and structures which must be challenged in Canada are less brutal and chilling than in many parts of the world, they are as complex and mystifying; moreover, the 'magical consciousness' employed to maintain ideological domination is often equally bizarre. The kinds of life experience faced by activists in Central and South America, such as those encountered by Domitila Barrios de Chungara in her autobiographical *Let Me Speak* (1978),[8] or the experiences faced in Zimbabwe as described and analyzed by Dr Toby Tafirenyika Moyana in his powerful account of that country's post-colonial liberation struggle in *Education, Liberation and the Creative Act* (1988), are in the main less harsh and widespread in Canada, but the liberation project is the same.

Whether or not the social movements reviewed here prefigure political developments which can carry this project through remains to be seen. In what unfolds, however, the ideas and insights to be employed should include those of Paulo Freire. While it remains true that Freire focused on education – pedagogy and the institutions and practices entailed – his life work has unceasingly and relentlessly directed attention to power, oppression, dominance and subordination, and liberative resistance. Much of the continuing debate about poststructuralist theories of subjectivity and ideology, which are well summarized by Peter McLaren (1989), has been adumbrated in Freire's practice and writings. To the extent that the new social movements are manifestations of the ongoing struggle against the dominant ideologies through which oppression is sustained, Freire's ideas and practices are germane.

They are profoundly germane most of all because of his unremitting insistence that within liberation struggles, ideas and practice must always be united. 'The first virtue, or quality, that I would cite for a progressive social worker', said Freire in a recent speech to the International Federation of Social Workers, 'is the convergence between what is said and what is done.' This is a timeless and fundamental challenge to those who seek a humane transformation to a better world, and is buttressed then by Freire's sustained insistence on 'the importance of the role of the subjective in the process of making history or of being made by history' (Freire 1990: 9). Understanding the limits of what is historically possible, understanding and engaging our subjective strengths – these ideas ensure Paulo Freire enduring relevance in all contexts where the great struggles for human liberation continue.

NOTES

1 See discussion of the Pro-Canada Network below.
2 This great endemic theme in Canadian history is once again, at this writing, passing through another of its recurring crises; the literature is vast and readily available in Canada.
3 One very possible and plausible outcome, in fact, may be some profound constitutional restructuring in which the Province of Quebec, where French-speakers predominate, separates from Canada.
4 *The Pro-Canada Dossier* is published nine times annually by the Network, 904–251 Laurier Avenue, West, Ottawa, Canada K1P 5J6.
5 For a definitive assessment of the concept of ideological hegemony see Giroux (1981).
6 For other examples see Adkins (1989) and Findlay (1984).
7 For an excellent review of Gramsci's ideas on the state and social change, see Carnoy (1987).
8 Besides Domitila's work, Lawrence R. Anschuler (1980) has also written an interesting case study. Sadly, *New Internationalist* 200, October 1988, reports that the preceding decade saw unfortunate developments in Bolivia, and for Domitila herself.

REFERENCES

Adkins, L. (1989) 'Convergence: the labor movement and the new social movements'. Unpublished manuscript, Department of Political Science, Queens University, Kingston, Canada.
Anschuler, L. (1980) 'The conscientization of Domitila: a case study in the political psychology of liberation', *Contemporary Crises* 4, 27–41.
Barrios de Chungara, D. with Viezzer, M. (1978) *Let Me Speak*, New York: Monthly Review Press.
Boggs, C. (1986) *Social Movements and Political Power: Emerging Forms of Radicalism in the West*, Philadelphia: Temple University Press.
Braungart, R.G. (ed.) (1984) 'Historical generations and youth movements', *Research in Social Movements, Conflicts and Change* 6.
Canadian Centre for Policy Alternatives (1984) *British Columbia's Operation Solidarity*, Ottawa: CCPA.
Carnoy, M. (1987) *The State and Political Theory*, Princeton, NJ: Princeton University Press.
Cunningham, F., Findlay, S., Kadar, M., Lennon, A. and Silva, E. (1988) *Social Movements/Social Change: The Politics and Practice of Organizing*, Toronto: Between the Lines Press.

Drache, D. and Cameron, D. (eds) (1985) *The Other MacDonald Report*, Toronto: Lorimer.
—— (1988) *The Free Trade Papers* Toronto: Lorimer.
Findlay, P. (1984) *British Columbia's Solidarity Movement*, Ottawa: CCPA.
Freire, P. (1990) 'A critical understanding of social work' (M. Moch, trans.), *The Journal of Progressive Social Services* 1, 1, 3–9.
Giroux, H. (1981) *Ideology, Culture and the Process of Schooling*, Philadelphia: Temple University Press.
Langille, D. (1987) 'The Business Council on national issues and the Canadian state', *Studies in Political Economy* 24, 41–86.
Majka, T.J. and Majka, L.C. (eds) (1984) 'Power, insurgency and state intervention: farm labor movements in California', *Research in Social Movements, Conflicts and Change* 6.
Martin, D. (1975) 'Reappraising Freire: the potential and limits of conscientization'. Unpublished MA Thesis, University of Toronto.
McLaren, P. (1989) 'On ideology and education: critical pedagogy and the cultural politics of resistance' in H. Giroux and P. McLaren, eds, *Critical Pedagogy, the State and Cultural Struggle*, Albany, NY: State University of New York Press.
Miliband, R., Panitch, L. and Savile, J. (1988) 'Problems and promise of socialist renewal', *Socialist Register*, pp. 1–11.
Milner, H. (1989) *Sweden: Social Democracy in Practice*, London: Oxford University Press.
Moyana, T. (1988) *Education, Liberation and the Creative Act*, Harare: Zimbabwe Publishing House.
Navarro, V. (1988) 'Social movements and class politics in the US', *Socialist Register*, London: Merlin.
Rosenblum, S. (1980) 'Swedish social democracy at the crossroad', *Contemporary Crises* 4, 267–82.
Rothschild-Whitt, R. (ed.) (1984) 'Worker ownership: a collective response to an elite-generated crisis', *Research in Social Movements, Conflicts and Change* 6.
Simard, M. (1988) 'Coalition politics: the Quebec labor movement' in Cunningham, F. *et al.*, *Social Movements/Social Change: The Politics and Practice of Organizing*, Toronto: Between the Lines Press.

Chapter 7

Freire – present and future possibilities

Edgar González Gaudiano and Alicia de Alba

(translated by Adriana Hernández)

> Gradually, through practice, I became an educator. Since that time I have been gradually acquiring a practice from which I have never departed: that of always thinking in the practice. In fact, to think in one's current practice is not only an efficient way to improve tomorrow's practice, but is also the effective pattern for learning to think correctly.
>
> (Freire and Frei Betto 1988: 72–3)

INTRODUCTION

There exists in the West an undeniable lack of knowledge of and appreciation for the contributions of Latin Americans to developments in educational theory and practice. Hence, it is encouraging to witness the increasing attention one such educator, Paulo Freire, is receiving.[1] Many contemporary educators across the globe have been influenced by this great Brazilian thinker who has enriched the field of pedagogy without any pretence to universalizing his discourse.

Rather than attempting a comprehensive review of the intellectual cross-cultural currents of Freire's work, we will address just its influence with respect to the most dispossessed groups within the Mexican population. Specifically, we refer to the concrete circumstances of indigenous Mexican groups and Guatemalan Indian refugees living in a country which, like Brazil, reveals at the dawn of the twenty-first century relentless suffering, and a proliferation of neo-colonialist practices that subordinate difference to the occidental referents of the hegemonic culture. Mexico resembles Brazil also in that it suffers despoliation of its natural resources and its workforce through the sophisticated corporate mechanisms of the international market system.

Analyzing Freire's thought in the context of educating Mexico's indigenous population enables us to recognize the potential for achieving a future cultural and educational hegemony for the safeguarding of human life and respect for difference, as well as the possibility of shaping a social utopia (albeit necessarily a provisional one) from which to rethink and transform educational and social practices into the next century.

FREIRE'S PEDAGOGICAL ROOTS

In 1969 the first Spanish-language edition of *Education: the Practice of Freedom* appeared, followed in 1970 by *Pedagogy of the Oppressed*: two of Freire's most published works[2] (by 1989, 38 and 39 editions respectively of these books existed in Mexico, reflecting a deepening of the critical educational project there).[3] Until that time educational studies were confined in Mexico largely to the field of educational technology, and educational practices were primarily an extension of the worst dimensions of North American positivism applied to education. Besides his methodological contributions to literacy, Freire's socio-political vision made possible an analysis of educational conditions in Mexico from the perspective of human agency. Efforts were made to rethink educational reform within a framework of ideology critique and a practice of freedom, proceeding from awareness that education is unthinkable apart from a political project, because the political is already 'co-extensive' with the educational. Not surprisingly, the First World has 'discovered' Freire as an outstanding proponent of Latin American pedagogical-political thought without recognizing that he belongs to a substantial Latin American intellectual tradition which includes such distinguished contributors as José Vasconcelos (Mexico), José Carlos Mariategui (Peru), Julio Antonio Mella (Cuba), Farabundo Martí (El Salvador) and Augusto César Sandino (Nicaragua).

Arguably, this distinguished tradition within Latin American education begins with Simón Rodríguez, the teacher of Bolívar, who maintained that the school should be a workshop where 'a distinct man [sic] is educated with a capacity to think and a potential to make' (Uslar Pietri 1981: 13, cited in Puiggrós 1988b: 17). Such a tradition is decidedly anti-imperialist and, among other things, contests the 'civilizing' project developed by First World educators for the growing Latin American populace. Ignorance of this tradition, however, is not exclusive to First World countries. Indeed, it exists also in the very countries which nurtured and developed these thinkers. This is not so surprising given that the expansive hegemony of social and political life determines which histories and traditions are to be rescued and legitimated within the pedagogic enterprise in general, and which are to be deemed 'dangerous memories'. Since, with few exceptions, Latin American educators who have been linked to socialist thought stand in opposition to the dominant social logic within the hemisphere, their field of action has been considered subversive. Consequently, they have been marginalized.

Socialist thought has influenced pedagogical development in accordance with the specific characteristics of particular historical moments in Latin America, engendering a project known as 'popular education'. The thought of Aníbal Ponce, for example, sought to integrate the positivism of José Ingenieros with the mechanistic economism developed by Kautsky. This produced a confrontation between bourgeois and proletarian conceptions:

> In a society without classes, that is to say, in a fraternal society of producers who work according to a plan, the school cannot be either the precarious

elementary school or the closed upper or secondary school. In order to prepare workers to be conscious of a society in which the relations of dominance and submission have disappeared absolutely, it is necessary to create a school that establishes with extraordinary precision the immediate purpose that corresponds to it. And, since the school of the bourgeoisie never pronounces a word that does not serve its interests, the proletarian school wants also to serve its own interests: with the evident difference that if the former corresponds to an exiguous minority, the latter embodies – on the contrary – the aspirations of the vast masses.

(Ponce 1934: 177)

In other cases, Julio Antonio Mella and Farabundo Martí, caught up in the political current of the Third International, formulated educational visions according with classical socialist paradigms and closely associated with national liberation struggles. Augusto César Sandino formed a school in Las Segovias for groups most marginalized by the Nicaraguan oligarchy, within a context of armed struggle against an incursion of North American marines. Sandino, whose own education was limited to elementary school, had nonetheless read Cervantes, Bolívar and Napoleon, and valued education highly. Speaking of the 'child-man' of the Nicaraguan resistance, Sandino wrote:

Everything in the child expressed the living protest against the current civilization and that which surprisingly was contained in his look still makes the memory of that scene cause a lump in my throat. He joined our forces because there was no way to convince him that he could not resist, because of his age, the roughness of the war . . . and today, instead of rags, he wears a beautiful uniform [and also possesses the] knowledge of reading and writing that he has acquired in our army. He is a 'child-man'.

(Sandino cited in Fonseca 1982: 199)

Other intellectuals, like Vasconcelos, linked themselves to the movement of the Mexican Revolution, incorporating political elements which had emerged from the best of the liberal tradition of the previous century; but it was José Carlos Mariategui who began the construction of an authentic Latin American Marxist pedagogy. Mariategui asserted

the problem of teaching cannot rightly be understood in our time if it is not considered as an economic and as a social problem. The mistake of many reformers has been their idealist abstract method, their exclusively pedagogic doctrine. Their projects have ignored the intimate meshing that exists between the economy and teaching, and they have tried to modify the latter without knowing the laws of the former. Consequently, they have not succeeded in reforming anything but the means by which they have complied with the economic laws they despise. The debate between the classicists and the modernists in teaching has not been ruled any less by the rhythm of capitalist development than has the debate between conservatives and liberals in politics.

The programs and systems of public education today that are now declining have depended on the interests of the bourgeois economy. The realist or modernist orientation has been imposed, above all, by the needs of industrialism. It is for a purpose that industrialism is the peculiar and substantive phenomenon of this civilization that, dominated by its consequences, claims from school more technicians than ideologists and more engineers than rectors.

(Mariategui 1928: 141–2)

Paulo Freire identified strongly with these early Latin American intellectuals. When he began his literacy work he attempted to develop a theoretical and transformative approach to what were largely underdeveloped nationalist educational projects. As Adriana Puiggrós points out:

The popular nationalist educational projects almost always lacked not only a theorization that would make their analysis and criticism possible, but also transformative proposals in the political-academic and didactic area. The traditional tie between teacher and pupil, inside the classroom, remained almost always untouched, positing the huge paradox of the existence of a process of democratization that would make possible access by the oppressed sectors to the educational system, but without great changes in the manner of participation once inside the system. In the nationalist government of João Goulart – who was overthrown by a military coup d'état in 1964 – the educator Paulo Freire made progress toward achieving a transformative orientation.

(Puiggrós 1988b: 27)

The pedagogical tradition to which Freire became indebted was also enriched by concrete Latin American approaches developed earlier; for example, Warisata in the Bolivian highlands[4] and the socialist education project in Mexico, both developed during the 1930s. The Bolivian project tried to put into practice theoretical conceptions of socialism, such as polyvalent education, integral formation, and concrete links with labor. The Mexican project attempted to fuse Marxist educational principles with national characteristics and needs, giving rise to the National Polytechnic Institute and the great social movement that the rural Mexican school comprised at that time. The Bolivian and Mexican examples were, in effect, mutually informing. Puiggrós (1988b) argues that during the 1940s and 1950s many educational reforms emerged in Latin America that tried to respond to large popular constituencies of workers: notably the Trabalhismo Brasileiro, the Chilean Popular Front of Aguirre Cerda, Peronismo in Argentina, the National Revolutionary Movement in Bolivia, and the movement prompted by the government of Jacobo Arbens in Guatemala.

We would emphasize that these movements stressed the popular democratic character of educational policies, in opposition to the long-standing liberal oligarchic educational model. It is necessary also to mention educational experiences springing from the success of the Cuban Revolution, which generated and galvanized mass movements on a broad front in the national crusade against illiteracy. Also worthy of mention are more recent educational developments in Nicaragua, beginning just two weeks after the success of the Sandinista-led insurrection against Somoza (July 19, 1979). The national literacy crusade was assessed to have reduced the rate of illiteracy among the population over ten years of age from 50.3 per cent to 12.9 per cent in just five months (Nicaraguan Ministry of Education 1983).

In the context of these various Latin American developments, Freire's pedagogy represents a very important contribution to answering the needs, interests, and aspirations of large segments of the population who seek social equality. Despite the fact that even today Freirean pedagogy is not yet fully worked out into a final form, it surpasses the prescriptions of dominant educational currents from the metropolitan center, and has cleared the way for framing a political project that enables Latin American populations to envisage the possibility of the liberation of the historical subject through a 'rewriting' of the world:

> Every reading of the word presupposes a previous reading of the world, and every reading of the word implies coming back to the reading of the world, so then to read-world and to read-word are constituted in a movement where there is no rupture, where one comes and goes. And to read the world together with reading the word, in substance, signifies for me a process of re-writing the world. To 're-write', with quotation marks, means to transform the world.
>
> (Freire and Frei Betto 1988: 78)

FREIRE'S PEDAGOGY

Within Latin American countries Freire's works have contributed to demystifying the ideological workings of pedagogical approaches based on technocratic rationality and conceptions of teaching as a form of technology. During the 1970s particularly, this latter approach fetishized education, creating an educational mirage distorting the social and political content of schooling and masking its imperialistic tendencies. Freire's pedagogy compensated for the aggregate of universalized formulas which often were applied with utter blindness to context, without restriction, and with little regard for the cultural specificity of the cultural sites involved. These were largely Eurocentric ideas that promoted a future without pedagogy and a pedagogy without future. Freire uncovered with decisive clarity the crippling falsehoods nested in our modes of colonized thought – internalized falsehoods that arose from the principal idea that the oppressed and 'immiserated' were incapable by themselves of generating emancipatory theories. Because of Freire's trail-blazing work, our dreams were regained without displacing the lucid thought of liberation. On the contrary, such dreams supported the idea of finding new paths and new strategies in our struggle against oppression that might save us from permitting ourselves to be dragged along by the most immediate convictions.

This is an idea in which the 'poem' and the 'theorem' can eventually find their place together. As Galeano put it:

> If, as we believe, hope is better than nostalgia, perhaps this rising literature might come to deserve the beauty of the social forces that, early or late, by good or by bad procedures, will probably change radically the course of our history. And perhaps that would help to preserve it for the youth to come, as the poet wanted, 'the true name of each thing'.
>
> (Galeano 1983: 20)

Freire contributed a critical vision of the dominant pedagogy which identified it as an ideological construct; he subjected the social domain to analysis of its discursive underpinnings, revealing its ontological consistency. The social tolerates the forms that constitute it, which it possesses, that are not manifested directly in phenomena. Freirean social analysis managed to lay bare the world of pseudo-concretion discussed by Kosik (1963).

Freire recognized that the essence of the dominant pedagogy should be sought in the sphere of ideology, since ideology comprises the space of representations wherein forms of representation that both manifest and shroud contradictory knowledge of the social are organized simultaneously and in concert. In this space, the consciousness of men and women of each historical period and each culture is produced as real, natural and commonsensical. To this extent there exists not one social system in general, but *specific systems* constructed by different groups inhabiting a totality of determinations and diverse relations, which must be understood in order to formulate a pedagogy of liberation. Consequently, one cannot speak of a *pedagogy* but must speak instead of *pedagogies* which respond to particular necessities, interests and conditions. Therefore, from both dominant and critical perspectives the response of schooling to social demands *must* be particular *and* multiple. Freire's intellectual legacy has enabled the discovery of *the proper consistency of multiple answers* to social demands and necessities. This is why his task has high theoretical-political value for Latin American educators:

> in the process of learning one only learns truthfully who appropriates what is learned, transforming what is apprehended, being able in this way to re-invent it; the one who is capable of applying the learned-apprehended to concrete existential situations . . . The task of the educator, therefore, is to problematize for the students the context that mediates them; and not to lecture about it, give it, extend it, deliver it, as if it were something ready made, elaborated, completed, finished . . . the problematization is . . . inseparable from concrete situations . . . it implies a return, a critical one, to action. It departs from the latter, and returns to it.
>
> (Freire 1973a: 28, 94–5)

Freire and education for socially marginalized and dispossessed groups

From these contributions of Freire we arrive at important questions for the education of socially marginalized and dispossessed groups. At the outset of this chapter we referred to education of Indians in Mexico. Before turning in detail to the education of Mexico's indigenous population we must address an important issue to clarify our position further. Like most Latin American countries, Mexico and Brazil share a history of systematic colonization and domination by First World powers. They also, however, possess large and highly diverse indigenous populations. One hundred and sixteen discrete indigenous groups live throughout Brazil and 56 throughout Mexico. They are presently under government assault as genocide and environmental spoiling become legitimate standard practices in Native America.

> Of the original 5 million square kilometres of the Amazon Basin, at least 600,000 are reportedly destroyed forever. This immense territory embraces a river basin which takes to sea 20 per cent of all non-salt surface water of the globe. Comprising nine countries, this basin has roughly 50 per cent of all living species, including 30,000 different kinds of plants and 2,000 species of fish.
>
> (PNUD 1988: 9)

Cultural diversity in Latin America is a recognized fact. Population figures indicate some 30 million natives. According to some linguists these speak 485 languages throughout thirteen countries. Others estimate there are 1,700 languages and dialect varieties (Nahmad Sitton 1982: 26). There is an absence of defined educational policies for these groups. Moreover, the politics of economic development that are applied seem to be oriented more toward cultural pillaging, hijacking, and destruction than toward protecting and celebrating the many important aspects of the autochthonous population.

First World countries are scandalized by the destruction of the Amazon forest, a destruction so devastating that it is capable of changing atmospheric conditions on a global scale. At a recent meeting of the PNUD (United Nations Program for Development) it was stated that 'The regional agenda should establish new patterns of development. It should touch upon global aspects but focus on specific routines' (PNUD 1988: 14). Despite the urgency and political import of such a warning, the origins of the problem are falsely located in the voracity of transnational enterprises alone. In a meeting of the Interamerican Development Bank in Miami during 1987, Chico Mendes – founder of the Brazilian Workers' Party – denounced the environmental destruction occurring in his country. Masquerading as a journalist in order to gain access to the meeting, he announced to the executive directors of the organization that deforestation of the Amazon was financed by the international banks (Micheli 1989: 9). A year later he was assassinated.[5]

The problem here of course is the destruction of the earth's most important natural reserve and, with this, the extermination of those indigenous groups who preceded the current 'legitimate' and officially recognized owners. A similar situation, albeit on a smaller scale, exists in Mexico as well. Great expanses of virgin forest in Mexico's southeastern states – states where native groups barely survive – are destroyed each year. Indeed, native groups throughout the Republic are forced to inhabit some of the most inhospitable regions. The process of progressive underdevelopment, to which the country has succumbed, has produced a crisis of immense dimensions in rural areas, particularly in areas occupied by indigenous groups.

Educators face what at times appears an insurmountable challenge. Clearly, education alone cannot counter the multiple dimensions (historical, cultural, political, social) along which the social order reproduces its characteristic lines of domination and oppression. Rather, education comprises a necessary though insufficient arena of social transformation. This is where Freire's pedagogy can intervene and ask whether existing educational prescriptions are capable of meeting the educational needs of socially less favored groups, or whether, on the contrary, they are complicit in maintaining the status quo. The 'natural' as well as the original focus of Freire's pedagogy is precisely on the existential realities of dispossessed Third World peoples.

The education provided for Mexico's most disadvantaged groups – its indigenous peoples – has moved from an 'integrationist' focus that regards the socio-cultural and linguistic patterns characteristic of Indians as obstacles to their development, to a perspective that recognizes such patterns as comprising a fundamental and necessary part of the nation's cultural heritage or national archive. At present both views orbit around a particular politics of social development associated with rural Mexico. During the last fifteen years, approaches that tend to respect, recover, and develop – at least at the level of political discourse – the traditions and cultural artifacts of indigenous groups have been strengthened significantly through programs of native bilingual-bicultural education.

At the same time Indian education is subject to diverse pedagogical approaches. Two stand out in particular. The first is a romantic approach that conceptualizes indigenous peoples in terms of nineteenth-century cultural anthropology. From this perspective Indian cultures are viewed as monolithic ethnographic monuments to be 'salvaged' for the metropolitan museum, giving rise to an educational proposal that ignores many conflicts and contradictions between the indigenous groups and the larger society. Consequently, this approach cannot provide indigenous social actors with the necessary elements for their transformation. It also tends to seek a functional equilibrium between educational content generated by the Indians' own socio-cultural patterns and the official curriculum of the country into which they have been assimilated discursively and coercively as subjects. As a consequence it is assumed that education can contribute a general vision of the global society without altering and 'othering' indigenous forms of 'reality maps' and the particular cultural, spiritual, and social interests that make up group identity.

Against this a more radical but marginal position also exists. It recognizes the fundamental importance of respecting the socio-cultural and linguistic patterns of the national ethnic groups and actively acknowledges that Indian cultures are situated 'antagonistically' within the larger context of capitalism – a situation which even those Indian groups in the interethnic regions of Mexico cannot escape, given the current incursion of capitalist rationality into the farthest reaches of Mexican cultural life. This pedagogical perspective takes into account the subordination of indigenous languages to Spanish; the erosion of traditional modes of community-based production by economic impositions such as credit and other commercial exchanges; permanent damage to indigenous cultural traditions, resulting from incursion of foreign cultures via mass media; and the damaging effects of the economy on youth who are forced to migrate from their communities to find work or enrol in educational programs.

These factors merge into a tight web of conditions which must be addressed in any educational attempt to foster critical analysis of determining factors and mediating responses within indigenous education. This task is necessary for building public spheres of resistance. At the same time education should seek to promote more critical forms of social and historical agency among students by strengthening and nourishing the symbolic and meaning-making systems con- tained in their languages and cultural practices. This requires developing a pedagogy that engages students in movement from 'naive' to 'critical' conscious- ness. Freire states that

> inter-subjectivity, or intercommunication, is the primordial characteristic of this cultural and historical world . . . [consequently, this] process of human communication cannot be exempted from socio-cultural conditioning.
>
> (1973c: 73, 82)

Freire's contributions have been adopted widely by Mexican educators, with particular impact on Indian education and adult literacy.[6] Indeed, Freire's theoretical and methodological principles have influenced the entire national system of education, especially basic-level programs. One area where his ideas are currently being applied to effect is in the education of Guatemalan refugees who have settled in three states in the south-east of Mexico.[7] Growing numbers of refugees are entering Mexico as a result of economic and political pressures and military conflicts afflicting Guatemala, creating sizeable displacements of people near Mexico's southern border. According to the last census by the Mexican Commission for Assisting Refugees (COMAR), some 43,000 people have crossed over. Most are from peasant communities and between them represent diverse ethnic groups of the Maya culture, including Q'anjobales, Mames, Qeqchies, K'iches, Kaqchikeles, Jakaltecos, Chujes, Ixiles, Chorties, Aguakatekos and Tz'utujiles. These refugees are spread among 126 encampments along the border of Chiapas state and five settlements in the states of Campeche and Quintana Roo. Their experience of exile is graphic.

> 'We left the land that saw us born, that saw us moving legs and arms to plough it and to take from it corn, beans, water, life . . .' reported Don Eugenio of the Elder's Council in the La Gloria camp, situated in the municipality of La Trinitaria, in Chiapas. 'We miss our lands, our houses, our first visions, our

hopes . . . to travel the ways in which our parents travelled. But now you see us happy, always moving forward, giving thanks that we are alive; we are not suffering any more, we do not cry, for what? The refugee only remembers that but he/she wants to live for these children, to prevent them from suffering what we suffered'.

(cited in Tovar de la Garza *et al.* 1989)

Freire, of course, understands exile, having lived it himself.

These peasant refugees from Guatemala have been acquiring Spanish as a means for communicating their different linguistic origins to one another. At the same time, Spanish has become a cohesive element in their recent circumstances as refugees, distinguishing them from the thousands who only speak one of the Mayan languages. Upon arriving in Mexico the refugees decided to develop schooling provision for their children, who comprise more than 60 percent of the total refugee population. This is a quite remarkable effort given that schools played only sporadic roles – if any at all – in the everyday life of their Guatemalan communities. In the midst of a generalized illiteracy and monolingualism, the refugees faced a daunting challenge. Initially they focused their educational project on young people or adults who had previously received between one and three years of schooling. The main difficulties were in preparing teachers and improvising materials. There was also a lack of school infrastructure, teaching resources and available spaces, as well as severe economic limitations facing attempts to cope with even the barest personal needs of the students. With the assistance of volunteers and educators grounded in Freire's educational approach, they are making strong progress.

This collective attitude of making children's education a top priority reflects one of the most significant factors in Freire's pedagogy. For Freire, education is a social engagement that provides conditions for understanding and improving through transformative praxis the whole of social life, and not merely individual advancement within the social structure.

Bringing Freire's pedagogical perspectives to this situation opens to refugee children the possibility of strengthening their own processes of identity formation and constructing a particular vision of their future which positions them as active subjects in history rather than as passive objects of history. Within such an 'unedited' Freirean pedagogy a future is built. Beyond silence and adversity the voices and smiles of children testify to the opportunity for constructing an emancipatory pedagogy of hope. A pedagogy based on dialogue should begin from faith in the future and hope because, as Freire says, hope

is at the root of the inconclusiveness of men, from which the latter move in permanent search . . . and this movement to search is justified only in the measure that it is directed toward being more, to the humanization of people.

(1970: 105, 94)

Freire tells us that education as transformative praxis is constructed at grass-roots level by ordinary men and women who, in their everyday practices, elaborate their own possibilities by engaging in a collective political-social project. This holds true for Indian education, adult education, and the education of refugees, where traditional values like freedom, honesty, courage, and citizenship have not lost the force of their meaning, and where critique and hope are fused in a struggle for the right to enter history and for the right of individuals to reclaim and make the world through linking the word to dreams of liberation. The oppressed must indeed engage in a new conquest of word and world, outside the structures of colonial or neo-colonial discourses. As Freire says,

> the problem of language cannot cease being one of the central preoccupations of a society that, being liberated from colonialism and rejecting neo-colonialism, dedicates itself to the effort of its own re-creation. In this effort to re-create society, the re-conquest of their Word by the People is a fundamental objective.
>
> (Freire 1973c: 238)

Freire's pedagogy, of course, is directed toward liberation of the oppressed. The burgeoning interest in Freire's work on the part of First World educators can, perhaps, be traced to the fact that he has shown them that they are also, in a strong sense, oppressed at the same time as they occupy their role as global oppressor. Puiggrós notes

> Men are products and producers of a reality that turns against them. Consequently, to transform the reality that oppresses them is a human task . . . But reality acts as much upon the oppressors as upon the oppressed. The oppressors are dehumanized and the oppressed are the ones charged with the liberation of both. With this destiny, the oppressed need to acquire a critical consciousness of oppression, overcoming the state of submersion in which their consciousness exists.
>
> (Puiggrós 1988a: 49)

The liberation of the oppressed necessarily entails a discourse of hope, a utopian basis for dreaming – dialectically – new narratives of freedom. A language of critique and hope is, by definition, utopian and, in its essence, deeply revolutionary. McLaren argues that

> Freire's utopian project addresses the need for a fundamental faith in human dialogue and community. In this sense, becoming literate is not just a cognitive process of decoding signs, but a critical engagement of lived experience in relation to others. Hence, literacy assumes a form of cultural action for freedom. 'To undertake such a work', writes Freire, 'it is necessary to have faith in the people, solidarity with them. It is necessary to be utopian'.
>
> (McLaren 1986: 16)

At the same time Puiggrós tells us

> Utopia is linked to conscientization; conscientization implies utopia, because

the more conscientized we are, Freire says, the more capable we will be of being announcers and denouncers, because all denouncement is an announcement, every conscious critique is infused with utopias. Consciousness is, at the same time, a process of breaking reality and demystification.

(1988a: 16–17)

Freire adds: 'For this reason conscientization obliges us to assume a utopian position toward the world' (1973b: 83).

FREIRE'S THOUGHT IN THE CONTEXT OF THE EDUCATIONAL CHALLENGES OF THE TWENTY-FIRST CENTURY

Once more men, challenged by the dramatic current age, pose themselves as a problem. They discover how little they know about themselves, about their 'place in the universe', and they worry about knowing more ... Installing themselves in the tragic discovery of their lack of knowledge about themselves they make a problem of themselves. They investigate. They answer, and their answers guide them to new questions. The problem of their humanization, in spite of having always been – from an axiological point of view – their central problem, assumes today the character of an unavoidable preoccupation.

(Freire 1981: 31)

The educational crisis that has affected the different regions of the world can perhaps be more clearly situated in the light of the economic, cultural, political, and social crisis that characterizes the approaching end of the millennium. In our view, it would be productive for educators to reflect on Freire's thought geopolitically – that is, in relation to the current world crisis of education – emphasizing Freire's contributions to utopian projects, possibility and transformative dialogue, and to understanding the importance of cultural contact in reproducing systems of domination.

Current discussions of the postmodern condition suggest that the metaphysical 'certainties' underwriting the grand narratives of modernity have been put under serious philosophical stress. At the same time, new bases currently in the process of being developed are not as yet clear. While we are not prepared to consider the postmodern condition as the 'end of history', it is evident that in spite of the many advances brought about via capitalist social relations and socialist projects throughout the world, these two modern social utopias have done little to resolve global social unrest, environmental degradation, and even the prospect of annihilating the human race. Elsewhere (de Alba 1989a) we have advanced a critique of much postmodern social theorizing. We argue that many postmodern social theorists suffer from a theoretical myopia. In criticizing the ethnocentrism of Western (European) rationality, they actually situate themselves within its very limits by ignoring the diverse roles ethnic minorities can play in the process of shaping a new political-social project for the new century.

With regard to the postmodern absence of utopia we find theoretical and political positions characterized by a marked pessimism. They not only reflect current postmodern society as the 'kingdom of the schizophrenic' and 'citadel of pastiche and irony' (Baudrillard 1983; Jameson 1983), but also have virtually arrived at a dead end in terms of developing a politics of liberation and counter-hegemonic public spheres. It is, perhaps, an indication of loss of belief in the possibility of building a utopian world order that the conquest of space has been mooted as a way out of current ills. Of course, this 'solution' itself reflects a profound social amnesia, ignoring as it does the destructive aspect of the very perspective through which space is understood. It quite fails to consider the ideological assumptions of colonization and conquest that inform official policies underlying space programs.

Others, however, are giving voice to an alternative approach wherein individuals assume material agency as social subjects in the task of transforming the future,[8] recognizing that a utopian approach calls for deconstructing present discourses and practices in order to enable a creative and committed rebuilding of the future. This 'utopia' is characterized by struggle, hope and possibility. Freire is a major figure in the attempt to establish this utopian response to current conditions.

From the time when *Education: The Practice of Freedom* and *Pedagogy of the Oppressed* were originally published, Freire has been acknowledged as much for his social critique – proceeding from the concrete reality in which men and women historically find themselves – as for his iron determination to be part of constructing a society committed to justice and liberation, in which liberatory education fulfils a key function. While Freire still works within a predominantly modernist perspective he is nonetheless pragmatically critical of the assumptions that inform its theoretical and practical positions. He believes that oppressed peoples of the Third World have much to contribute in this critical moment, as they come to analyze the complex dynamic of domination from the standpoint of liberation through cultural contact. In developing this perspective Freire has become one of the foremost Latin American social theorists, seeing very clearly that the problem of domination embraces the dominators as well as the dominated. Moreover, it is important to understand the logic of domination beyond the symbolic and material deconstruction of both oppressors and oppressed, and to examine the need for building a new regime of the possible which explores the utopian moments inherent in the various political, social, economic, and cultural projects of modernity.

Prior to the final curtain call for the Soviet bloc we maintained (de Alba 1989a) that the gravest problems besetting contemporary global relations are better understood through analysis of the relationship between North and South than by constructing the world politically through the standard binarism of East and West. From the first perspective we can see clearly the drastic disparity in wealth between rich and poor and the ideological, cultural, and political relations resulting from the disorganization of capital in the late capitalist era. We have also witnessed the creation of a Third World in the backyard of the US and exploitation of Latino populations inside that nation as sweatshops return to New York City and other centers where migrant labor can be purchased cheaply.

From the standpoint of the East–West binarism, the politics are those of confrontation between the superpowers which, following World War II, carved up and distributed the world between themselves. On this Freire comments:

> disgracefully, we see more and more in the sub-worlds in which the world is divided that the ordinary man, the oppressed, the diminished, and the controlled, is being transformed into a spectator, directed by the power of myths created for him by powerful social forces which, confronting him, destroy and annihilate him.
>
> (1969: 34)

While the superpowers discussed global disarmament and the possible arming of space (e.g., the Star Wars project), many constituencies within rich and poor nations alike pondered the paradox of the confrontations involved: science and technology, military armament and conquest of space, on the one hand; and starvation, malnutrition, social injustice, and the challenge to regimes of domination presented by liberation struggles, on the other. Even with the demise of the Soviet bloc and the removal of the threat seemingly posed to the 'integrity' of political, cultural, and economic dominance by the US and its allies, we still face the same essential paradox – whether in the form of ongoing US sabre-rattling focused on Iraq; or in the less readily apparent process of control and exploitation whereby the First World imposes technology transfer on the Third World, and IMF and World Bank policies are set which further entrench a 'development' agenda powerfully in favour of elite nations; or in enviro-ecological policies which, to be sure, are necessary for saving the planet, but which equally (and in the absence of adequate untagged aid and policies of global wealth and resource sharing) effectively deny poor nations the right to exploit natural resources for survival.

To understand such situations better and to transcend the political impasses they generate, we need an education that enables students to develop a genuine critique of global power relations. That is, we need a truly radical or critical pedagogy.

Freire's view of education, like Gramsci's earlier, seems to us central because of its potential for criticizing and transforming global power relations. Both Gramsci and Freire place an analytical emphasis on historical and cultural formations and on the relationship between knowledge and human agency. Within this perspective individuals, subjects, groups, social sectors, and nations play simultaneously the roles of educator and student. We recall here Freire's maxim: 'nobody educates anybody – nobody educates her/himself. Men and women educate each other, through the mediation of the world' ('*Nadie educa a nadie – nadie se educa a si mismo. Los hombres se educan entre si, con la mediación del mundo*'). As Freire says in *Pedagogy of the Oppressed*, 'Authentic education is not carried on by "A" *for* "B" or by "A" *about* "B", but rather by "A" *with* "B", mediated by the world – a world which impresses and challenges both parties, giving rise to views or opinions about it' (1970: 82).

FINAL REMARKS

Although cultural contact – global and regional – among different social groups is produced and developed within and through conflict and inequality, it is crucial to recognize that new meanings and significances are constantly being generated in the process. New cultural features of possibility are always appearing. Those people and groups rendered 'marginal' or 'peripheral' by the dominant forces of capitalist production have, in this 'moment' of global cultural crisis, much to contribute toward building a new cultural platform for the construction of counter-hegemonic public spheres that we will need to build for the new century. The process of cultural contact merits specific analysis that we will not attempt here. Even so, it seems necessary to point out not only the importance of accomplishing that task, but also the need to approach it with an attitude of openness that helps us understand that in cultural contact there exists a concrete and real possibility of learning in the sense that both Freire and Gramsci recognize. We maintain that perhaps it is not nations like Mexico alone that can achieve much by adopting a pluricultural condition, but that rich and powerful countries as well could benefit greatly from genuinely looking to the complexity and plurality of the diverse countries in the world – particularly the poor and oppressed, the underdeveloped Third World peoples. From such an attitude they may come to understand that these 'Others' have significance far beyond being merely sources of cheap labor-power and raw materials. 'Elite' nations can indeed learn from these diverse cultures new and enhanced ways of living, communicating, relating to the natural world, and addressing social organization that will afford new perspectives from which to approach the twenty-first century. Perspectives in which plurality is valued allow us to glimpse a future through multiple eyes (compare de Alba 1989a: 14–15).

We propose embracing the diversity and plurality offered by cultural contact. Cultural contact presents possibilities for rethinking education from an historical and structural perspective that fosters pursuit of liberation as a social function of education. Within this stance a *dialogical* relationship assumes a central and privileged place, encouraging us to listen to, hear, and affirm multiple voices. Dialogue is a relational stance that necessarily challenges current postmodern practices of substituting concrete and lived discourses of cultural contact with simulacra and pastiche. If 'liberating' or 'critical' pedagogy is directed only to the oppressed, cultivating only the importance of knowing the logic and culture of the dispossessed and marginalized, it implicitly puts the educator in the position of the dominator. Consequently, it does not escape the Cartesian rationality of merely reversing the binary opposition of colonizer/colonized. For this reason we insist that it is as necessary to know and understand the culture of the dominator and the social relations and material relations which inform it as it is to know and understand the culture of the dominated. We see, then, a need for *dialogic* education not only among the 'oppressed' but among and between classes, groups, and nations of oppressed and oppressors alike.

Our view recognizes Freire's grounding in a tradition of Latin American educational thought that has thus far been preoccupied with liberation of Third World peoples. Yet we sense strongly the possibility and importance of establishing serious dialogue among educators from both North and South. As we see it, the basic problems facing humanity continue to stem from its own disorganization, maldistribution of wealth, and prevailing relations of domination and economies of power and privilege. We concur, then, with Marx's observation that the fundamental challenge continues to be that of overcoming the domination of humanity by humanity.

NOTES

1 Henry Giroux's appreciation and amplification of Freire's work has been acknowledged and valued by Mexican educators among others within the Latino world.

2 The other works by Freire best known in Mexico are: *Extension or Communication?: Conscientization in the Rural Field*, first published in 1973 together with *Letters to Guinea-Bissau; Notes About a Pedagogic Experience in Process* (1977); and *The Importance of Reading and the Process of Liberation* (1984). All are published by Siglo XXI. To date they have run to sixteen, seven, and six editions, respectively.

3 Freire's works appeared at a time when Mexican public life was in a process of great change, largely as a result of the student political movements in 1968 and 1970, but also because of the flight into Mexico of distinguished Latin American intellectuals following political upheavals in several countries throughout the continent.

4 These developments were early influences on current practices of indigenous education in Mexico. Statements deriving from these movements were adopted by the First Indian Congress that took place in Patzcuaro, Mexico, in 1940. The Native School of Warisata allowed for participation of community members in all institutional and educational matters (created by the Parliament of Amautas). These initial developments matured, giving a start to what was to become the Peasant Schooling Nucleus. The socio-pedagogical schemas that were developed at this time became the foundation for rural education in Bolivia and other Latin American countries. See, for example, Montoya Medinacelli (1983: 57–82), and Rodriguez *et al.* (1983).

5 Other sources (e.g., the Brazilian Institute for the Environment) blame mining companies from France, the US and England, claiming their activities in extracting caseita, gold, and petroleum are destroying the forest. Specifically, British Petroleum, Brascan, the French group Rhons-Poulrenc, Pecten, Shell and Texaco are mentioned. For further information see the excellent synthesis prepared by Susanna B. Hecht (1989). Hecht's account of the devastation of the remote Brazilian state of Acre, on the border with Bolivia, identifies the network of economic interests that cross this Amazonian region.

6 According to information from the National Institute for Adult Education there were 4,200,000 illiterate persons over 14 years of age in Mexico in 1988. This represents 8.11 percent of that age population.

7 For further information on the general situation of refugees in Mexico, see Manz (1986), Quezada (1985), Quezada and O'Dogherty (1986), and Varese (1986). Concerning education specifically, data can be found in the magazine *Refugiados* (*Refugees*) no. 32, edited by UNHCR (United Nations High Commission for Refugees), and especially in the reports prepared for COMAR (the Mexican Commission for Assisting Refugees) by a group of researchers including Edgar González Gaudiano.

8 Commenting on the mediating role of the world, Freire says:

The importance for problematizing education, as a humanizing and liberating activity, resides in the fact that men who submitted to domination can struggle for their liberation. The world is no longer something which is talked about with false words but the mediator of the subjects of education, the object of transformative action of men, from which their humanization follows.

(1981 [1970]: 95)

REFERENCES

In these references the date of the first publication of the work is identified, and where this is not available, the year in which it was written or of the first located edition is given. These dates are cited in the quotations included in the text so as to situate the reader historically. Nonetheless, the page numbers indicated correspond to the edition consulted, as reported in the body of the bibliographic entry.

Aguayo Quezada, S. (1985) *The Central American Exodus: Consequences of a Conflict*, Mexico City: SEP-Cultural.

Aguayo Quezada, S. and O'Dogherty, L. (1986) 'Guatemalan refugees in Campeche and Quintana Roo', *International Forum (Foro International)* XXVII, Oct.–Dec., 2, 286–97.

Baudrillard, J. (1983) 'The ecstasy of communication' in J. Baudrillard, *Postmodernity* (Jordi Fible, trans.), Barcelona: Kairos, 1985.

de Alba, A. (1989a) 'The pluri-cultural condition in the curriculum field in Mexico'. Paper presented at the Society for Applied Anthropology Annual Meeting, Santa Fé, New Mexico, April.

—— (1989b) 'Coincidences between critical thought in Mexico and radical pedagogy'. Paper presented to the Center for Education and Cultural Studies, Miami University of Ohio, Oxford, Ohio, April.

de Alba, A. and Gutierrez, M. (1986) 'Pluri-culturality in the Mexican elementary school: a challenge toward consolidating national identity', in *Educación Primaría*, (ed.) Secretaria de Educación Publica, Mexico: SEP, pp. 1–101.

Fonseca Amador, C. (1982) *Viva Sandino*, Vol. 2, Managua: Nueva Nicaragua (Colección Pensamiento Vivo).

Freire, P. (1969) *Education: The Practice of Freedom*, 14th edition (Lilian Ranzoni, trans.), Mexico: Siglo XXI, 1974. (First Spanish edition: 1969, Siglo XXI in conjunction with Tierra Nueva, Montevideo, Uruguay. The author's explanatory note is signed Spring 1965, Santiago de Chile.)

—— (1981) *Pedagogy of the Oppressed*, 27th edition (Jorge Mellado, trans.), Mexico: Siglo XXI, 1981. (First Spanish edition: 1970, Mexico City: Siglo XXI/Montevideo: Tierra Nueva. The author's signature is dated Fall 1969, Santiago de Chile.)

—— (1973a) *Extension or Communication?: Conscientization in the Rural Field*, 9th edition (Lilian Ronzoni, trans.), Mexico City: Siglo XXI/Montevideo: Tierra Nueva.

—— (1973b) *Conscientization*, Bogota: Association of Educational Publications.

—— (1973c) *Letters to Guinea-Bissau*, 3rd edition (Antonia Alatorre, trans.), Mexico City: Siglo XXI, 1981. (First Spanish edition: 1977, Mexico City: Siglo XXI in conjunction with Siglo XXI, Spain. This contains letters to Mario Cabral and the group in Bissau, dated between January 1975 and Spring 1976.)

Freire, P. and Frei Betto (1985) *This School Called Life*, trans. Estela dos Santos, Buenos Aires: Legasa, 1988. (Text of interviews with Paulo Freire and Frei Betto, directed by journalist Ricardo Kotscho.)

Galeano, E. (1983) *Voices of Our Time*, San José, Costa Rica: EDCU.

Giroux, H. (1983) *Theory and Resistance in Education: A Pedagogy for the Opposition*, South Hadley, MA: Bergin and Garvey.

Hecht, S.B (1989) 'Chico Mendes: chronicle of a death foretold', *Perfil de la Jornada*, April 28.

Jameson, F. (1983) 'Postmodernism and the society of consumption' in *Postmodernity*, H. Foster (ed.) (Jordi Fible, trans.), Barcelona: Kairos, 1985.

Kosik, K. (1963) *Dialectic of the Concrete*, 5th edition (Adolfo Sanchez Vasquez, trans., Milan: Valentino Bompiani), 1965, prologue by Adolfo Sanchez Vasquez, Mexico City: Grijalbo, 1979.

McLaren, P. (1986) 'Postmodernity and the death of politics: a Brazilian reprieve' (Bertha Orozco Fuentes, trans.) in *Sociedad, Cultura y Educación*, Mexico City: ENEP-Aragon, UNAM, 1989. A revised edition appears as Chapter 11 below.

Manz, B. (1986) *Guatemala: Changes in the Community; Displacements and Repatriation*, Mexico City: Praxis.

Mariategui, J.C. (1928) *Seven Essays of Interpretation of Peruvian Reality*, Mexico: Era, 1979.

Micheli, J. (1989) 'Politics and ecology from the Amazon', *La Jornada*, March 13, 9.

Montoya Medinacelli, V. (1983) 'Bilingual education in integrated projects' in N.J. Rodriguez, K. Masferrer and R. Vargas Vega (eds), *Education, Ethnic Groups and Decolonization in Latin America. A Guide for Intercultural Bilingual Education*, vol. 1, Mexico: UNESCO-Instituto Indigenista Interamericano (III).

Nahmad Sitton, S. (1982) 'Indo-America and education: ethnocide or ethnodevelopment?' in Arlene Scanlon and Juan Lezama Morfin (eds), *Towards a Pluricultural Mexico. From Castilinization to a Bilingual and Bicultural Education*, Mexico City: Porrua.

Nicaraguan Ministry of Education (1983) *Education in Four Years of Revolution*, Managua: Ministry of Education.

PNUD (United Nations Development Program) (1988) *Report of the Regional Workshop on Managing the Environment and Sustainable Development*. Belem du Para: PNUD, December 12–13.

Ponce, A. (1934) *Education and Class Struggle*, Akal 2nd pocket edition, Madrid: Akal, 1981. This edition follows the text of Las Obras Completas (the complete works) of Aníbal Ponce, edited in Argentina in 1974, revised and annotated by Hector P. Agosti. We also consulted the 1976 United Mexican Editors edition that contains Emilio Troise's 'Marxist Ponce'. Troise points out that the book abridges the course given by Ponce in 1934. The date of the first edition of the book has not been located.

Puiggrós, A. (1988a) 'Prologue' in *This School Called Life* (Estela dos Santos, trans.), Buenos Aires: Legasa.

—— (1988b) *Democracy and Authoritarianism in Latin American Pedagogy*, Mexico: GV Editors.

Rodriguez, N.J., Masferrer, K.E. and Vargas Vega, R. (eds) (1983) *Education, Ethnic Groups and Decolonization in Latin America. A Guide for Intellectual Bilingual Education*, vol. 1, Mexico: UNESCO-Instituto Indigenista Interamerico (III).

Tovar de la Garza, E.C., González Gaudiano, E., Lucero Marquez, A.F. and Salgado Ruelas, M. (1989) *Who Are the Refugees? Towards a Pedagogy of Hope*. Report of activities during visits to the encampments and settlements of refugees by the group responsible for the Mexican Commission for Help to Refugees (COMAR) bilingual-bicultural education project, Mexico, May.

Uslar Pietri, A. (1981) *Robinson's Island*, Caracas: Seix Barral. Cited by Adriana Puiggrós (1988b), *Democracy and Authoritarianism in Latin American Pedagogy*, Mexico: GV Editors.

Varese, S. (1986) *Multiethnicity and Exile: Cultural Factors in the Situation of Guatemalan Refugees in Mexico*, Mexico City: UNRSD/ACNUR, pp. 186–7.

Zemelman, H. (1987a) *Critical Use of Theory: Round About the Analytical Functions of Totality*, Mexico: El Colegio de Mexico, University of the United Nations.

—— (1987b) *Knowledge and Social Subjects: Contribution to the Study of the Present*, Mexico: El Colegio de Mexico.

Chapter 8

Critical literacy, feminism, and a politics of representation

Jeanne Brady

INTRODUCTION

For a multicultural democratic society to thrive, any discourse about literacy needs to acknowledge the multiplicity of voices that engulfs us. Yet, if we aspire to a goal of developing a critical citizenry, whose actions are informed by democratic principles of justice that address issues of oppression and discrimination and allow for the creation of multiple spaces where hope is shared, we need a view of literacy that provides a language for naming and transforming the ideological positions and social conditions that obstruct these possibilities.[1] In other words, it needs to address the question of social usage, which suggests at least three forms of literacy: functional, cultural and critical. In this case, literacy would be linked to developing particular skills and knowledge that offer students a range of subject positions that would be necessary for realizing democratic public life. For example, beyond functional literacy, people need forms of literacy that provide multiple languages that allow communication across lines of cultural difference. They also need modes of critical literacy that challenge the idea of identity as singular, autonomous, and uniform; that is, a mode of critical and cultural literacy that provides the pedagogical conditions for understanding how identities are constructed through different subject positions, how literacy as a critical and cultural discourse functions in this case as a form of enunciation or address, and a location from which expression and action proceeds.

Put more sharply, literacy needs to be viewed within an ethical and emancipatory discourse providing a language of hope and transformation that is able to analyze, challenge and transform the ideological referent for understanding how people negotiate and translate their relationship with everyday life. It is also a form of social praxis that is directed at self and social transformation. In other words, it offers an alternative form of literacy to the dominant discourse, enabling a critical reading of how power, ideology and culture work to disempower some groups of people while privileging others. Hence, the concept of literacy is central to any notion of educational reform that presupposes a particular reading and transformation of the world. Literacy in this sense is informed by the broader project of educating students to advance the imperatives of a cultural democracy.[2]

A critical literacy and pedagogy of empowerment is not a new concept, but has evolved progressively over the past two decades (Shannon 1989, Graff 1981). Its roots are grounded in the work of Paulo Freire, the Brazilian educator and philosopher. Freire is viewed by many educators and social theorists as the most influential theorist in critical literacy and pedagogy, in virtue of his ability to interrelate theory, ideological commitment and political practice (Freire 1970, 1972, 1978a, 1985; Freire and Macedo 1987; Freire and Shor 1987).

EXTENDING CRITICAL PEDAGOGY

In what follows I will explore present critiques of Freire, not in an attempt to reject or discredit his work but, rather, to extend and build upon what he has done in order to enrich and deepen its most emancipatory possibilities. More specifically, I want to examine some of the theoretical lacunae in Freire's work, especially in light of some of the theoretical gains that have been made by feminists and a number of other theorists in recent years.

Much of Freire's earlier work was developed within problematic elements of modernism. In his attempt to create a language of critique and possibility, Freire often has been constrained by binarisms and totalizing narratives that worked against his most valuable insights. One instance has been Freire's theoretical inability to name and address the often more extensive, multiple, and contradictory forms of domination and struggle that inhabited the larger social reality. Tied to an over-emphasis on class struggle, Freire ignored the various forms of domination and social struggles being addressed by feminists, minorities, ecologists, and other social actors.

The most glaring example can be found in Freire's earlier work, where the subject and object of domination are framed in a thoroughgoing patriarchal discourse.[3] Not only are women erased in Freire's language of domination and struggle, there is no attempt even to acknowledge how experience is gendered differently. There is more at stake here than simply the refusal to treat identity and experience in gendered terms. There is also an unwillingness to address the complex, multiple, and contradictory nature of human subjectivity. Consequently, Freire often falls into a theoretical discourse which legitimates a modernist notion of the unified human subject and its attendant emphasis on universal historical agents. A number of ideological trappings characteristic of modernism inhabit Freire's early work, particularly *Pedagogy of the Oppressed*, *Pedagogy and Process*, and *Education for Critical Consciousness*. In fact, underpinning Freire's emphasis on a totalizing narrative of domination, his support of a unified subject, and a unified historical agent, we find a creeping essentialism in which gendered differences seem frozen in a pseudo-universal language that subsumes experience and cultural practice within a patriarchal discourse. Before examining these issues in more detail, however, I want to comment specifically on how Freire's pedagogy has been taken up by educators in the West.

Freire is best known for his work with literacy programs in Brazil, Chile, and

Guinea-Bissau. However, his work has gone far beyond its origins in Latin America and other Third World countries to be 'reinvented' by educators and cultural workers in North America. In recent years, Freire's work has frequently been appropriated by academics, public school teachers, community organizers and workers in adult education. Unfortunately, in a great many instances the political venture that informs Freire's work has been 'forgotten' and what remains in these appropriations is a caricature of Freire's project. In the first place, a number of Western educators have reduced his politically charged pedagogy to an insipid and dreary list of methodologies dressed up in progressive labels that belie the truncated nature of the ideology that informs them. As McLaren notes,

> The critical theory to which Freire's work speaks must be extended in order to allow women as well as minorities to emerge as critical, social actors on the stage of human transformation and struggle. Futhermore, the conceptual frame- works that purport to uncover and transform the constructions of subjectivity need to be purged of their phallocentrism, Eurocentrism, and masculinist ideologies.
>
> (in press)

Instead of situating Freire's work in a politics that provides the basis for transformative pedagogical practices, a number of Freirean-based educators have largely displaced the political aspect of Freire's work for the safety of a list of prescriptive rules that allegedly add up to a model of critical pedagogy. While not unaware of the theoretical pitfalls that this approach produces, even such well-versed 'Freireans' as Ira Shor appear to have fallen into this theoretical trap. For example, in a text designed to apply the Freirean approach to job training education, Shor promotes what he calls a nine-point agenda for critical education. Situated within a topology that urges teachers to develop educational practices that are participatory, dialogic, situated, critical, and desocializing, Freire's work is denuded of the colonial context that informs it and the historically specific theoretical assumptions that give it its meaning (Shor 1988). With a few exceptions, the same approach to Freire's work can be found in the book *Freire for the Classroom: A Sourcebook for Liberatory Teaching* (Shor 1987). In a revealing criticism of this book, Gail Stygall (1989) argues against the simple application of Freire's work to a North American context.[4] In her view, *Freire for the Classroom* is silent on a number of issues as a result of the depoliticization and decontextualization of Freire's work. According to Stygall,

> it fails to provide an analysis of the changes required in applying Freirean peda- gogy in post-industrial societies; it avoids close scrutiny of the institutional sites of literacy training in this country, our schools; and with the exception of a handful of articles, the volume presents no adequate theory of language.
>
> (1989: 114)

At issue here is not merely the erasure of politics as part of a transformative politics, but also the under-theorization of a critical discourse of literacy. Consequently, theory is subsumed within a reductionist methodology and, while displaying the best of intentions, the appropriation of Freire's critical literacy by many North American theorists results in pedagogical applications that are often patronizing and theoretically naive. Simply to take a discourse developed by Freire for pre-literate peasants in Latin America and transpose its formative pedagogical assumptions to a population of students who belong to a highly industrial society, have been reared under the banner of Western rationality, and are steeped in the legacy of colonialism, without making problematic the politics of place, location, and translation that inform such a pedagogical process borders on imitating the very colonial logic Freire was initially fighting when he launched his literacy campaign in Brazil. Pedagogical models based on recipe-like prescriptions of Freire's work, and applied from one setting to another, are at odds with Freire's pedagogical and political project.

In short, what must be made a significant concern in taking up Freire's theory of literacy and critical pedagogy is the ways in which the process of negotiation and translation, when enacted in different cultural and historical settings, often contradicts the use of Freire's work as a revolutionary pedagogical practice, by sometimes trivializing the political project and in some cases eliminating it altogether. I want here to elucidate how some feminist and post-colonial theorists have begun to rewrite Freire's work in a manner less inclined to reify it as a methodology or romanticize it as a tradition that merely needs to be learned and applied. Recent work by theorists such as Kathleen Weiler (1991), Peter McLaren (McLaren and Leonard 1992), Henry A. Giroux (1992), and Abdul JanMohamed (1993) has begun to engage both the strengths and limitations of Freire's work. In this context, the relation with Freire's work is one not of submission and repetition, but of transformation and critique (Strategies Collective 1988). In what follows I want to highlight some of the important insights produced by this work.

FEMINIST CRITIQUE OF FREIREAN THOUGHT

A feminist re-reading of Freire has argued against his exclusive focus on class as the only form of domination and called into question the abstract quality and limitations of certain terms – grounded in universal truths and assumptions – that narrow the collective experience of oppression. Feminists like Kathleen Weiler have argued that Freire's use of such terms as oppression, humanization, reason, and experience fails to engage the multiple forms of oppression experienced by people of different groups, and overlooks the political and pedagogical importance of addressing issues of identity and difference as they are structured through the contradictory practice of domination, struggle and possibility within and between different groups of oppressed people (Weiler 1991). Feminists have made clear that even though Freire recognizes the subject positions of the oppressed, he does not recognize the specific gendered realities of expression and exploitation. This is evident not only in the gendered language that populates his early works such as *Pedagogy of the Oppressed*, but also in his notion of reproduction as being exclusively linked to the project of economic reconstruction, especially in

Pedagogy and Process. By focusing on reproduction around agriculture, Freire ignores the complexity of reproduction for women around the issue of women's work, i.e., health care, birthing, family matters. In effect, feminists like Weiler and bell hooks have acknowledged that Freire's work needs to be supplemented by a theory of power that 'restores a sense of "both-and": a view of politics as fully dialectical' (Brunt 1990: 157).

A feminist notion of difference reflects both diversity and unity and focuses on the lives of people who work and live in a multiracial, multicultural society. Again, Kathleen Weiler addresses the issues of difference as a central theme to expand on Freire's liberatory pedagogy. She points out the critiques of the essentialist position of a common women's experience based on the writings of lesbians, women of color, and postmodern feminists around the acknowledgement that no single women's experience can be conceived as universal. By identifying the possibility for multiple and sometimes contradictory positions, she illuminates how Freire fails to address 'the overlapping and multiple forms of domination revealed in "reading the world" of experience' (Weiler 1991: 469). At issue here is the need for critical educators to reject the notion of identity as fixed or static, and to recognize and develop a project of multiple forms of liberation.

Indeed, a critical theory of literacy must come to understand how identities are constructed within multiple and often contradictory subject positions, how such identities shift, and how the struggle over identity takes place on many fronts, involving many different types of battle.[5] As Peter McLaren notes, Freire's theory of literacy and identity formation must be extended and deepened by acknowledging how the specificities of different historical and social conditions configure to produce, within a changing matrix of agency and determination, a range of diverse identities and subjectivities (McLaren, in press). Educators must engage the specificity of the subject positions of teachers, students and others as they are defined by class, race, gender, and other subject-producing forces. We must reject outright the notion that there is a universal subject and a set of common experiences that equally define all oppressed groups, along with those humanist discourses that enshrine 'man' as the repository of human will and agency.

A number of feminists have also addressed the issue of authority and the role of the intellectual as developed in Freire's work. While few feminists, with the notable exception of bell hooks, have recognized that Freire does not equate all forms of authority with authoritarianism, feminists have nonetheless provided a critique of Freire's notion of authority that is as theoretically compelling as it is pedagogically useful.

Freire acknowledges that power is productive and not merely negative, and thus can be used to construct democratic forms of authority. He does not, however, consider adequately how the politics of teacher location inscribes educators within different degrees of strength or marginalization as a result of how they describe themselves and are seen by others. It is not enough to respect the specificity of the voices that students bring to the classroom or any other educational site. It is also imperative to deconstruct the place from which teachers speak and are 'spoken'

(Kintz 1990). The places from which teachers speak always carry privileges for some and create hardships for others. These varied locations and the pedagogy of place they engender can be more fruitfully understood by analyzing how some feminist theorists have addressed the issue of teacher authority.

How authority is exercised by teachers is not an issue that can simply be generalized through an abstract discussion of the productive nature of power. Issues such as race, class, gender, and sexual orientation, as well as the particular material and ideological gravity of particular institutions, all affect how authority is produced, sustained, received, and legitimated.[6] Weiler specifically reiterates this criticism from a feminist perspective and in doing so takes issue with Freire's overly abstract image of the teacher around questions of authority in relation to knowledge and power. Weiler notes that 'Freire fails to address the various forms of power held by teachers depending on their race, gender and the historical and institutional settings in which they work' (Weiler 1991: 460).

Weiler highlights the need for critical educators to address the concerns raised by a number of feminists around the central issues of difference, positionality, and subjectivity. She is not content, however, merely to illuminate the discursive and ideological limits that structure the ways in which authority and power come together within the range of subject positions available to teachers. She also argues, correctly I believe, that any discourse on authority must address and transform the hierarchical structures of schooling that support a patriarchal society and ultimately serve to deny women authority.

> [T]he issue of institutional authority raises the contradictions of trying to achieve a democratic and collective ideal in a hierarchical institution, but it also raises the question of the meaning of authority for feminist teachers, whose right to speak or to hold power is itself under a patriarchal (and racist, homo-phobic, class specific) society.
>
> (Weiler 1991: 460)

It is thus necessary for feminist teachers to accept and exert authority, not in an attempt simply to gain and maintain power, but rather in a positive way that empowers both themselves and their students while working simultaneously to transform the conditions of institutional power. Weiler uses a feminist exploration of authority to advance Freire's position by providing a richer and more developed concern for authority that addresses the contradictions between the hierarchies of knowledge and power without denying the specificities of difference and the politics of identity.

> An acknowledgement of the realities of conflict and tensions based on contradictory political goals, as well as of the meaning of historically experi-enced oppression for both teachers and students, leads to a pedagogy that respects difference not just as significant for students but for teachers as well.
>
> (Weiler 1991: 462)

There are at least three important pedagogical concerns not addressed by Freire that need to be raised in the interests of deepening the possibilities of a critical pedagogy.

First, teacher authority becomes emancipatory to the degree that it recognizes the importance of what I want to call a feminist pedagogy of place. Schools are by and large structured around ideologies, delivery systems, and goals that are largely competitive, hierarchical, and instrumental. Informed largely by a rationality that supports patriarchal practices, teachers' authority must recognize the important limits these forces place on producing knowledge, developing non-competitive forms of learning, giving students access to the conditions necessary for producing knowledge, and building classroom social relations that are democratic and just.

Second, authority in its emancipatory forms is never transparent or innocent. It is always a site of struggle involving issues of both access and definition. The issue of who speaks, for whom, under what conditions, and in what manner, is intimately tied to a politics of representation that can only be understood by acknowledging how race, class, and gender shape power that legitimates certain forms of authority based on issues of exclusion and marginalization. Women and racial minorities need to represent *themselves*. This suggests that any discussion of authority must be rooted in an identity politics that acknowledges the need for people to represent themselves within relations of power that dignify and support the specificity of their struggles, histories, and collective memories. This is not meant to romanticize experience, particularly the experience of those who are oppressed. It is meant to suggest that such experiences must relate to having the authority to speak, and being held responsible for what one says and does in ideological and political terms. These issues have to be factored into any notion of democratic authority.

Weiler contributes to this analysis by identifying the notion of personal experience as a fundamental category in Freirean pedagogy that needs to be explored and expanded. She argues her position from a feminist perspective which emphasizes personal feelings and experience as a guide to knowing about the world. At the same time she addresses the limitations and contradictory moments of using feelings or emotions as a source of knowledge. According to Weiler,

> [t]here is a danger that the expression of strong emotion can be simply cathartic and can deflect the need for action to address the underlying causes of that emotion . . . shaped by the dominant discourse.
>
> (1991: 463)

Given this, she argues that feminist teachers need to understand how the authority of the dominant culture participates in the construction of emotions in shaping the identities of teachers, students, and others. Authority does not simply produce knowledge, but also plays a central role in constructing a pedagogy of affective investment, in producing and policing desires (McLaren 1988). This does not suggest, however, that the sphere of the affective be linked to the forces of domination. On the contrary, Weiler and other feminists argue strongly that emotions and affective investments have an important role to play in shaping and understanding relations to ourselves, others, and the world around us. Moreover, the affective realm, with its privileging of compassion, empathy and solidarity, reveals the limits of an exclusionary rationality that believes that meaning is only constructed through rational thought.[7]

Third, the notion of feminist authority must provide the conditions for students to become empowered within a pedagogy of place that allows them to speak without being terrified over the implications of what they say. The various discourses of feminism must work to create critical public spaces in which diverse discourses come into play, within an attempt to cultivate a critical spirit and form of ethical address that recognizes the importance of feminism as one among many discourses that can be used to promote human agency, collective struggle, and social justice.

THE POLITICS OF POST-COLONIALISM AND POSTMODERNISM

A number of post-colonial theorists have aptly taken up Freire's work in a critical way. In doing so they address some of the major problems involved in appropriating and 'reinventing' Freire's theories, transferring them to different cultural and historical settings. Central to such critiques is the recognition that many uses of Freire's work reveal an inadequate understanding of both the anti-colonial project that informs his pedagogy and his dialectical theory of language. More specifically, lost in the translation of Freire's work is an understanding of his reliance on anti-colonial and post-colonial discourses and how they radically structure his view of the relationship between theory and practice. In part, this means his work is often appropriated and re-created in ways that empty it of any understanding of the legacy of colonial struggle that informs it as a counter-narrative; at the same time, the sites of privilege and power in which Freire's work is used generally represent locations and sites of theorizing which are both complicitous with and unreflective about the legacy of imperialism. As Giroux points out,

> a politics of location works in the interest of privilege and power to cross cultural, political and textual borders so as to deny the specificity of the other and to reimpose the discourse and practice of colonial hegemony.
>
> (1992: 15)

Abdul JanMohamed has also commented on the risk intellectuals from the First World run when they appropriate the work of Third World intellectuals like Freire. According to JanMohamed, such intellectuals must be clear about 'mapping the politic of their forays into other cultures' (in press: 3). Giroux seeks to take this position a step further by requiring educators to

> make problematic a politics of location situated in the privilege and power of the West and how engaging in the question of the ideological weight of such a position constructs one's specific reading of Freire's work.
>
> (1992: 16)

This means that educators must negotiate and deconstruct the borders that define the politics and privilege of their own location. In developing this argument Giroux calls upon cultural workers to become border crossers, as part of a self-conscious attempt to step outside the safety zone of the cultural, theoretical, and ideological confidence that both informs their work and structures their relationship with the oppressed 'Other' (Giroux 1992). JanMohamed further reinforces this point by arguing that Freire's

> pedagogy implicitly advocates the nurturing of intellectuals who will cross borders and in the process develop strong antagonisms . . . In so doing, they in effect become archaeologists of the site of their own social formation . . . Their contemplation of the condition of their lives represents a freedom, or at least an attempt to achieve freedom, from the politics of imaginary identification and opposition, from conflation of identity and location, and so on – in short, from the varied and powerful forms of suturing that are represented by the instrumental in the construction of their sedimented culture.
>
> (JanMohamed 1993: 113)

By refusing to deconstruct their own politics of privilege and location, educators continue to maintain and produce forms of domination and oppression that are deeply rooted in the legacy of colonialism. As Giroux points out,

> From the comforting perspective of the colonial gaze, such theorists often appropriate Freire's work without engaging its historical specificity and ongoing political project. The gaze in this case becomes self-serving and self-referential, its principles shaped by technical and methodological considerations.
>
> (1992: 21)

Giroux elaborates further on the difficult task of using Freire's work. Not only does it change over time, it also carries with it a shifting political project. As cultural workers and border intellectuals we must likewise constantly re-examine the sites and spaces in which we work as historical, social, and political border-lands which offer possibilities for refiguring knowledge, values, and identities so as to develop relations that can produce resistance to and relief from structures of domination and oppression. At stake here is the need for educators who use Freire's work to change the terms on which borders are both named and crossed. In his attempt to extend Freire's work from a post-colonial perspective, McLaren argues that resistance to domination and oppression entails the development of a new language that avoids the binarisms of logocentric discourse (McLaren, in press). Hence, there is a need to make clear what the terms of reference are that educators use to speak from a particular place, to create the conditions for others to speak, and to reconfigure through specific pedagogical practices the relations between the centers and margins of power, *within* the school as well as *between* the school and the larger society.

Within varied post-colonial discourses, there is much concern over how Eurocentric practices displace the theoretical and political gravity of 'Third World' discourses as part of an effort to appropriate (domesticate) them and to rewrite them as part of a Western hegemonic project. Post-colonial and feminist theorists have sought to rewrite the language of difference and culture outside the monumentalist view of Eurocentrism. In doing so they have challenged the notion of an authentic culture and of humanist 'man' as a unified, autonomous subject, while simultaneously emphasizing the role that cultural difference can play as part of a broader goal of creating diverse public cultures and further animating the conditions necessary for democratic life. In this case, Freire's original concern for making the issues of agency and identity central to the notion of difference have been expanded, so as to increase the range of democratic antagonisms that underlie multiple forms of struggle and resistance.

Within this perspective, language does not become the passive vehicle of prescriptive methodologies. On the contrary, it becomes an active form of cultural production for 'getting at' and understanding the things that shape our identity; it allows us to understand zones of cultural difference, and to create spaces where people can move beyond wooden topologies that lock them into rigid boundaries and identities. Moreover, in Freire's work, language becomes a referent for understanding how institutional practices privilege certain forms of identity, how one reads the world, and also how one refigures one's own identity within a specific set of historical, social, and economic configurations.

Finally, it is important to stress that Freire's approach to literacy, as it has developed over the last twenty years, represents, in the words of Cornel West, 'a world-historical event for counter-hegemonic theorists and activists in search of new ways of linking social theory to narratives of human freedom (West 1992: 1).' His work has helped rewrite the role of the committed and passionate intellectual who makes the concrete central to struggle without ever sacrificing the importance of theory and analysis. Although Freire's work has been subjected to criticism, it is necessary to note that its richness, depth, and rigor have become a model for radical educators and cultural theorists all over the world. Freire's work is exemplary, in respect of its revelation of the man who produced it and of the ethical address it constitutes through its call for democratic dialogue, collective empowerment, and social struggle. Freire's discourse has always been grounded in the noble utopian project of creating the conditions for human beings to understand and make history as part of a broader project of constituting themselves as political subjects and ethical agents. Freire provides a legacy of dangerous memories that allow us to take up his work with love, care, and a sense of criticism that dignifies its own homage to resistance and engagement.

NOTES

1 For valuable historical accounts and analyses of the literacy movement in North America, see Willinsky (1990) and Shannon (1989). For an excellent analysis of the range of conservative and right-wing views of literacy, see Mitchell and Weiler (1992). One of the most comprehensive analyses of literacy as a form of cultural politics can be found in Green (1991).

2 For analysis of the relationship between literacy, democracy, and critical citizenship, see Giroux (1988) and Freire and Macedo (1987).

3 This is particularly true of Freire's most famous book, *Pedagogy of the Oppressed* (1972). It is also important to point out that Freire has in numerous interviews and articles recognized the patriarchal ideology that was inscribed in his earlier work, and has both repudiated it and thanked feminists for bringing it to his attention. For a most recent example of Freire's views on this subject, see the splendid interview with Freire in Olson (1992).

4 For a more extensive critique of Shor and his use of Freire's work, see Gale (1992).

5 One of the best sources engaging the politics of identity and difference from the perspective of a number of political positions can be found in Rutherford (1990).

6 For a brilliant analysis of this issue from a feminist and critical theory perspective, see Jones (1991); see also Sholle (1992).

7 For excellent discussions of this issue, see Welch (1990) and Flax (1990).

REFERENCES

Brunt, R. (1990) 'The politics of identity' in S. Hall and M. Jacques, eds, *New Times: the Changing Face of Politics in the 1990s*, London: Verso.

Flax, J. (1990) *Thinking Fragments: Psychoanalysis, Feminism, and Postmodernism in the Contemporary West*, Berkeley: University of California Press.

Freire, P. (1970) *Cultural Action For Freedom*, Cambridge, MA: Harvard Educational Review.

—— (1972) *Pedagogy of the Oppressed*, Harmondsworth: Penguin.

—— (1978a) *Education for Critical Consciousness*, New York: Seabury Press.

—— (1978b) *Pedagogy and Process: Letters to Guinea-Bissau*, London: Writers and Readers.

—— (1985) *The Politics of Education*, London: Macmillan.

Freire, P. and Macedo, D. (1987) *Literacy: Reading the Word and Reading the World*, South Hadley, MA: Bergin and Garvey.

Freire, P. and Shor, I. (1987) *A Pedagogy for Liberation*, London: Macmillan.

Gale, I. (1992) 'Towards a dialogic pedagogy: an interactive model of composition instruction'. Ph.D. dissertation, University of South Florida.

Giroux, H. A. (1988) *Schooling and the Struggle for Public Life*, Minnesota: University of Minnesota Press.

—— (1991) 'Paulo Freire and the politics of postcolonialism', *Journal of Advanced Composition* 12, 1, 15–25.

—— (1992) *Border Crossings: Cultural Workers and the Politics of Education*, New York: Routledge.

Graff, H. (1981) *Literacy and Social Development in the West*, Cambridge: Cambridge University Press.

Green, W.C. (1991) 'After the new English: Cultural politics and English curriculum change'. Ph.D. dissertation, Murdoch University.

JanMohamed, A.R. (1993) 'Some implications of Paulo Freire's border pedagogy', *Cultural Studies* 7, 1, 107–17.

—— (in press) '"Worldliness-without-world, homelessness-as-home": toward a definition of the border intellectual', *Boundary 2*.

Jones, K. (1991), 'The trouble with authority', *Differences* 3, 1, 104–27.

Kintz, L. (1990) 'On performing deconstruction: postmodern pedagogy', *Cultural Critique* 16, 87–107.

McLaren, P. (1988) 'Schooling the postmodern body: critical pedagogy and the politics of enfleshment', *Journal of Education* 170, 3, 53–83.

—— (in press) 'Critical literacy and post-colonial praxis: a Freirean perspective', *College Literature*.

McLaren, P. and Leonard, P. (eds) (1992) *Paulo Freire: A Critical Encounter*, New York: Routledge.

Mitchell, C. and Weiler, K. (eds) (1992) *Rewriting Literacy: Culture and the Discourse of the Other*, New York: Bergin and Garvey.

Olson, G.A. (1992) 'History, praxis, and change: Paulo Freire and the politics of literacy', *Journal of Advanced Composition* 12, 1, 1–14.

Rutherford, J. (ed.) (1990) *Identity, Community, Culture, Difference*, London: Lawrence and Wishart.

Shannon, P. (1989) *Broken Promises*, New York: Bergin and Garvey.

Sholle, D. (1992) 'Authority on the left: critical pedagogy, postmodernism and vital strategies', *Cultural Studies* 6, 2, 271–89.

Shor, I. (ed.) (1987) *Freire for the Classroom: A Sourcebook for Liberatory Teaching*, Portsmouth: Boynton/Cook.

—— (1988) *Working Hands and Critical Minds: A Paulo Freire Model for Job Training*, Chicago: Alternative Schools Network.

Strategies Collective (1988) 'Building a new left: an interview with Ernest Laclaw', *Strategies* 1, 12.

Stygall, G. (1989) 'Teaching Freire in North America', *Journal of Teaching Writing* 8, 113–25.

Weiler, K. (1991) 'Freire and a feminist pedagogy of difference', *Harvard Educational Review* 61, 4, 449–74. A modified version of this article is given as Chapter 1 above.

Welch, S. (1990) *A Feminist Ethic at Risk*, Minneapolis: Fortress Press.

West, C. (1992) 'Preface' in P. McLaren and P. Leonard, eds, *Paulo Freire: A Critical Encounter*, New York: Routledge.

Willinsky, J. (1990) *The New Literacy*, New York: Routledge.

Chapter 9

Politics, praxis and the personal
An Argentine assessment

Adriana Puiggrós
(translated by Fiona Taler)

(In this chapter Adriana Puiggrós, a leading Latin American social and educational theorist, replies to Peter McLaren's questions.)[1]

PM: We met for the first time in Mexico City in 1989, although we had been corresponding for some time before that. But it wasn't until our subsequent meetings in Buenos Aires and Parana City that I learned something about your personal history. Your father, Rudolpho Puiggrós, was the President of the University of Buenos Aires and a well-known and respected author of the history of Latin American politics and was one of the founders of EL DIA, a vital organ of critical journalism in Mexico. Your family was targeted for assassination in 1974 by Lopez Rega, one of Isabel Perón's ministers. After bombs exploded both in your office at the University of Buenos Aires, where you were working as Dean at the School of Philosophy and Literature, and in the apartment complex where you lived with your family, you and your parents went into exile in Mexico City. A year later this 'dictadura militar' murdered your brother Sergio, in Argentina. You completed your doctorate when in exile at the Autonomous National University of Mexico City, the largest university in Latin America (with over 300,000 students). Then you returned to Buenos Aires in 1984 where you now teach as professor of Argentine and Latin American History of Education and as researcher for the National Council of Science and Technology.

Your maternal grandparents were Russian Jews who escaped with their daughter from the great purges of Stalin by crossing the Urals on foot, eventually traveling on a Japanese boat to Singapore, and then making the journey to South Africa and finally to Argentina in 1931. I remember the comment you made that it was ironic that your grandparents escaped communism only to have their daughter marry a famous Argentine communist – your father, Rudolpho. Learning about your history reminded me of the early struggles of Freire – his imprisonment and his exile for seventeen years. Which brings me to the point of our interview. Can you describe your first encounter with Freire's work? At what point in your life did you first become aware of his writings?

AP: Initially I became aware of Paulo Freire's work by word of mouth and via newspaper articles around 1966. Only in 1970 did I read *Education: The Practice of Freedom* (Freire 1972) for the first time, since Freire's thought faced great difficulties becoming known in Argentina.

PM: What were these difficulties?

AP: Freire's thinking was introduced by activists of the Catholic left wing, advocates of 'liberation theology' who, following the Bishops' Conference in Medellín in 1968, sought to build a new philosophy within the church. Influenced particularly by Monsignor Hélder Camara, Bishop of Olinda and Recife in Brazil, they were committed to socialist revolution and trying to establish links between Marxism and Christianity. It was among these groups that the revolutionary Peronist left wing, active in Argentina between the end of the 1960s and the late 1970s, evolved. Despite the fact that the influence of the Christian left on Argentine youth, especially middle-class youth, was strong at that time, Freire's readership was strictly limited. Moreover, literacy work, which had spread widely in other Latin American countries, was limited in Argentina to minimal and isolated initiatives.

PM: How were you influenced?

AP: In those days I was an associate lecturer at the University of Buenos Aires. In a lecture I gave in 1972 I included reference to Freire's works together with a paper that described liberation pedagogy, combining the strong and distinctively Latin American Marxism in which I had been educated myself with elements of Frantz Fanon's work. A key feature of this approach was the difficulty it posed to establishing the differences between a colonial and a hegemonic system; a difficulty shared by a large section of the left and Argentine popular nationalism.

PM: Explain the differences here.

AP: The differences were no mere side issue. These differences were the key to understanding Argentina's distinctive situation, and where its economy, politics, social organization and culture differ from, or are similar to, those of other Latin American and Third World countries. Cultural colonialism, one of the axes of Freire's critical stance, involves one culture invading the consciousness of another, eliminating that culture and imposing another language and world view in its place.

PM: There is certainly a history of that in Latin America.

AM: Yes, one of the landmarks giving rise to modern history, five hundred years ago, was indeed a colonialist event: the beginning of the conquest of America. The founding scene of Latin American education consists in the 'conquistadores' reading to the indigenous people, in Spanish, a list of their rights and obligations. By this ritual, incomprehensible to the Incas, Nahuas, Guaranís, and other native peoples, a colonialist pedagogy was established. Later, however, came national liberation movements which developed into the struggle for independence in Latin America during the nineteenth century. These struggles were led by liberal politicians together with progressive sectors of the Latin American populations who sought the modernization and democratization of their societies.

PM: How did these movements impact education?

AP: One of the main aims of liberal political projects in education was to help integrate new nations, molding the population into the form of the citizen. The role of these projects was contradictory: they fought against 'barbarity' – that is, popular political culture – contributing to the development of societies, but developed them in an unjust manner.

PM: What were the consequences of this development? In what ways was education influenced?

AP: The development of Latin American education has been *uneven* in the way it has reached the people; *combined* in the sense that it has included discursive fragments derived from other cultures, from differing educational approaches to schooling, and from other stages of technological development; and *asynchronic* in the sense that its rate of development has differed in each country, region, and social sector.

The political, social, and cultural specifics of each society were very important in shaping the kind of 'articulation' produced between the discourse of public school and the discourses of popular education. An example is evident in the political-cultural differences resulting from the 'collision' between the indigenous population and public schooling in Mexico and that between immigrants and public schooling in Argentina. In Latin America the classic tasks of ideological transmission and enforcing the dominant 'habitus' (Bourdieu and Passeron 1977) were achieved in the context of deep inequalities. The school enacted simultaneously its unifying function and that of creating and maintaining distinction. These mechanisms are not, of course, the exclusive heritage of Latin American education systems, but are typical rather of the founding model of modern school systems.

PM: How has Freire's work shed light on these dilemmas?

AP: Achieving unification and distinction together (articulating two seemingly contradictory functions) necessarily requires exercising hegemony; that is, it involves removing some differences and consolidating others, linking everything into a central system. One of the main differences between central and peripheral school systems is the weakness of the hegemonic function among the latter – which subverts the political-pedagogic modes of articulation in that framework. Consequently, when we refer to the 'combined' character of education systems in Latin America, it must be remembered that this term does not imply a complementary exchange between forms that are culturally different yet politically equal but, rather, an exchange that involves dominance and antagonism. As we will see shortly, the antagonism within the pedagogic relationship was one of the most salient ideas in Paulo Freire's pedagogical critique.

PM: In what ways is the pedagogic relationship manifest in Latin America?

AP: The 'combined' character of Latin American education systems reflects deep rifts in the social and cultural fabric. These appear like *imprints* in the system.

PM: Give us an example.

AP: One that especially stands out among them is the 'gap' between the school habitus and the habitus of those educated within other pedagogical forms (such as within the family, in matched/paired groups, in ethnolinguistic groups, etc.). The high level of scholastic failure, in terms both of understanding and school retention, among a large part of the Latin American people shows that certain sectors of the society have not been 'sufficiently integrated' into the hegemonic system.

Even so, school systems have attained a very important place in all of Latin America. They have come to comprise the *legal* education system and in many countries reach a very high proportion of the population. Their development depended on a range of conditions being met.

PM: Such as. . . .

AP: The most notable were:

- the existence of projects to build nation states, directed by social sectors having the potential to establish a hegemony;
- bases for achieving the demand for mass conformity in the face of a project of national integration within a social order grounded in inequalities and differences: that is, to establish social accords, implicit or explicit, formal or informal, among 'directors' and 'directed';
- establishing the belief that the school system is able to promote movements within the society such as social mobility, morality and 'recovery' or 'redemption', and economic progress;
- faith that agreements can be reached across generations so that projects can build from generation to generation;
- agreement among the key social *subjects* (or forces/players) that there is a need for the state to play a formative role, that the periphery is moving toward development, and that the modern education system is also moving in that direction (Amin 1989: 34);
- the existence of a dominant culture able to penetrate deeply into the rest of the cultures; a culture that expresses itself pedagogically through a *habitus* capable of transcending the gap that separates it from the habitus of these other cultures and imposing itself upon them (Bourdieu and Passeron 1977: 113).

The incomplete, unequal, and unjust development of Latin American societies and the unfinished nature of the nations themselves did not impede the spread and growth of school systems, in that some of these necessary conditions could nonetheless be met. The ways in which and extent to which these conditions were met – in different combinations and degrees – gave rise, precisely, to different educational processes andpedagogical discourses among the various Latin American countries.

The differences can be ordered along a spectrum. At one end we could locate those countries where a hegemonic modern pedagogical discourse existed which defeated other discourses, subordinating them to its logic and incorporating their elements. At the other end would be those countries where a modern pedagogical discourse could not fracture and articulate the 'hard core' of other cultures and thus establish a dominant relationship over them. Everywhere, however, vestiges of colonialism remain encapsulated in Latin American education. They were never completely expunged from the hegemonic orders that proceeded to be built in each country after the formal creation of nation states.

In those countries where the bourgeoisie effected a more elaborate development of the state, a more diversified economy and a more comprehensive education system, the project of creating a nation state took on a symbolic presence that was more diffused and better sustained than in other countries, although it remained incomplete in all of them. In general, the Latin American bourgeoisie is characterized by shortcomings in national and social consciousness and a structured, dependent character. There are exceptions in those 'national bourgeoisies' which participated in moments of the rise of popular nationalism, especially in Mexico. But for a century the pedagogical discourse of public schooling had fundamental ideological effects. It helped forge the idea of the nation – albeit a dependent nation – within the collective imagination of large sectors of the urban population and, in some cases, among rural sectors as well.

I have been arguing in support of the view that situations of internal cultural colonialism, typical of Latin America, are not created independently of national school systems. Rather, they are a function of the *failure* of those very school systems, insofar as they constitute a large part of their being as *resistance* to pene- tration by modern pedagogical discourses.

In Brazil, constituting public education had been a late development. Despite this, by the time Freire was building his educational position at the start of the 1960s there already existed a school system of the type associated with nation states – although deep cultural rifts remained and large segments of the population were not attending school. Paulo Freire was director of the Department of Education and Culture of the SESI (Industrial Social Service) in Pernanbuco between 1946 and 1954, during the popular nationalist government of Getulio Vargas. Hence Freire's early work comprised part of a program aimed at extending a hegemony of modern culture. That government had begun around 1930 a process of building a national state via a strategy of articulating discursive fragments derived from diverse social and political 'subjects' (Laclau 1978). In 1947 Vargas implemented the Youth and Adult Education Campaign. This operated until 1954 (the year of Vargas's suicide), and prompted an important social mobilization process. At that time public instruction was aimed at rural sectors as well as at technical-industrial training of mass workers.

The differences between the popular nationalist regime in Brazil from 1930 to 1945 and the popular nationalism occurring during the same period in Argentina (Peronism) can explain the different paths taken by liberation pedagogy in the two countries. The sheer range of contradictions evident in Brazil (a combination of regional, racial, ethnic, cultural, and socio-economic differences) resulted in a smaller political-cultural concentration than in Argentina. There, as we will shortly see, Peronism acted upon a society that had been undergoing a process of cultural, political, and linguistic integration for decades. Amid the web of cultural relations in Brazilian society, colonialist enclaves persisted strongly. In Argentina, by contrast, they had all but disappeared. Between 1945 and 1955 the popular masses had gone through a profound process of cultural homogenization.

Let me, finally, draw a conceptual distinction. The pedagogic discourse of the colonist tries to fill the minds of its recipients with another culture. It functions, however, as an external element which – according to Freirean thought – can be eradicated if the recipient becomes 'conscientized' to the invasion he or she suffers. By contrast, hegemonic pedagogic discourse needs to break up (fragment) the recipient educatee's culture and establish multiple bonds with the fragments. Many educatees participate in the schemes of dominant pedagogical discourse in a resigned and subordinated manner.

PM: What do you see as the main contributions Freire has made to education specific to Argentina?

AP: The fact that Freire's work encountered such difficulties in coming to influence Argentine education is really symptomatic of two things. First, Freirean discourse was not yet a pedagogical *theory* but existed rather as a series of ideas that were highly corrosive and had not transcended an identity as highly effective political-pedagogic strategies tied to a specific locale and historical moment. Second, it was evident that these ideas contained enormous potential for effecting a crisis within modern pedagogy: a pedagogy whose central axes are the banking relationship; belief in the importance of the positions of *educator* and *educated*; recourse to a logic of similarity, identity and homogeneity for building educational discourse; and the myth of the separation between education and politics. Putting liberation pedagogy into practice cast doubts over a pedagogy that had been hegemonic for a century – despite the fact that some of its theoretical trappings, such as the overgeneralized use of the term 'colonialism', were impediments to liberation pedagogy spreading through more modern Latin American societies.

Take the case of Argentina. There, from the beginning of the struggle for independence from Spain (1810) to the fall of Perón's second government (1955), certain bourgeois sectors displayed progressive and industrial intentions, supporting these with corresponding education programs. But they were always overruled by projects stressing the export of agrarian commodities and the import of manufactured and capital goods: projects which were speculative and generated external debt. On the other hand, national education projects centered on popular demands for cultural transmission have always been linked to attempts to achieve a national economy that is relatively self-centered. The best examples of this came from the first Peronist governments (1945–55; 1973–76). The failure of those proposals in the hands of the old school system was an aspect of the failure of popular nationalist states in their attempts to overcome the old social model [viz., colonial or neo-colonial dependence and subordination: *Ed.*].

Let us look briefly at the origins of Argentina's school system. In the 1880s the first pillars of educational legislation were put in place. From then until 1910 various struggles emerged between different educational projects. These culminated in the establishment of a habitus, a curriculum (explicit and hidden), and hegemonic rituals under the direction of political pedagogues whom we will call 'normalizers'. They espoused a view of education linked to a 'vision' of an agricultural exporting country that was culturally and politically limited, rather than to the vision of an industrialized progressive country dreamed by the 1837 generation (whose main representative was Domingo F. Sarmiento, a strong admirer of Horace Mann) and a good proportion of Argentina's delegates who attended the South American Pedagogical Congress in Buenos Aires at the end of 1882.

In 1910 – as expressed in the words of José María Ramos Mejía, president of the National Council of Education, in 1908 – it was a common belief in the corpus of Argentine society that:

> The power of the State to keep the people on the right road and at the same time to maintain its own unity and strength, resides, as I have said in the first place, in the school.

(Ramos Mejía 1910)

A few years earlier, in 1905, Law No. 4874, as proposed by Senator Manuel Láinez, had been decreed. That law amended Law No. 1420 (from 1884) which dealt with free and compulsory common education in terms of the national government's responsibilities for provincial primary education. The policies of cutting back and of strengthened federalism that came with Law 1420 were replaced by others through which central – and real – power took in hand the inability of the provinces to contribute to educational provision and at the same time brought within its compass the basis of a national education system. The decision to centralize came from a political-pedagogical conviction: the people must be kept on the right track. There were several grounds for this, according to someone as representative of oligarchic thought as Ramos Mejía. The most import- ant, however, was the 'deeply felt need' that 'impels us to open the doors of our country to anyone in the world who wants to inhabit Argentinian soil' but whose 'moral consequence has not delayed in making itself felt'.

For 'establishment' intellectuals, achieving national unity was a pressing need. This, they felt, was threatened by ideological and cultural plurality. It was argued that differences along these lines were the cause of the bad political and social behavior of new inhabitants in the central Argentine cities. The state was an indispensable means of carrying out actions tending to limit, keep on track, and subject immigrants to the rules of the game as established by the oligarchy. The latter had called for European migration to deal with the problem of under- population of the national territory. The source of oligarchic riches was not dependent, however, upon a workforce or technical advances, but rather upon the easy rents coming from extensive exploitation of the land. Thus Argentina received its immigrants in a very different way from the United States. In Argentina, those getting off the ships found themselves facing a closed economic system, where almost all of land ownership was in very large *latifundios* (landholdings) and where industrial development was limited. Immigration was accepted by the Argentine ruling classes as an unfortunate necessity, as an unpleasant and dangerous remedy for 'natural ills' – namely, large expanses of land that were not exploited but which its owners, paradoxically, were unwilling to divide up, as well as underpopulation and the mestizo characteristics of the population. The oligarchy saw integrating immigrants as a political-pedagogic matter. For this reason they created laws to repress the political and union activity of migrants and charged public schooling with reaching every corner of the nation to impose the culture of the oligarchic state.

At the same time, however, from the end of the nineteenth century, the dominant trend among immigrants was toward integration. Almost all the Spanish, most Italians, and great portions of other immigrant groups [though possibly not the English], preferred to send their children to public (state) schools, even if this risked losing their language, customs and traditions. Immigrants shared with the Argentine oligarchy the belief in a myth: that national unity was possible only through socio-cultural homogeneity. Argentine society as a whole was unable to conceive of national unity as a product of the articulation of differences, preferring to be accomplices to educational strategies that tended toward concealment, censure or elimination of these differences.

The complementarity between government and civil society was very important in implanting public education; enough to meet the tasks of basic primary education necessary in a country to which tens of thousands of illiterate people were migrating – many of them not Spanish speakers. The compulsory require- ment of education had to be assured in many ways. Instruction was provided on the ships which brought the European migrants. In port and in the immigrants' hotels, signs were posted stating the current rules and obligations concerning public education, along with the penalties for not observing them.

Within civil society various other means of educating evolved which complemented public schooling. First there were popular education societies and popular libraries belonging to groups of Italians, Spanish, Germans and others, as well as attached to guilds, neighborhoods, progressive political groups, and so on. Their role was one of augmenting public education, with the exception of those under an anarchist banner, which, at least on account of their philosophy, were antagonistic to the state. Popular education societies covered the gamut of educational demands which the state system failed to meet or, rather, that the bureaucracy with its 'normalizing' mentality did not identify as shortcomings: for example, women's education, training of workers, and the education of truants or dropouts and illiterate individuals. When associated with political groups, typically the socialist party or anarchist groups, popular education societies provided ideological-political knowledge. In other cases they linked with schools, supporting their teaching activities and carrying out complementary tasks inside and outside the schools. The raison d'être of the popular education societies was essentially to integrate with the public schools, functioning as support groups. They never comprised a parallel education system.

No Argentine government, whether conservative, popular nationalist, or development-oriented, doubted its obligation to ensure the fulfilment of compulsory schooling until the advent of neo-conservatism from the mid-1970s. From the beginning of the century, publicity and social pressure were used to coerce parents to send their children to school. A structure of school agents motivated parents who were either neglectful or ignorant of their obligation to send their children to school. They assumed the model of North American 'truant officers', Scottish 'compulsory officers', and English 'attendance officers' (whose reports were observed by Marx in *Capital* in reference to the exploitation of child labor). Observation of the law regarding child and female labor was policed through inspection of all workshops and factories by the Bureau of Compulsory Schooling and Penalties (*Oficina de Obligación Escolar y Multas*). Popular education societies also played an important role in motivating parents to send their children to public school, *which was not only a medium for the political and cultural subjugation of immigrants, but also a site of relationship between state and civil society.*

The demands of the newly emerging working and middle classes, outgrowths partly of external and partly of internal migration, as well as antagonism between the port of Buenos Aires (the center of power) and the interior of the country, were determining factors in the decision to centralize educational power in the nation state. The political-educational concentration (of power) was consolidated during the first half of the century. Administration of the system fell on central organisms. Decision-making mechanisms were vertical. Local, regional, and provincial structures had their power stripped away. Educational organizations of civil society, especially the popular education societies, lost their real power. Rigid norms were established for the teaching profession. Private school activity for monetary gain was subordinated to the national government.

Law 1420 of 1884 had imposed a secular form of state education which was a bastion of the oligarchy and liberal sectors during the period of mass migration. However, in coming to power through elections, the popular-nationalist government of Hipólito Yrigoyen (1916–22) cast doubt on the infallibility of government and public schooling in being able to guarantee political-cultural imposition. Nearing the 1940s, Argentina's Catholic church, among the most conservative in Latin America, had gained ground and was imposing obligatory instruction in the Catholic religion in all public schools.

The significance of that development can be seen in relation to the process of ritualization. At the beginning of the century, secular and nationalist rituals were established within the school system. A large part of civil society participated spontaneously in these rituals. The nation, its symbols and heroes, were venerated in public and private spaces. The day-to-day running of the school was influenced by secular symbols and practices like the use of the flag, the coat of arms, the national anthem and other patriotic songs; regulating behavior (lining up, standing up in the presence of an adult, not speaking without permission, greeting an adult in chorus, standing to listen to the national anthem, following conventions in covering exercise books and setting out correctly the title page, margins and illustrations, and beginning each page correctly); the choice of pictures and other objects to decorate the classroom; and school functions. As you have observed in your book, *Schooling as a Ritual Performance* [McLaren 1986], school rituals are a substitution for religious rituals, where what is substituted or displaced is subordinated. That subordination has political significance.

Nationalism and secularism, however, were tactical rather than ideological positions within the political culture of the Argentine oligarchy. The oligarchy never seriously intended to subordinate the church, and never allowed its legal separation from the state; in fact, it is still part of the state. At the start of 1940 the Argentine government attained an ideal balance between the state, the nation, the church, and the interests of class education. Patriotic rituals were not actually substituted but, rather, had religious rituals added to them, so that symbols relating to public and secular school co-existed along with images from the calendar of saints' days.

In 1946 General Juan Perón took power through popular elections; the first non-fraudulent elections since 1916. Perón's government made an agreement with the church, and religious studies continued to be taught in all public schools. However, a third kind of ritual was introduced and superimposed on the two former types: namely, the ritual of popular nationalism.

PM: I am interested in the phenomenon of Peronism, especially after attending the seminar which you gave on the myth of Peronism in the summer of 1992. Can you expand on this?

AP: In a strategy typical of Latin American popular nationalism, the Peronist government assumed care of educational needs which traditionally had been catered for by popular education societies or had otherwise been left unmet. Examples include education of the working class, women, adults, and the general democratization of access to all forms of primary and intermediate schooling (a consequence of the improving economic and social status of workers). The positive response of the government toward meeting these needs was a 'promissory' act, since in a dependent, underdeveloped country with a weak civil society the government is the only organ with the capacity to provide for mass education.

At the same time, it is necessary to appreciate that the popular nationalist state tends to take control of society's entire educational processes, appropriating the pedagogical elements present in social, political and cultural discourse, public and private alike. In the case of Peronism, state discourse reached into all homes by various means such as party militants, public schools, and through direct com- munication between the popular president-leader and the working masses at meetings in the public squares – which had been turned into important political- pedagogical sites. Govern- ment plans took on many different guises in order to reach all Argentinians. One could say, to use a phrase from Argentine author Julio Cortázar, that following Peronism 'there are no more desert islands' in Argentina.

In order to turn this brief history toward explaining the difficulties Freire's ideas met in finding acceptance by Argentine educationists in the 1960s and 1970s, it must be stressed that the model of popular nationalist education was geared basically to building up *the nation* on the basis of a new subject; what Laclau (1978) calls *the people* as subject. This project involved the articulation of many discursive fragments coming from diverse popular sectors and media (e.g., women, children, the elderly, working-class youth, etc.) into a national discourse which would promote independent capitalist development. This was undertaken in greater depth than had been attempted by the earlier government of Hipólito Yrigoyen between 1916 and 1922. At the same time, however, fulfilling that end required a large measure of symbolic violence, that is, establishing a 'banking' model as the organiz- ational norm of political-educational processes. This coercive element gradually took over the whole of Peronist pedagogical discourse, bringing about a separation of the base from the political leaders/directors. But we must point out that this coercion was possible only through the consensus of the entire socio-economic stratum that benefited from the regime's policies, and which still adhered – as did the opposition also – to the theory that political-pedagogical uniformity is the only way for an independent nation to consolidate and for that same group to be elevated as a 'power bloc'.

After Peronism was ousted by the military coup of 1955, liberal Catholicism began a campaign against state education and in favor of subsidies to private schools. The state began to put schemes in place intended to free it from educational forms designed for the popular sectors and to limit official response to educational needs – with the exception of primary education. Civil society did not have popular institutions capable of generating new democratic alternatives. The experiences under Peronism rekindled in the dominant bloc a mistrust of the state and a preference for their own education system, without, however, removing their demands that this same state should subsidize the greater part of private education. This demand for subsidies to private schooling had a dual function: it strengthened the elite education system and weakened the public education system.

The equation pushed by the dominant bloc between 1955 and the mid-1980s was as follows:

- Public primary education was to be generalized from the public school system, but with a Catholic orientation, and met from the smallest possible investment.
- From the intermediate level up there should be a strong selection mechanism and the public should be encouraged into the private system.
- A private school system comprising both secular and religious institutions would exist, subsidized by the state, and highly profitable for investors.

As is evident from all this, during the late 1960s and early 1970s, the time that Freire's work was becoming known, Argentina was not ripe for tackling the matters Freire was addressing. The literacy rate was equal to that of developed countries; almost the entire population had been to school long enough to have absorbed the influence of school patriotism; the newspapers, radio and national cinema reached to the furthest corners of the country. But above all, a comprehensive process of articulation had taken place in the great national political-cultural discourses; an articulation of the differences that simultaneously divided and ordered society.

Here, then, there is a difference by comparison with the situation in Brazil. In Brazil, despite the wide reach of public schooling, trabalhismo ['workerism'] – a movement led by Getulio Vargas – did not comprise all-embracing social discourses. Rather, it promoted modernization of Brazil without being able to fracture or rearticulate the many discourses peculiar to the diverse groups that are still active within the country: such as ethnic, religious, cultural, ritualistic, social, and regional groupings. In Argentina, on the other hand, the modernization brought about by Peronism depended on a process of subordinating, adjusting, and fitting together all political-cultural differences. Public education has played a leading role in this process since the turn of the century.

A hypothesis could be proposed here that Freire's ideas on literacy (which in fact comprise a political-cultural strategy) would be especially applicable in a society where modern pedagogical discourse has not developed sufficiently to be able to incorporate the educational-cultural 'production' of all sectors within a single hegemony. This hypothesis is supported by recent events in Argentina. Precisely when the activities of the last military dictatorship (1976–83), and of Saúl Menem's neo-conservative government, managed to fracture the school system, important educational experiments among the popular sectors based strongly on Freire's methodology began to surface. At the moment Argentina is closer to Brazilian society than to English, Italian, or French society, which, for a century, were the mirrors reflecting it.

PM: How has Freire's work woven itself into your various projects over the years?

AP: I met Paulo Freire in Buenos Aires in 1974. At that time (1973–76) Peronism was in power for the third time, having won the elections after eighteen years of exile. But by now it was highly fragmented internally and the discourse, which in earlier times had been able to articulate needs and demands from very diverse social levels, was now split into tendencies which could even be mutually antagonistic. The university was governed by the more radical Peronist groups, the so-called Peronist left, which had been infiltrated by liberation pedagogy. I was Dean of the Arts Faculty of the University of Buenos Aires. The Ministry of Education had invited Freire to give a seminar to a group of Ministry and university leaders. From the Arts Faculty we had asked him to supervise reforms we were carrying out within the Department and the Institute of Research in Educational Science which belonged to the Faculty. Freire was very interested in our work which, as one of its key pivots, called for a change in the power relations between educators and educatees, and for linking teaching and research with a national popular-democratic project.

Freire insisted, however, that it was necessary to take into account the political and cultural conditions in which these reforms were taking place. At the end of his visit a colleague and I talked with him through an entire night. I recall Freire being very concerned about the situation in Argentina, especially about the experiments in participation he had seen in the area of adult education within the Ministry of Education and at the university. He was impressed by the enormous student/teacher mobilization which accompanied and propelled the university reforms. We were very enthusiastic, as everyone is who finds themselves in the midst of those rare moments of political-cultural creativity. Like those who are privileged to participate in the fleeting materializations of a utopia, we did not understand that the time span for innovative production is always very short, and we thought we had conquered the universe – just like Paulo himself in 1963 during the popular national government of João Goulart, when he established his first dialogues with the *campesinos* [peasants] of Río Grande do Norte. He had hundreds of *campesinos* learning to read and write, propelled by the dialogic relationship and the advance of a progressive wave in Brazil. However, by the time he visited Argentina, Paulo Freire had been in prison and was living in exile. He had suffered the pain of running up against the limits, of realizing that deep changes are only produced convulsively in a society, asynchronically. He was aware that there would never be a single 'great day of resurrection or liberation' in Latin American societies, and that there was still much work to be done. He also knew that between the fancy of intellectuals and the needs of the people there are very serious rifts and irretrievable differences. It was probably for these reasons that he talked to us all that night, sharing his perception of the imminent end to our experiments. These are deep reforms, he said to us, and this degree of depth cannot be tolerated by the conservative social sectors: the bureaucrats, the people within and outside the government who are opposed to the transformation of this society.

I recall arguing with him until dawn, maintaining that we could still go ahead. I also recall the memo I sent him two months later from my own exile in Mexico. It said: 'Paulo, you were right.' The executive power had intervened in the national universities and these were occupied by the army. The inspector of the Faculty of Arts, Father Sánchez Abelenda, a very conservative Catholic priest, went through all the classrooms in several faculties of the University of Buenos Aires carrying an olive branch in his hand and exorcizing 'the evil spirits of Freud, Marx and Piaget'. Many of the university leaders – and many political and trade union leaders – suffered fascist attempts on our lives; these were the first steps in preparing for the installation of the military dictatorship in March 1976.

I saw Freire again on a few occasions and continued to learn much from him: one always learns when talking to Paulo. I was also concerned during those years about the harassment he endured from the left in Latin America and particularly the left in Brazil. They were trying to imprison him inside his conceptual parameters and that was very hard. They discounted Freire's contributions because the categories he used did not belong to the Marxist world. A centerpiece of this dispute was his use of the category '*pueblo*' [people], the complexity of which could not be grasped by the traditional left.

PM: The traditional left here has also been inhospitable to those of us who have tried to bring new categories and frameworks of analysis into the political project of educational and social transformation.

AP: I think that reductionism has been one of the most salient mechanisms of discourse building among the traditional left. They confined historical-social processes to categories given in a matrix that actually followed a positivist logic, although it was couched in Marxist terminology. The category 'social class' was the only one accepted as a true theoretical mode for classifying the population, as the only valid dimension of social differentiation.

The category '*pueblo*' is very important in Freire's conceptual universe, precisely because it allows complex social, cultural and political subjects to be included, subjects that do not always coincide in Latin America. This complexity is incompatible with the simplicity demanded by 'social class' as a category, which implies the existence of some socio-economically homogenous sector of the population that exists in opposition to another. Such homogeneity implies that only elements falling within a narrow spectrum will be admitted under a particular class grouping, but at the same time it hints at *continuity* between ideology, politics and socio-economic organization within society. That is, consciousness is a reflection of structure.

So far as Freire's discourse in the 1960s and, especially, the 1970s is concerned, there were important conceptual differences from Marxism. The basic category for socio-pedagogic analysis, *'pueblo'*, is wider in Freire's thought than 'social class'. It does not exclude class, but allows for identifying subjects that are the outcome of multiple articulations between discontinuous elements. The main characteristic of *'pueblo'* is that it is a theoretical semi-structured space which allows *specific* articulation between subjects to be recognized. In Freire's work *'pueblo'* is used without giving it a conceptual definition. One could say it is used intuitively and is derived from the personalism of the French philosopher Emanuel Mournier, from Jacques Maritain, from Gabriel Marcel and the Brazilian Tristão de Ataíde. These had influenced Freire's work. The most important feature is that *'pueblo'* acts as an operator allowing words that are 'contained' in the dispossessed to burst into pedagogical discourse.

The *generative word* is an expression of a *subject* in literacy work, not of an object. Therefore Freire conceives the very process of literacy as a process of building up discourse, a process of articulating differences rather than an imposition by the colonizer of a closed discourse upon another discourse. The education process, for Freire, becomes legitimate through being a space where new subjects can emerge.

Conversely, indoctrination not only makes people adapt to the reality in which they live, but also hides that reality from them and makes them incapable of emerging from it and being able to change it. *'Pueblo'* is a conceptual element within pedagogical discourse that permits the object to emerge as a subject, within a process where Freire conceives the educator as more than a mere reproducer of dominant ideology and gives her or him the flexibility to engage in cultural interchange with the educatee.

A decade after the appearance of Freire's first books another Latin American author, the Argentine historian and political scientist Ernesto Laclau, undertook important research into popular nationalisms. In his work Laclau recovers the richness of the category *'pueblo'* and explains popular nationalisms as discursive formations whose central axis is the special articulation between the categories *'pueblo'* and *'nation'*, according to the specific features of the historical-social condition in each case that arises.

Returning to the question, it was particularly important for me to read Freire again, in the late 1980s when I was in Mexico, in the light of Laclau's deconstruction of the categories of people and nation; noting that Laclau had met them not via Freire's pedagogy but rather as a result of the impact that popular national discourses had made on his Marxist roots. Because of my dual position as a Latin American pedagogue/educationist and an intellectual whose political life story was similar to Laclau's, both authors were of great importance to me.

PM: What do you see as the general strengths and weaknesses of Freire's work, particularly as it relates to your own?

AP: I think Freire offers us elements that enable us to break with modern pedagogical discourse. He constructs a new set of pedagogical images. I have noted earlier that during the 1960s Freire's developments were still linked to the political-social conditions within which they were produced. Freire himself said in *Education: The Practice of Freedom* that Brazil was living through the transition from one epoch to another, and that it was not possible for the educator to detach herself or himself from the new 'cultural climate' that was emerging (1972: 47). But when Freire, from his exile, together with educators he had influenced, tried to bring liberation pedagogy into general use, they met serious problems of an epistemological and political nature. This is the stage we are at. I believe Freire's discourse has enormous potential because it probed the limits of modern pedagogy. Now we have to deepen and develop it conceptually, moving it from the imaginary plane to a symbolic plane. Theorizing can also be helpful in using Freire's pedagogy to frame political-pedagogical strategies. Failure to pursue its theoretical development and its engagement and articulation with other theories could be dangerous for Freire's theory. It would result in his theory being appropriated and his experience being transferred without effecting the required theoretical-methodological changes. Conversely, greater theoretical development will clarify the unassailable gap that presently exists between theory and practice, revealing that it is precisely in acknowledging existing divisions between these two 'registers' that a major advance in constructing new pedagogies is to be found.

'Practicism' has been one of the key characteristics among many groups of educators who claim to be following Freire. The reckless, unreflective use of his ideas as if they were *tactics* rather than ideas capable of becoming constructs has had unfortunate political and pedagogical consequences for Latin American education. I am coming increasingly to believe that in order to implement practice successfully there is nothing better than a sound theory.

PM: 'Practicism' exists here, too, especially among those who deride theory and pride themselves on being 'activists', and it has had a debilitating effect not only on the potential for Freire's work to effect change in the North American context but on the ability of students and teachers to confront the harsh realities associated with postmodern culture and new global forms of capitalism.

AP: Let me briefly discuss the deep fracture I believe Freire has forced in the history of modern Latin American pedagogy. Various axes stand out as supporting the theoretical structure of Latin American pedagogical thought, and as elements which Freire has called into question. I will look at three of these here.

1 The *educator* (it could be the teacher, the party, the state, adults, humanity, the Anglo-Saxon culture, mass culture as directed by TV . . .) and the *educatee* (the student at school, the son or daughter, the activist, the citizen, etc.) are positions that essentially relate to the subjects filling them. In his third thesis on Feuerbach, Marx points out that the educator

too must be educated. In this Marx undertakes a critique that deals not with the subordinate position of the educated with respect to the educator, but rather with the class identity of the educator and the contents of her or his culture. Freire advances further in stating that the positions of 'educator' and 'educatee' are not givens. They are in fact positions that are constituted historically and politically and are interchangeable. The educator can be the educatee and vice versa. These are the conditions that make dialogical education possible, and also that defeat reproduction theory.

In the light of Freire's argument, reproductivist critique (reproduction theory) is shown clearly to be a circular way of thinking, an internalized expression of modern pedagogy itself (Puiggrós 1984, 1991a, 1991b). It does not recognize education as a site of struggle, or modern pedagogy as the outcome of articulation between the different forces that feature in the battle for hegemony. Reproduction theory posits education as a mechanism for reproducing dominant ideology, and in so doing it freezes the educator and educatee within theory in positions that necessarily correspond to dominant class/dominated class. When Freire posits the interchangeability of the educator/educatee positions, he unfreezes the theorizing of this situation, allowing each term in this educational relationship to be recognized as a subject formed by multiple distinguishing features. These subjects grow inside pedagogical discourse; it is within the process of discursive production that the educator/educatee relationship is created. Consequently that relation has specificity; it is educational.

The specific character of the pedagogical relationship is rejected when Freire analyzes the dominator/dominated relationship in the *cultural* register rather than as a mere reflex of dominance relations that exist in other planes of social life. The political aspects become internal elements of the pedagogical relation, rather than fixed and eternal as posed by functionalism. It is a quasi-Foucauldian perspective where a 'microphysics' of educational power can be glimpsed.

2   Within modern pedagogy the precondition for the existence of the *educator* is precisely the existence of an *empty subject*, the educatee, who lacks knowledge, has no form, but needs to be encultured, formed, 'subjected'. That is, the basis of the pedagogical relationship is the acceptance of a lack of knowledge in the one and possession of knowledge in the other. Once this is established as legitimate, the pedagogical relationship is shaped by a relational bond of political domination. This emerges as a contradiction that could be permanent if conceived outside the context of struggle for hegemony: each generation would receive the same cultural legacy from the previous one; nothing would change; there would be no history; education, defined as a process of 'subjection' of the individual to the culture, would be entirely possible.

However, social conflict cuts across the pedagogical relationship thus conceived and history shows, fortunately, that colonizing moves by educators which take learners to be a tabula rasa are seldom successful. This view can be supported by using arguments from reproduction theory, but using them in a different sense, thus:

- one of the myths of modern pedagogy, but not a necessary condition for the education relation, is that the educator must possess the whole culture and the educatee be devoid of discourse, so that the roles can be played and the education scenario realized;
- but if, as Bourdieu suggests, the educator transmits an arbitrary cultural element, only a segment and not the whole culture,
- and the educatees are exposed to countless educators, as happens in modern society, then cultural arbitrariness ensures the impossibility of totalizing each of the discourses: producing facsimiles or clones is a topic confined to science fiction.

3   Freire paints a picture where literacy teaching is possible only so far as the educator recognizes that the educatee has a different culture and is not a cultural void, and opens herself or himself to the discourse of the educatee. That means education is possible only as a consequence of the 'incompleteness' of the educator's discourse, and recognition that other discourses reside among those being educated. Let us consider two opposing positions within modern pedagogy, Durkheim's functionalism and the Marxist view of reproductive education.

According to the first, it is possible for each generation to transmit its culture, which is considered culture par excellence, to the following generation. It is seen as necessary that systematic transmission is ensured so that the social order is not altered. According to the second, it is recognized that the dominant class transmits its ideology to the dominated class through education, even though Marxist critique may reject that process as being the mechanism that maintains the social order. Both are typical modern positions. Both conceive education as no more than a function to 'homogenize' or 'uniformize' society in the mold of the 'citizen', and entail a theoretical-political search for synchrony and continuity among educational, political, socio-economic and ideological elements.

Extending Freire's position beyond what is contained in his texts, we could reach the view that dialogical education, conversely, is opposed to banking homo- geneity and opens the way to envisaging the possibility of a pedagogical discourse emerging from articulation of *differences*. Now, it must be recognized that when we talk of 'differences' we still presuppose inequality, which is an inherent condition of pedagogical relationships. However, contrary to modern pedagogy we consider that the character of this proposed pedagogical discourse, based as it is on dialectical antagonism, is the only way open to producing the *new*.

This last statement immediately poses the problem of relationship with the teacher *Paulo Freire*. I believe Freire deserves that we, his readers, adherents and other people he has influenced, should incorporate him critically into our work, rather than merely imitate him, try to 'apply' his ideas, or make him into a myth. He had the necessary courage and intelligence to lay the foundation of what you, Peter, have called 'a new democratic pedagogical imaginary'.

For those pedagogues who are willing to further the development of Freirean pedagogy, a program of hard work is currently unfolding to meet major conceptual challenges. It is essential to develop further and more deeply the 'deconstruction' of modern pedagogy, and to identify the routes taken by those who have brought it to the very edge of the abyss: people like John Dewey, Francisco Ferrer y Guardia, A.S. Neill, or the Russian revolutionary pedagogues in the years before the Soviet revolution. Within the Latin American tradition it involves following tracks that start way back at the beginning of the nineteenth century in pursuit of popular education; a trek undertaken by Bolívar's master, the Venezuelan Simón Rodríguez, arriving finally at Paulo Freire's liberation pedagogy. This way we advance toward building what Henry Giroux calls 'border pedagogy'. We will contribute to a pedagogy that is capable of opening up as a space where political- cultural associations and differences can be produced. This can be achieved by allowing all kinds of 'antagonisms' (generational, linguistic, domestic, traditional, etc.) to be expressed, and by offering an opportunity for them to be resolved democratically.

NOTE

1 The interview took place in Cincinnati, Mexico City and Buenos Aires, and was completed through written correspondence.

REFERENCES

Amin, S. (1989) *Disconnection*, Buenos Aires: Ediciones del Pensamiento Nacional.
Bourdieu, P. (1979) *Distinction: A Social Critique of the Judgment of Taste*, Paris: Minuit.
Bourdieu, P. and Passeron, J.-C. (1977) *Reproduction: In Education, Society and Culture*, Barcelona: LAIA.
Freire, P. (1972) *Education: The Practice of Freedom*, Mexico City: Siglo XXI.
Laclau, E. (1978) *Politics and Ideology in Marxist Theory*, Mexico City: Siglo XXI.
McLaren, P. (1986) *Schooling as a Ritual Performance*, London: Routledge and Kegan Paul. Revised edition in press.
Puiggrós, A. (1984) *Popular Education in Latin America*, Mexico City: Nueva Imagen.
—— (1986) *Democracia y Autoritarismo en la Pedagogía Argentina y Latinoamericana*, Buenos Aires: Editorial Galerna.
—— (1991a) *Imagination and Crisis in Latin American Education*, Mexico City: Alianza Ed.
Ramos Mejía, J.M. (1910) *La Educación Común en la República Argentina*, Buenos Aires: Kraft.
—— (1991b) *Sujetos, Disciplinia y Curriculum en los Orígenes del Sistema Educativo Argentino*, Buenos Aires: Galerna.

Chapter 10

Education and hermeneutics
A Freirean interpretation

Michael Peters and Colin Lankshear

INTRODUCTION

From its traditional home in biblical exegesis, classical philology and juris-
prudence, hermeneutics underwent something of a renaissance under the
influence of Schleiermacher and Dilthey, who raised it to the status of a general
theory of interpretation and methodological problematic for the *Geisteswissenschaften*.

Recently there has been a revival of interest in hermeneutics on the continent
and, in the hands of Heidegger and Gadamer in particular, it has undergone a
change of direction and status at least as important as its nineteenth-century transformation.

First, it has departed from its 'objectivist' pursuit of a secure epistemological
and methodological basis for the scientific investigation of meaning to develop in
an ontological direction. Second, in its subsequent ontological development,
hermeneutics has surpassed the realm of theory to attain the status of a philosophy.

These two interrelated changes amount to a modern transformation and
reorientation of hermeneutics which can briefly be summed up in what Ricoeur
(1981) has called the move from the 'epistemology of interpretation' to the
'ontology of understanding'. Hermeneutic philosophy does not aim at the
acquisition of knowledge through the employment of a hermeneutic method, but
rather begins more radically with the phenomenological explication and
description of human *Dasein* in its temporality and historicality.

The revival and transformation of hermeneutics by Heidegger and Gadamer has
not gone entirely unnoticed in the English-speaking world. As early as 1971,
Charles Taylor wrote his seminal paper, 'Interpretation and the sciences of man',
which, drawing on the work and inspiration of Gadamer, Ricoeur and Habermas,
sought to make clear three general conditions involved in the interpretation of a
text or text analogue. 'The object of a science of interpretation', argues Taylor,
'must . . . have a sense distinguishable from its expression, which is for or by a
subject' (1971: 27). He emphasizes the fact that the hermeneutical sciences break
with, and challenge, certain commonly held notions about our scientific tradition:

> We cannot measure such sciences against the requirements of a science of

verification: we cannot judge them by their predictive capacity. We have to
accept that they are founded on intuitions which all do not share, and what is
worse, that these intuitions are closely bound up with our fundamental options.
These sciences cannot be *wertfrei*; they are moral sciences in a more radical
sense than the eighteenth century understood. Finally, their successful
prosecution requires a high degree of self-knowledge, a freedom from illusion,
in the sense of error which is rooted and expressed in one's way of life; for our
capacity to understand is rooted in our own self-definitions, hence in what we
are.

(ibid.: 71)

Since that time the English-speaking world has paid greater attention to
hermeneutics and its recent developments.

Texts in sociology – for example, Outhwaite (1975), Bauman (1979) – have
appeared characterizing the approach to understanding in terms of its founding
fathers, and philosophers and social theorists have begun to take seriously the
theoretical contribution of hermeneutics to understanding and resolving certain
epistemological difficulties inherent in the empiricist problematic. Rorty (1980),
for instance, in *Philosophy and the Mirror of Nature*, follows Gadamer in opting
for a hermeneutical notion of knowledge based on the model of conversation. For
Rorty, hermeneutics, as 'abnormal' discourse about as-yet incommensurable
discourses, escapes the captivating mirror-imagery surrounding post-Kantian, epi-
stemologically centered philosophy, and indicates the future cultural directions
philosophy might follow given the demise of traditional foundationalism.

In the realm of social theory and in the wake of a breakdown of what he calls
the 'orthodox consensus' in sociology, Giddens (1982) has argued for a
reformulated social theory that is 'hermeneutically informed'. Further, Kuhn
(1977) and Hesse (1980) have noted the ways in which developments in the theory
of the text are crucially relevant to issues at the forefront of post-empiricist
philosophy of science. Introducing a series of readings in interpretive social
science, Rabinow and Sullivan interpret the present crisis in the social sciences as
stemming from the widespread positivistic assumption that in order to reach
paradigmatic status social sciences must 'follow the path of the modern
investigation of nature' (1979: 4).

In the field of education, by contrast, there has been little or no explicit
recognition of either the importance of hermeneutics – its potential for
transforming the way educational problems are identified and approached – or its
intellectual heritage and philosophical underpinnings (see, however, Vandenberg,
1979).

It is not our purpose here to attempt to redress this imbalance, or to document
ways in which contemporary hermeneutics might profitably be applied to
educational issues. Rather, we have a much more modest aim: to bring out and
elucidate the substantial hermeneutical ingredient in the work of Paulo Freire.
Although Freire himself does not explicitly recognize or attempt to chart the

importance of hermeneutics to education, the way he defines his problems and the manner in which he addresses them are hermeneutical through and through. This is no mere accident. Freire drew heavily on the phenomenological-existentialist tradition in developing a praxis for 'teaching' illiterate adults in Third World settings. His pedagogy is designed to attack the dual related problems of illiteracy and oppression within a single process of adults learning to read and write.

Something of his hermeneutics is revealed in the dialectical relationship he proposes between 'reading the text', on the one hand, and 'reading reality' on the other. Freire advances a *dialogical* philosophy which professes to treat the word – both metaphorically and literally – as primitive.

In the next section of this chapter we will locate the space of Freire's philosophy in relation to *being* and *time*. The third section will investigate these notions as they have surfaced in contemporary hermeneutics. Our aim is not to trace the development of Heidegger's or Gadamer's analysis but, rather, to provide just enough exposition to establish the role and importance of the concepts of 'being' and 'time' in hermeneutical thought. For these constructs are central to the philosophies of both Freire and Gadamer, yet underpin very different hermeneutics in the two cases. The final section discusses major differences between Gadamer and Freire, noting key points at which Freire moves beyond Gadamer to propose a *critical* hermeneutics, linking interpretation and action in a philosophy aimed at revolutionary social change.

'BEING' AND 'TIME' IN FREIRE'S PHILOSOPHY

A diverse range of traditions has contributed to Freire's intellectual development and his evolving educational theory. In this chapter we are especially concerned with Freire's development of the pedagogy of the oppressed and specific intellectual influences bearing upon it. Two are of particular note here. First, Freire's thinking reveals his debt to a humanist existentialism derived from Buber, Jaspers, Sartre and Marcel. Second, the shift in his educational theory from an early liberalism to revolutionary socialism was strongly influenced by currents in modern theology and the (related) existence, in Brazil and other Latin American countries, of radical Catholic movements for social change. Of crucial importance were the theological conceptions of 'humanization' and 'socialization' developed by Teilhard de Chardin and Henrique de Lima Pe Vaz (Mackie 1980: 97–100). Given the important influence of these two traditions on Freire's work, it is hardly surprising that the notions of being and time should figure prominently in his educational theory.

Being, that is, *human* being, is not a metaphysical abstraction for Freire. Rather, he conceives it in material and historical terms. The being that humans have is a concrete, physical and objective presence; an existence or *being in the world* in an everyday sense of that phrase. To this extent humans have a being in the world, *are* in the world, in just the same sense that animals, rocks, and trees are in the world. This, however, is by no means the full extent and nature of human being. For humans are crucially different from rocks, trees, and even animals. This difference is conveyed in Freire's idea that whereas animals are merely *in* the world, humans are both *in* the world and *with* the world (Freire 1976: 3). Humans enter into relationships with the world in a way that animals (and, far more, rocks and trees) cannot, and this capacity is the very essence of being human – or, to put it the other way, of human being. Animals, says Freire, are creatures of 'mere contacts' (ibid.) in that they *come into contact* with (other things in) the world, but do not *relate to* the world. Humans, by contrast, are 'beings of relations in a world of relations' (ibid.: 109). Beings of relations, but 'What sorts of relations?', we might ask.

We can approach this question by identifying what it is that humans enter into relationship *with*. Freire suggests there are two broad 'objects' of human relations: the world, and other human beings. 'To be human', he says, 'is to engage in relationships with others and with the world' (ibid.: 3). This may at present obscure finer points such as the fact that individual human beings can enter into relationships with themselves – e.g., make their own ideas, beliefs and circumstances the object of their own inquiry or evaluation – and conflate what is at least a triadic social-cultural-natural reality into a dichotomized 'others' and 'the world'. Nevertheless, it is sufficient for suggesting the *kinds* of relations of which humans are capable: such as investigation, action, communication, evaluation, transformation, criticism, adoration, denigration, destruction, exchange, etc. Human beings consciously make the world and other people objects of their investigation, contemplation, action and comment. In doing so they communicate with others, transform the natural world, build relationships of various kinds with their fellows, and create, modify, and (sometimes) destroy institutions. Humans, says Freire, relate to their world in a critical way (ibid.).

We achieve these interactions, this critical orientation – in short, our status as beings of relations – through consciousness of the world and of others in the world. In true phenomenological style, Freire isolates *intentionality* or being *conscious of* as the hallmark of consciousness (cf. Husserl 1981). In an act of reflection – thought – persons become conscious of themselves and their reality. In both cases intentionality serves to distinguish us from other animals.

Whereas animals merely apprehend the objective data of their reality by *reflex* humans apprehend – and may thus *comprehend* – these objective data through reflection (see Freire 1976: 3). Humans alone consciously separate themselves from their reality and, furthermore, from their activity. They alone are capable of treating their actions as the object of their reflection (Freire 1972: 70). Moreover, and importantly, man (sic),[1] unlike animals, can 'treat . . . his very self as the object of his reflection' (ibid.) and, as we will see, as the object of his own action.

Freire talks of consciousness as intentionality *toward* the world, for both reflection and self-reflection are the basis of *knowing* – of coming to know ourselves and our reality objectively. Such reflection must, however, be always considered in relation to our *actions* for it to constitute authentic knowledge. In other words, according to Freire authentic knowledge is a praxis. To know implies to act in conjunction with reflection. This reference to action suggests an important dimension of human consciousness which we will mention briefly here and later develop as a theme in its own right. This is the dimension of time, which Freire identifies as one of the fundamental human discoveries.

Aware of time, of the fact that there is a before, during and after, humans achieve agency. They are capable of *action*, since they not only make things happen in the world but know that they do so. They can see themselves as causes of effects and events in the world, in the immediate present and over time. It is this capacity for action *and* reflection, and particularly for initiating a dialectic of action and reflection, that makes humans beings of praxis; that makes us capable of authentic knowledge and critical consciousness. In addition, awareness of our temporality makes of us *historical* and *cultural* agents. We can recognize that much of our reality, including much of what we (presently) *are* ourselves, is the consequence of human action in the past. Moreover, we can conceive of a changed world, a changed human reality, in the future; changed as a consequence of our own actions in the present. In an early articulation of this idea Freire says:

> As men emerge from time, discover temporality, and free themselves from 'today', their relations with the world become impregnated with consequence. The normal role of humans in and with the world is not a passive one. Because they are not limited to the natural (biological) sphere but participate in the creative dimension as well, men can intervene in reality in order to change it. Inheriting acquired experience, creating and recreating, integrating themselves into their context, responding to its challenges, objectifying themselves, men enter into the domain which is theirs exclusively – that of history and of culture.
>
> (1976: 4)

These ideas lead directly to Freire's notion of being in its full sense: namely, as a process of *becoming*. Authentic being is consciously directed at becoming more fully human. In other words, in order genuinely *to be* we must continually engage in becoming; in becoming more and more fully human. In Freire's view, being is not a finite, completed state. Rather, it is a never-completed, dynamic *process*. Human being, conceived as human becoming, is precisely the ongoing process of becoming (more fully) human. This sounds profound; even mystical. What does it mean?

Freire claims that it is the historical and ontological vocation of humans to become more fully human (1972: 31, 41). In proclaiming it an *ontological* vocation he is asserting the metaphysical view that it is of the human 'essence' – written, as it were, on our very nature – to strive after ever fuller humanness. In proclaiming it *historical*, he identifies 'becoming' as an active process of creative participation in and with the world. As we have seen, Freire conceives the domain of history as that of humans' integration with their context – the world – in acts of creation and recreation informed by experience inherited from other people as well as acquired in interaction with the world. Humans enter the historical (and cultural) domain by intervening in reality in order to change it. The crucial idea is that humans create their humanity – they become human – in the very process of intervening in reality in order to change it; in making and remaking the world. In this process of making and remaking the world, humans make and remake *themselves*, their human *being*. Just as the world is never complete – and, indeed, *because* the world is never complete but always there to be remade – so human being is never complete(d). The world, in the acts of human creation and re-creation, is constantly in the process of becoming. To participate more and more in making and remaking the world is to become more and more fully human – although not quite. There are certain normative conditions which must be met for human engagement with the world to be truly humanizing.

To introduce two ideas that go to the very heart of this chapter, humanizing interaction with the world involves 'speaking true words' in a process of 'dialogue' (Freire 1972: Ch. 3, 60–5ff). Here Freire employs an elaborate and rich conception of language which represents a nexus between Marxist, existentialist, and hermeneutical thought; a conception of language that is quite foreign to the Anglo-American philosophical tradition. While his notion of dialogue subsumes our everyday idea of two or more people communicating with each other in words, it goes far beyond that. According to Freire, *the word* (properly understood) has two components: action and reflection in dialectical relationship. To speak a true word involves both components. 'There is no true word that is not at the same time a praxis. Thus, to speak a true word is to transform the world' (ibid.: 60). That is, the word is work. If either reflection or action is absent when humans 'speak' to the world, they fail to transform reality in the act of 'speech'. Word without action is mere verbalism; word without reflection is mere activism. Neither has *human* significance, according to Freire. Both are inauthentic words.

In speaking true words (and *only* in speaking true words) humans transform the world. And in so doing they 'nourish human existence', which 'cannot be silent' (ibid.). More than this, in speaking true words humans *become*. Just as for Marx, so too for Freire: humans create themselves in work, and work involves a dialectic of reflection and action. It is a praxis. In a key passage Freire says:

> To exist, humanly, is to *name* the world, to change it. Once named, the world in its turn reappears to the namers as a problem and requires of them a new *naming*. Humans are not built in silence, but in word, in work, in action–reflection.
>
> (ibid.: 61)

Each time humans remake the world it re-presents itself as in further need of remaking. Each human transforming action creates the need for reflection upon the change effected. This in turn calls for further action in light of this reflection, and so on. Consequently, humans are continually presented with opportunities to further make themselves, to become more fully human through their (trans-forming) work.

The process of human becoming is not, however, just a matter of an isolated individual speaking a true word. Neither can it be a privileged group of people naming the world at the expense of others who have to accept the world thus named. Rather, humans become in a process of *dialogue*. Just as ordinary language is a public and not a private phenomenon – there can be no such thing as a private language, in the technical sense of 'private language' – so speaking true words is necessarily a shared, public engagement. The very idea of a dialectic between action and reflection is meaningless unless a context of *communication among humans* is presupposed. For one thing, reflection implies standards, evaluation, critique. These imply a public context. Humans, that is, can speak true words only in a context of human communication.

Such a context, however, is not necessarily a context of *dialogue*. Communication can be established within a group where some are reduced to the status of silent observers, by-standers. Yet Freire maintains that humans become (only) in a process of dialogue. The point here is that becoming is the ontological vocation of human beings: of *all* human beings equally. To deny any human beings the right to name the world on equal terms with other humans is to dehumanize those people, to subvert their ontological vocation, to rule them out of the process of becoming. This is for them to be made by others, as objects, rather than for them as subjects to make themselves, and in making themselves to become, and thus to *be*, human. Consequently, human becoming must be a process in which all people have an equal right to their voice. It is this idea that Freire captures in his notion of dialogue. In its everyday sense 'dialogue' implies a genuine exchange of words or ideas, between two or more persons who enjoy an equal role in the conversation. Likewise, in speaking of dialogue as the process in which humans become, Freire is drawing attention to the importance of equal, active participation in naming the world: in making and remaking reality through transforming action–reflection. Dialogue, says Freire,

> is the encounter between men, mediated by the world, in order to name the world. Hence, dialogue cannot occur between those who want to name the world and those who do not want this naming – between those who deny other men the right to speak their word and those whose right to speak has been denied them.
>
> (ibid.: 61)

Furthermore,

> If it is in speaking their word that men transform the world by naming it, dialogue imposes itself as the way in which men achieve significance as men. Dialogue is thus an existential necessity.
>
> (ibid.)

Human becoming presupposes critical consciousness and liberation from constraints which prevent people from speaking their word. The process in which humans simultaneously attain critical consciousness and achieve liberation is precisely one of dialogue. The possibility of becoming more fully human depends upon us becoming conscious of our own incompleteness, of the unfinished nature of reality, of the various constraints to our recognizing this and, upon recognizing it, to entering the active process of making reality and our own human selves. This is to become *critically* conscious. Critical consciousness contrasts with naive consciousness. Bearers of naive consciousness regard the world as complete, static, 'given'. They see their own circumstances as unalterable, the quality of their lives as a 'given'. They regard themselves as completed beings – in the sense that they can only be what they already are. Their role is to be passive, accepting, resigned to existing circumstances. The process by which people who presently bear naive consciousness win through to critical consciousness comprises Freire's pedagogy: the pedagogy of the oppressed. This is a social process of dialogue between 'educator-educatees' and 'educatee-educators': a dialogue among equals. In the course of dialogue the efficacy of a more critical consciousness is actively tested against the world: by undertaking collective transforming action on the world informed by collective reflection upon an aspect of reality important to the educatees. In the very process of testing reflection against the world by means of a transforming act, the people perform and achieve an act of liberation. This act comprises speaking a true word, since it involves action based upon reflection. And the action will, in the ongoing dialogue, be subjected to further reflection. Consequently, it is a humanizing act: an act in which humans *become*.

We may summarize this exposition by saying that in order *to be*, in any genuine or authentic sense, we must *become*. This process of becoming – involving as it does the development of critical consciousness – cannot, however, take place in isolation. The process of becoming is essentially a socio-cultural process achieved only in dialogue. It is a communal or group becoming – *a cultural development*. This brings us some way toward understanding cultural action and cultural reflection as dialectical elements of cultural *knowledge* and of *becoming* culturally.

Let us now briefly consider the second concept, 'time', and its relation to 'being' and to development of critical consciousness. According to Freire, critical consciousness is distinguished from naive consciousness on several related dimensions. One of these is perception of time. The critical thinker perceives time very differently from the naive thinker and, in so doing, achieves an entirely different awareness of the bounds of human possibility. The bearer of naive consciousness 'sees "historical time as a weight, a stratification of the acquisitions and experiences of the past", from which the present should emerge normalized and "well-behaved"' (Freire 1972: 65). In naive thinking the present is merely the extension of the past, bearing the shape or imprint of the past and not differentiated from the past. Past and present together comprise a static, fixed 'block'. Naive thinkers are submerged in a limitless 'today', says Freire. Since the present is the extended shape of the past, the naive thinker sees life in terms of accommodating 'to this normalized "today"' (ibid.). Reality is 'there': fixed and given. The human task is to adjust to it, to fit within the limits it imposes. In naive consciousness there can be no conception of reality as dynamic, as something to be shaped and created, to be entered into. Just as present reality is the (undifferentiated) shaped and determined extension of the past, so the future will be the (undifferentiated) shaped and determined extension of the present. Submerged in time, the naive thinker is reduced to passive adjustment.

In critical thinking, by contrast, historical time is not perceived as a weight bearing down upon us and confirming us within a determined, given 'today'. Rather, time is perceived more as space between events and, as noted above, is clearly differentiated into past, present and future. Moreover, the critically conscious person knows that it is precisely human activity in the space between events that shapes reality. Reality is seen as process and transformation, not as a static entity (ibid.: 64). Humans are *in* time, but not *submerged* in time. They can enter into the gaps between events, thereby shaping the events that occur subsequently. They can enter into reality in the present and, acting on what they 'inherit' from the past, shape future reality. They are not lost in a limitless 'today'. Instead, they inhabit the space between 'yesterday' and 'tomorrow'; between what has just happened and what will happen next. The shape of 'tomorrow' will reflect what we do 'today'. Aware of their historicity, critically conscious humans are in a position to affirm their agency, their subjecthood.

Critical consciousness begins with the awareness of our own temporality and of the fact that 'reality is a process undergoing constant transformation' (ibid.: 48). Freire talks of people emerging from a naive consciousness, from the '"weight" of apparently limitless time', from 'a permanent "today"', to discover temporality and thereby free themselves from a powerful constraint to becoming more fully human. Unlike the bearer of naive consciousness, critically conscious people are aware of both their own temporality and that of reality. They are in a position to confront the 'limit situations' that overcome them, by performing 'limit acts' (ibid.: 71–2). Awareness of temporality marks a crucial difference between being objects of the historical process, known and acted upon, and becoming subjects of history who know and act to transform their reality. Unlike animals, humans have the possibility of becoming subjects of the historical process since they culturally create their time. We 'humanize reality' by adding to it something of our own making, 'by giving temporal meaning to geographic space, by creating culture' (Freire 1976: 5). The ultimate outcome of this process of cultural creation is *human being* itself.

According to Freire's philosophy, then, *human development* is based upon a certain quality of awareness: awareness of our temporality, our 'situatedness' in history, and of our reality as being capable of transformation through action in collaboration with others. As we have noted, this is precisely to be critically conscious. Progress from naive to critical consciousness involves conscientization. This is the process by which we learn to perceive social, political, and economic contradictions and become involved in the struggle to overcome them; to identify 'limit situations' for what they are and confront them with 'limit acts'. In this very process we enter history as subjects, humanizing ourselves, becoming more fully human. This, for Freire, is *authentic* education itself. Far from being a (mere) preparation for life, education as conscientization is an *induction into* life; into human *life* as humanized existence. We will return to the theory and practice of education as conscientization in the final section.

'BEING' AND 'TIME' IN CONTEMPORARY HERMENEUTICS

The ontological significance of the notions of 'being' and 'time' is really a contemporary feature of hermeneutics. Although it might be argued that such notions were at least implicit in both Schleiermacher's and Dilthey's treatment of hermeneutics – for example, in Dilthey's emphasis on 'life', 'lived experience', and the historicity of understanding (Dilthey 1976) – the move from the epistemology to the ontology of understanding and interpretation took place at the hands of Heidegger, who subsequently influenced Gadamer.

Ermarth (1981) characterizes the modern transformation of hermeneutics as a progressive movement involving three phases. The first phase, that of Schleiermacher and Dilthey, stresses the historical specificity of the object, or alien other, to be understood; the second, Heideggerian phase stresses the historicity of the concrete subject as *Dasein*; and the third phase, represented in Gadamer's work, goes beyond both to emphasize the historicity of the 'understanding event', which fuses the horizons of self and others.

It was Heidegger who broke with the romanticist emphasis in hermeneutics on method – on hermeneutics as the general method of the humanities – to suggest that our existence in the aporia of Being[2] is essentially hermeneutical. There is no doubt that Dilthey's insight into the structure of understanding, which led to an emphasis on the context of life, and which in part inspired the *Verstehen* approach in the social sciences, exerted a strong influence on the young Heidegger.

At first as a student of Catholic theology (compare Freire himself), and later of philosophy under Rickert, Heidegger was introduced to various notions of spirit and being, and to the works of Nietzsche, Kierkegaard, Dostoevsky, Hegel and Dilthey – works which stand centrally in the hermeneutical tradition (Heidegger 1981). 'The question of Being' was an early (viz., 1907) concern for Heidegger, as he himself notes (ibid.). Indeed, it predated his introduction to the formal study of philosophy at the University of Freiburg. Heidegger was to formulate and reformulate this question several times throughout his writings (see Sheehan 1981). His concern for Being was given shape and impetus in his theological studies and in his critique of Jaspers' *Existenzphilosophie*. Macquarrie actually goes so far as to say that Heidegger 'replaces god with Being' (1968: 51). It was not, however, until he became acquainted with Husserl's work, subsequently studied under Husserl, and reworked the approach to phenomenology that Heidegger gained philosophical access to the meaning of Being.[3] In Heidegger's own words:

> the expression 'phenomenology' is the name for the *method* of *scientific philosophy in general* . . . Philosophy is the science of Being. For the future we shall mean by 'philosophy' scientific philosophy and nothing else . . . If philosophy is the science of Being, then the first and last basic problem of philosophy must be: What does Being signify? Whence can something like Being in general be understood? How is understanding of Being at all possible?
>
> (1982: 3–15)

The thrust of Heidegger's work moves toward a more comprehensive hermeneutic, enveloping older conceptions, leading back to the point 'where meaning first
emerges into the open at the very origin of human experience' (Kisiel 1969: 358).

While Heidegger adopted phenomenology as a method to get at primordial
sources, his conception of phenomenology differs from Husserl's. In line with his
view of the original philosophical purity of the Greek language, Heidegger
engages in a hermeneutical exegesis of the Greek words *phainomenon* and *logos*,
deriving the notion of 'letting something show itself as it actually is' (Heidegger
1962: 50ff). In this sense, then, rejecting Husserl's bracketing of reality/existence
while retaining the latter's emphasis on the structures of the 'lived world' and the
relationship of the lived world to time, Heidegger identifies phenomenology first
as ontology and then as hermeneutics. He says, 'phenomenology is the name for
the method of ontology, that is; of scientific philosophy' (1982: 20), and elsewhere
adds, 'The meaning of phenomenological description as a method lies in *interpretation* ... The phenomenology of dasein is a *hermeneutic* in the primordial
significance of this word, where it designates this business of interpreting' (1962:
61-2). As Kisiel explains, 'In Heidegger's terms, *Dasein*, human existence in its
situation, stands in the "event of unconcealment", and accordingly understands. It
is in this "event", then, that the heart of the hermeneutical is to be found' (1969:
358).

The metaphysical purpose of Heidegger's magnum opus, *Being and Time*
(1927, trans. 1962), is the fundamental analysis of *Dasein*, a search for an answer
to the question of the meaning of Being. *Dasein* is distinguished from all other
beings in that it is the ontological being – in other words, it is the being which alone
has understanding of Being. Kisiel explains the point here in a refreshingly
non-technical way:

> In a move which is decisive for the concept formation of all of Heidegger's
> thought, the opening pages of *Being and Time* unravel the interrogative
> relationship that man has with his being into two interrelated axes of the
> comprehensive relation of dasein. If man questions what it means to be, then
> 1) he must already have some understanding of what it means to be and 2) he
> must have a tendency or capacity to question what it means to be. These two
> dimensions of the interrogative relation to being are designated by the terms
> *understanding* and *existence*.
>
> (1981: 100)

Since *Dasein* is characterized by its understanding of Being, the meaning of
Being can only be interpreted from within this current pre-understanding: it must
start with a fundamental 'hermeneutic of *Dasein*'. Such a hermeneutic reveals the
basic ontological characteristics of *Dasein* as *existentiality*, *facticity* and *fallenness*,
which constitute an inseparable, indissoluble, unified structure Heidegger calls
Sorge (that is, care). Heidegger (1962) begins his analysis with facticity or 'being
in the world', considered as a unitary phenomenon. *Dasein*, or human being, is
always already in the world, my world. Existentiality refers to human being as an

anticipation of its own possibilities, or its power of becoming or of going beyond the given. Fallenness, the third interrelated characteristic of *Dasein*, means that we habitually forget Being in the scattering of our everyday activities, mistaking it for particular beings.

This all-too-cursory exposition provides us at least with a basic outline from which to approach Heidegger's second stage of analysis (1962), where he develops the concepts of time and temporality in relation to *Dasein*.

In Part II of *Being and Time* Heidegger argues that 'the primordial ontological basis for *Dasein's* existentiality is *temporality* (1962: 277). In other words, the structural unity of *Dasein* (*Sorge*) is grounded in its own temporality. Briefly, the ontological characteristics of *Dasein* mentioned above actually constitute in some sense the three dimensions of our temporality. To facticity belongs the past; to existentiality belongs anticipation of the future; and to fallenness belongs the present. Such an analysis becomes the basis of an investigation which reveals the a priori structures that determine the transcendental horizon of Being in temporality. The task of hermeneutics, therefore, is considered to be ontological – disclosing the meaning of Being in general – rather than epistemological – the acquisition of knowledge through the employment of a hermeneutic method.

Where for both Schleiermacher (1977) and Dilthey the knowing subject's own subjectivity is something to be methodologically overcome in reaching historical understanding, for Gadamer (1975a), following Heidegger, the knowing subject's subjectivity – which is constitutively involved in the process of understanding – becomes something that, as it were, opens up the past. Tradition, a form of authority defended by Romanticism against the Enlightenment, is the source of our prejudices. In Gadamer's words, 'we owe to romanticism this correction of the enlightenment, that tradition has a justification that's outside the arguments of reason and in large measure determines our institutions and our attitudes' (1975a: 249). But as Gadamer describes it, tradition is not something other or alien to us that we can distance and free ourselves of in an objectifying process. We always stand in a tradition; it is always part of us.

Gadamer demonstrates through historical interpretation and analysis that the concept of prejudice acquired a negative value as a result of Enlightenment attitudes toward church authority and tradition which were, themselves, discredited and distorted in contrast to reason. Only the methodologically disciplined use of reason, witnessed for example in Descartes's idea of method, can safeguard us against all error. Modern science's preoccupation with a commitment to truth and method is thus a product of this Enlightenment attitude and shares with it the prejudice against prejudice. The pre-Enlightenment meaning of the concept of prejudice was simply 'pre-judgement' – a judgement 'given before all the elements that determine a situation have been finally examined' (ibid.: 240) – and, accordingly, the concept could have equally either a positive or a negative value.

Gadamer seeks to rehabilitate authority and tradition as those positive prejudices which are the very conditions of understanding. He maintains it is our prejudices which constitute our being:

Prejudices are not necessarily unjustified and erroneous, so that they inevitably distort the truth. In fact, the historicity of our existence entails that prejudices, in the literal sense of the word, constitute the initial directedness of our whole ability to experience. Prejudices are biases of our openness to the world. They are simply conditions whereby we experience something – whereby what we encounter says something to us.

(1976: 9)

It is clear that Gadamer is concerned with truths that go beyond the range of methodical knowledge (1975a: xiii). He is not concerned to elaborate a system of rules which describe or direct the methodological approach of the *Geisteswissenschaften*. His purpose is philosophic in the sense that the primary object of this investigation is the question 'how is understanding (*verstehen*) possible?'.

In seeking an answer to this question Gadamer follows the direction pointed out by Heidegger. Heidegger's influence on Gadamer, however, is not confined merely to indicating that the hermeneutical approach should be ontological rather than epistemological – that it should focus on the 'Being of history' rather than the 'possibility of science'. It also characterizes a much broader conception of *verstehen* which rejoins a longer tradition of hermeneutics in theology and law (Kisiel 1969).

Following Heidegger's ontological critique of consciousness (*Dasein* as 'being in the world'), Gadamer construes our involvement in tradition, in history, as an *active* process constitutive of understanding.

Tradition is not simply a pre-condition into which we come, but we produce it ourselves, inasmuch as we understand, participating in the evolution of tradition and hence further determine it ourselves. Thus the circle of understanding is not a 'methodological' circle, but describes an ontological structural element in understanding.

(1975a: 261)

The focus on understanding considered not so much as an action of subjectivity but as entering into an occurrence of transmission, in which past and present are constantly being mediated, leads to an acceptance of Heidegger's 'hermeneutic of facticity' – a radical finitude and temporality beyond which one cannot go. Temporal distance, however, is not something to be overcome – the naive assumption of historicism – for 'true historical thinking must take account of its own historicality' (Gadamer 1975a: 267).

At one point Gadamer states his position in summary form:

My thesis is – and I think it is the necessary consequence of recognizing the operativeness of history in our conditionedness and finitude – that the thing which hermeneutics teaches us is to see through the dogmatism of asserting an opposition and separation between the ongoing natural 'tradition' and the reflective appropriation of it. For behind this assertion stands a dogmatic objectivism that distorts the very concept of hermeneutical reflection itself. In this objectivism the understander is seen ... not in relation to the hermeneutical situation and the constant operativeness of history in its own consciousness, but in such a way as to imply that his own understanding does not enter into the event.

(1976: 28)

Understanding is not reconstruction, re-enactment or restoration of meaning. It is a mediation of the past into the present – Gadamer talks of it as 'fusion of horizons' (1975a: 269ff). In one sense this is the very center of his magnum opus, for he tells us that while he did not intend 'to deny the necessity of methodical work in the human sciences' (ibid.: xvii), the hermeneutics he develops is 'an attempt to understand what the human sciences truly are beyond their methodical self-consciousness, and what connects them with the totality of our experience of the world (ibid.: xiii). In asking the philosophical question 'how is understanding possible?', his purpose is:

to discover what is common to all modes of understanding and to show that understanding is never subjective behavior toward a given 'object', but towards its effective history – the history of its influence; in other words, understanding belongs to the being of that which is understood.

(ibid.: xix)

It is necessary to recognize the importance Gadamer attributes to language (1975a) – the inherent linguisticality of interpretation and of tradition – for language is the medium of the hermeneutical experience. Understanding as a fusion of horizons is essentially a linguistic process. The prejudices Gadamer speaks of as constitutive of our being can now be seen to be embedded in our language and transmitted in the language that we use. This tradition is immanently operative in the use of language, and as such the ontological structure of understanding is revealed in 'being in language'. The notion of understanding as a fusion of horizons in language has more in common with the dialectic of question and answer, and with a dialogue between two persons, than with the traditional model of hermeneutics as a body of techniques or method of interpretation performed by a knowing subject upon an historical object.

CONCLUDING DISCUSSION

Freire and Gadamer share a number of important philosophical emphases and orientations. Among these, as we have sought to show, is the common acceptance of the ontological dimension of understanding which gives primal significance to the notions of 'being' and 'time'. These two notions are at the root of other critical similarities: the common emphasis on the importance of language and tradition; the focus on the interpretation of texts and text-analogues; the shared assumptions concerning the historicity of reason and the rationality of history.

Yet in their respective treatment of these related themes Gadamer and Freire differ quite markedly. The differences, we believe, grow out of the way in which each of them views the ontological significance of the notions of 'being' and 'time'. In brief, whereas Gadamer's treatment tends to be idealistic and conservative, Freire's, in sharp contrast, is materialistic and critical. To a large extent the differences between them are the differences of the major intellectual influences at work on them; they can be put down to the fact that Gadamer's Heideggerian influences lead him in a quite different direction from that pointed by Freire's increasingly Marxist orientation.

This can be illustrated quite simply: where for Marx (and Freire) humanity is ultimately in control of history, for Heidegger (and Gadamer) humanity is not. In Heideggerian terms, history is governed within 'the destiny of Being' (see Zimmerman 1984) – a theme that is translated into the realm of language by Gadamer. While Gadamer talks of the principle of 'effective history' exemplified in the influence of history on human beings, it occurs at the pre-reflective level and is not open to reflective appropriation or critical appraisal. By contrast, Freire's approach here is to endorse an agency view of history, which, perhaps in a less philosophically sophisticated manner but 'historically' more relevant way, emphasises the Marxist view of a liberatory praxis – a view committed to change, to seeing human beings as the subjects of history. The Marxist view of history is not left in an abstract academic space; Freire uses and refines it in a praxis of cultural action where traditions are seen to be open to rational appraisal and criticism. Traditions in the form of 'generative themes' (Freire 1972) are coded and decoded according to existential situations. They can be rejected as oppressive; to be transformed into cultural traditions more congruent with human needs and purposes. The practical and revolutionary testimony of Freire's notion of cultural action for freedom can be seen in the Freirean-based literacy campaigns undertaken in Brazil and, more recently, by the people of Guinea-Bissau, Grenada, and Nicaragua.

Significantly, the issues that divide Gadamer and Freire are, to a large extent, exactly the same issues that divide Gadamer and Habermas (see Deprew 1981). Apel (1980) and Habermas (1971, 1979) both accept in general Gadamer's focus on subjectively intended meaning as characteristic of the *Geistewissenschaften*. They object, however, to Gadamer's 'uncritical' acceptance of tradition and to the (alleged) idealism of his hermeneutics, in which language is regarded as a transcendental absolute unconstrained by particular socio-historical conditions and structures.

Specifically, they challenge Gadamer's assumption regarding the a priori superiority of tradition and the 'categorization of language'. In their view this implies a refusal to acknowledge that language can be and is used as an instrument or medium of domination, and implicitly denies any regulative principle of progress in knowledge. According to them, the idealism that follows from the autonomy of language and tradition in Gadamer's hermeneutics does not take account of the *material* socio-historical conditions or forces – characterized by the level of economic development reached and the prevailing forms of political domination and control – which set parameters for the development of consciousness and exchange of meaning. Consequently, the idealism inherent in Gadamer's hermeneutics apparently carries no practical implications for material practices aimed at transforming the world – the ultimate text-analogue that has yet to be completely 'read' and 'written'.

Apel and Habermas contend that the unconstrained or unimpeded dialogue typifying Gadamer's hermeneutics is at best only the *anticipation* of an authentic state of human existence which is yet to be realized, and Gadamer presents no notion of or prescription for how to reach that state. They argue that we need criteria for distinguishing between understanding and misunderstanding *before* we can demonstrate the possibility of understanding. Against this Gadamer claims that 'there can be no communication and no reflection at all without a prior basis of common agreement' (1975b: 315). He regards the view from critical theory that we can reinstate authentic dialogue by emancipatory reflection as naive and self-contradictory. His objection to Habermas here is captured in the question: 'what justification can be offered for the standpoint of critical hermeneutics itself?'. In other words, Gadamer believes that Habermas must demonstrate that the standpoint from which a critique of ideology operates is not itself ideological.

We may note in passing here that for Freire dialogue – what he refers to elliptically as 'speaking true words' – is a praxis which contains the two dimensions of reflection and action as they are combined in transforming the world. In one sense, then, Freire dialectically supersedes the ontological–epistemological division separating Gadamer and Habermas, for not only is dialogue essentially creative and transformative, it is both an existential necessity *and* a methodology (dialogics) for overcoming oppression.

Gadamer rejects the claim that his emphasis on tradition as a factor entering into all understanding implies an uncritical acceptance of tradition and a socio-political conservatism (ibid.: 108). He argues that 'the confrontation of our historic tradition is always a critical challenge of this tradition . . . Every experience is such a confrontation' (ibid.). Given Gadamer's position, however, we must see this confrontation as taking place *within* the confines of linguistic tradition. In other words, it operates within the assumptions, prejudgements, or prejudices of that tradition. Consequently, there can be no notion of coming to grips with the ideological basis of that tradition itself, and the way in which it is related to certain socio-historical structures within which some humans exploit and oppress others.

This, by contrast, is the very point at which Freire *begins*. His is a *critical* hermeneutics which is both ontological and epistemological. As ontological it is tied to Freire's conviction that our vocation as human beings is to become more fully human. It is epistemological in that Freire offers a methodology for investigating generative themes, as part of the praxis through which humans become more fully human. In both its (unified) ontological and epistemological aspects this hermeneutics is *critical*. It is critical because we are called on to perform *evaluative* acts in the praxis of naming the world.

Echoing Kosik (1976), Freire claims that human beings

> in their permanent relations with reality, produce not only material goods –
> tangible objects – but also social institutions, ideas, and concepts. Through
> their continuing praxis, humans simultaneously create history and become
> historical-social beings. Because – in contrast to animals – humans can
> tri-dimensionalise time into the past, the present, and the future, their history,
> in function of their own creations, develops as a constant process of
> transformation within which epochal units materialise.
>
> (1972: 73)

The task of naming the world is a process of evaluating the world humans have
made with a view to making it better. Reading the world – the ultimate
text-analogue – with a view to remaking it is necessarily an evaluative act. This
world-to-be-evaluated comprises humanly constructed ideas, concepts,
institutions, as well as material objects. Human practices and the ideas, beliefs, and
values which shape and sustain these practices are, then, up for evaluation and
subsequent transformation. This means that tradition, *including linguistic
tradition*, cannot be taken as a given. It is part of the very world we are called upon
to evaluate and remake as our ontological vocation. We *have* to understand
tradition as an integral part of the text to be understood, interpreted and rewritten.
Consequently, we have to be able to appraise tradition rationally and understand
the ideological role it plays within our current reality.

The beginning point for Freire's critical hermeneutics is the fundamental theme
of our historical epoch, *domination*, and its negation, *liberation*. Domination must
be understood as a totality of humanly constructed practices and relations, masked,
sustained, and legitimated by ideas, beliefs, concepts and theories – that is,
ideology in general. Liberation must also be seen as a human construction: a
totality of practices and relations created by human beings. The dialectical
interaction between these opposite (created) tendencies is the dynamo of historical
continuity within our epoch. History is made and remade as humans build and
rebuild, defend and legitimate, the ideas, practices, institutions, and relations of
one mode against the other. In its ontological dimension, hermeneutics proclaims
the relations, processes, and practices of *dialogue* to be the essence of education
as the practice of freedom; hermeneutics in its epistemological dimension provides
the methodology for awakening critical consciousness through investigation of the
'generative themes' of our epoch.

For Freire, critical consciousness *is* a critical hermeneutics. It involves the
dialectical movement of thought exemplified in the analysis of concrete,
existential, 'coded' situations. Examples of 'coded' situations actually employed
by Freire in the process of educating for critical consciousness are included in
Education: The Practice of Freedom (1976: 61–84). According to Freire, decoding
an existential situation

> requires moving from the abstract to the concrete; this requires moving from

the part to the whole and then returning to the parts; this in turn requires that the subject recognize himself in the object (the coded concrete existential situation) and recognize the object as a situation in which he finds himself, together with other subjects.

(1972: 77)

The reading of a text and the reading of reality – a text-analogue – follow the same process. Both are designed to enable subjects, reflecting and acting together, to perceive the *totality* which is their reality, to identify the *limit situations* which confront them – which would determine them as objects, negating their freedom to determine their next step, their future, themselves – and to overcome them in the process of transforming the world, which is precisely the process of making their own history. Thus Freire's hermeneutics is always critical of prevailing tradition and intimately tied to an emancipatory intent.

To overlook the hermeneutical ingredient in Freire is to overlook the distinctively educational and revolutionary process implied by his philosophy: where reading and writing transcend their traditional conceptions to become, in Freire's hands, an interrelated set of genuinely transformative educational practices. The text is no longer a privileged educational object to be 'banked'. It is *constructed* from the lives of the people and *interpreted* within the wider con-text, linking an understanding of the immediate reality to understanding of the world and of history in a process of critical reflection and action. For Freire the model is one of dialogue, involving the dialectical process of 'reading' the text/reality and 'writing' it anew.

Freire adopts a *critical hermeneutics* as the basis of emancipatory praxis. The intent is to encourage subjects or agents reflecting and acting together to recognize in an objective manner the material structures and constraints that are used by others to oppress and exploit them. If educators ignore this hermeneutical ingredient they will fail to conceptualize properly the methodological basis of Freire's approach to pursuing emancipation, as well as the way in which it is grounded in an ontology of understanding. We believe it is educationally important that these matters be recognized clearly and accurately. This chapter is intended to serve as a first step to following them further.

NOTES

1 In Freire's more recent works, as noted by other authors in this volume, there is a clear shift away from male-gendered language. We try here to do minimum violence to Freire's texts while accepting the proper requirements for non-sexist language.
2 We employ the following conventional terminology: Being (*Sein*); being (*Seienden*); *Dasein*, literally 'being there', meaning human being. For an understanding of the term *Dasein*, see Kisiel (1981) and Hofstadter (1982). According to Heidegger (1982), Being specifies itself in four fundamentally different ways. Heidegger analyzes these four ways by reference to four traditional theses about Being advanced during the course of Western philosophy. (These are: Kant's thesis – Being is not a real predicate; the thesis of medieval ontology derived from Aristotle – to the constitution of the Being of a being

there belong essence and existence; the thesis of modern ontology – the basic ways of Being are the Being of nature and the Being of mind; the thesis of logic – the Being of the copula.)

3 Compare here Husserl's influence on Freire, in particular Freire's emphasis on 'intentionality' as the hallmark of consciousness – a feature which, interestingly, Heidegger actually rejects.

REFERENCES

Apel, K.-O. (1980) *Towards a Transformation of Philosophy* (G. Adey and D. Frisbey, trans.), London: Routledge and Kegan Paul.

Bauman, Z. (1979) *Hermeneutics and Social Science: Approaches to Understanding*, London: Hutchinson.

Deprew, P.J. (1981) 'The Habermas–Gadamer debate in Hegelian perspective', *Philosophical and Social Criticism* 8: 425–46.

Dilthey, W. (1976) *Selected Writings* (H.P. Rickman, ed., trans. and intro.), Cambridge: Cambridge University Press.

Ermarth, M. (1981) 'The transformation of hermeneutics: nineteenth century ancients and twentieth century moderns', *Monist* 64: 175–92.

Freire, P. (1972) *Pedagogy of the Oppressed*, Harmondsworth: Penguin.

—— (1976) *Education: The Practice of Freedom*, London: Writers and Readers.

Gadamer, H.-G. (1975a) *Truth and Method* (G. Barden and I. Cumming, trans.), New York: Continuum.

—— (1975b) 'Hermeneutics and social science', *Cultural Hermeneutics* 2, 4: 307–16.

—— (1976) *Philosophical Hermeneutics* (D.E. Linge, ed. and trans.), Berkeley: University of California Press.

Giddens, A. (1982) *Profiles and Critiques in Social Theory*, London: Macmillan.

Habermas, J. (1971) *Knowledge and Human Interests* (J. Shapiro, trans.), Boston: Beacon Press.

—— (1979) *Communication and the Evolution of Society* (T. McCarthy, trans.), Boston: Beacon Press.

Heidegger, M. (1962) *Being and Time* (J. Macquarrie and E. Robinson, trans.), New York: Harper.

—— (1981) 'A recollection' in T. Sheehan, ed., *Heidegger: The Man and the Thinker*, Chicago: Precedent.

—— (1982) *The Basic Problems of Philosophy* (A. Hofstadter, trans., intro. and lexicon), Bloomington: Indiana University Press.

Hesse, M. (1980) *Revolutions and Reconstructions in the Philosophy of Science*, Bloomington and London: Indiana University Press.

Hofstadter, A. (1982) 'Introduction' to M. Heidegger, *The Basic Problems of Philosophy* (A. Hofstadter, trans., intro. and lexicon), Bloomington: Indiana University Press.

Husserl, E. (1981) 'Inaugural lecture at Freiburg in Breisgau' in P. McCormick and F. Elliston, eds, *Husserl: Shorter Works*, Notre Dame, IN, and Brighton, Sussex: University of Notre Dame Press and Harvester Press.

Kisiel, T. (1969) 'The happening of tradition: the hermeneutics of Gadamer and Heidegger', *Man and World*: 2, 3, 358–95.

—— (1981) 'Toward the topology of Dasein' in T. Sheehan, ed., *Heidegger: The Man and the Thinker*, Chicago: Precedent.

Kosik, K. (1976) *Dialectics of the Concrete*, Boston: Reidel.

Kuhn, T. (1977) *The Essential Tension: Selected Studies in Scientific Tradition and Change*, Chicago: University of Chicago Press.

Mackie, R. (1980) 'Contributions to the thought of Paulo Freire' in R. Mackie, ed., *Literacy and Revolution: The Pedagogy of Paulo Freire*, London: Pluto Press.

Macquarrie, J. (1968) *Martin Heidegger*, Richmond: John Knox Press.

Outhwaite, W. (1975) *Understanding Social Life: The Method Called Verstehen*, London: Allen and Unwin.

Rabinow, P. and Sullivan, W.M. (eds.) (1979) *Interpretive Social Science: A Reader*, Berkeley: University of California Press.

Ricoeur, P. (1981) 'The task of hermeneutics' in P. Ricoeur, *Hermeneutics and the Human Sciences* (J.B. Thompson, ed. and trans.), Cambridge: Maison des Sciences de L'Homme and Cambridge University Press.

Rorty, R. (1980) *Philosophy and the Mirror of Nature*, Oxford: Blackwell.

Schleiermacher, F. (1977) *Hermeneutics: The Handwritten Manuscripts* (H. Kimmerle, ed.; J. Duke and J. Forstman, trans.), Missoula, MT: Scholars Press.

Sheehan, T. (1981) 'Introduction: Heidegger, the project and the fulfilment', in T. Sheehan, ed., *Heidegger: The Man and the Thinker*, Chicago: Precedent.

Taylor, C. (1971) 'Interpretation and the sciences of man', *Review of Metaphysics* 25, 1. Reprinted in P. Rabinow and W.M. Sullivan, eds, *Interpretive Social Science: A Reader*, Berkeley: University of California Press. Page references are to the reprinted article.

Vandenberg, D. (1979) 'Existential and phenomenological influences in educational philosophy', *Teachers College Record* 81: 166–91.

Zimmerman, M. (1984) 'Karel Kosik's Heideggerian Marxism', *Philosophical Forum* XV, 3: 209–33.

Chapter 11

Postmodernism and the death of politics
A Brazilian reprieve

Peter L. McLaren

> For me education is simultaneously an act of knowing, a political act, and an artistic event. I no longer speak about a political dimension of education. I no longer speak about a knowing dimension of education. As well, I don't speak about education through art. On the contrary, I say education *is* politics, art and knowing.
>
> (Freire 1985b: 17)

INTRODUCTION: SOCIAL THEORY AND THE RETREAT INTO THE CODE

Contemporary social theory exists in a state of crisis. In recent years, its methods of inquiry have been shaken by the ascendancy of 'postmodern' theoretical perspectives that carry with them the primacy of critique and deconstruction. Epistemologies that rely on foundational principles are now exceedingly vulnerable to criticism and in peril of outright rejection or dismissal, having been opened up to the conditions of their own impossibility. What were once accepted – albeit disparate – procedures for arriving at ontologically and metaphysically secure 'truth claims' have now shifted from the inevitability of epistemological relativity to judgemental relativism and a burgeoning nihilism.

Postmodern theoretical trajectories take as their entry point a rejection of the deep-grained assumptions of Enlightenment rationality, traditional Western epistemology, or any supposedly 'secure' representation of reality that exists outside of discourse itself. War is declared on the myth of the subject, and the concept of praxis is marginalized in favor of rhetorical undecidability and textual analyses of social practices.[1] As a species of criticism, postmodernist discourse resigns itself to the impossibility of an ahistorical, transcendental, or self-authenticating version of truth. The reigning conviction that knowledge is knowledge only if it reflects the world as it 'really' exists has been inexorably annihilated in favor of a view in which reality is socially constructed or semiotically posited. Furthermore, normative agreement on what should constitute and guide scientific practice and argumentative consistency has become an intellectual target for what Habermas calls 'a capering deconstructivism' (Habermas 1985: 97).

The discursive trail from consciousness to language, from the denotative to the performative, and from the hypothesis to the speech-act has opened new epistemological territory occupied by a plethora of discourses, many lacking any firm moral, ethical, or political grounds for legitimation. The dilemma in which contemporary social theory finds itself has provoked Jean-François Lyotard, one of the pre-eminent exponents of postmodernism, to announce: 'Postmodern science ... is theorizing its own evolution as discontinuous, catastrophic, nonrectifiable, and paradoxical' (1984: 60).

The term 'postmodernism' remains hotly contested among contemporary social and cultural theorists and currently exists as a disciplinary archipelago consisting of post-structuralism, deconstruction, and critical hermeneutics scattered throughout the sea of social theory. The term is generally conscripted to describe what is often ambiguously referred to as a rejection or debunking of modernism's epistemic foundations or metanarratives. It has also been variously used to describe the dethronement of the authority of positivistic science as the monopoly of truth and knowledge; the critical deconstruction of Enlightenment rationality (specifically its attack on a unified goal of history, the totalizing subject, and logocentrism); the decline of the idea of a self-reflective transcendental subject; and the impossibility of context – transcending legitimation and criticism and even of philosophy itself.

I am using the term 'postmodern' not so much as a periodizing label to designate the inauguration of a new age, culminating in cultural decline associated with the *post-histoire* of the French Nietzscheans, as to refer broadly to various rationalities or discourses underlying new developments in social theory, such as structuralism, deconstructionism, poststructuralism, discourse theory, and speech–act theory in the context of their general 'refusal of history' and lack of a well-articulated political project or politics of hegemonic refusal. I am not suggesting that postmodern continental philosophy (poststructuralist French critical theory, or neo-Wittgensteinian challenges to Western *meta-récits*) or new developments in social theory such as critical pragmatism do not have their transformative moments or have not been made to serve laudable political ends. Rather, I am referring both to the lack of an explicit, well-defined, and unhesitant political posture in certain strands of this work and to the generally ahistorical employment of these new approaches. I would also like to make it clear that I am not attempting to dismiss postmodernist political theory as mere relativism, nor do I wish to imply that this approach – even its 'ludic' varieties – claims nothing exists outside of the text.

I do wish to argue, however, that postmodern social theory (with the partial exception of its nascent 'resistance' varieties) suffers from some major theoretical ailments: first of all, in attempting to understand the product of historical agency in a post-culture of cannibalized reality, of detranscendentalized self-simulacra, it lacks a well-developed theory of the subject, and without such a theory it cannot further the discourse of social change; secondly, in the absence of an adequate language of social change, postmodern social theory has failed to be guided by a substantive political project. In other words, in as much as history is seen as an unwelcome diversion, postmodern social theory has excluded from its practice the ability to think in utopian terms.[1]

Given the demise of the episteme of representation and the announced incommensurability of language games, it could easily be argued that postmodern social theorists find it more expedient to criticize that which is taken for granted than to construct new political platforms. But the problem goes far beyond mere cynicism, lack of critical effort, or a failure of the imagination. I wish to claim that, in some fundamental way, the erosion of the political in leftist social theory is linked to a logic endemic to the very nature of postmodern theorizing. And in doing so, I shall assert that much of the critical posture assumed by postmodern theorizing cannot bear its own critical weight. Anthony Giddens (1984: 32) has described this posture as the structuralist and poststructuralist 'retreat into the code', wherein the primacy of the semiotic overshadows concern for the social or the semantic. Similarly, the anti-subjectivist and overdeterministic tendencies of much semiotic theorizing fail seriously to consider human agency as a mode of resisting cultural hegemony. Consequently, human subjects rarely speak; instead, they are presumably 'already spoken' or culturally inscribed by historically sedimented discourses and linguistic traditions which serve as mediative constraints to individual action (Lears 1985: 592).

The advent of poststructuralist advances in social theory has in no small way contributed to a deepening rupture within the emancipatory impulses of leftist social theory in general and radical pedagogy in particular. In fact, the 'relentless refusal of the search for meaning and its substitution of the semiotic idea of "signification"' (Aronowitz 1985: 126–33) – which numerous critics consider to be the penultimate postmodern moment – threatens to cripple the very concept of the political in the human and social sciences. That is, in their rush to 'playfully' decode the social order, ludic postmodern critics often become fixated on understanding why things are the way they are as distinct from what must be done for things to be otherwise. In other words, they fail to take seriously the urgency of translating theoretical insights into a mode of collectively constituted thought and action that seeks to transform the asymmetrical relations of power and privilege that inform and regulate daily life. Put yet another way, the current interest in how social life is constituted as a social text as opposed to how it can be materially reconstituted speaks to a failure on the part of contemporary postmodern theorists to understand textuality and materiality as dialectically re-initiating relations, and to situate their work in an organizing problematic that allows it to become the starting point for transforming conditions of oppressive and inequitable moral and social regulation and providing straightforward guidelines for concrete strategy and action. As long as we view social reality and the values embodied in that reality as 'only' socially constructed or semiotically posited, social action in the service of facilitating political mobilization is seen as uncompromisingly totalizing or even sectarian; it loses all authority and intrinsic meaning and therefore fails to elicit our commitment. Involvement in addressing specific political constituencies is therefore reduced to an arbitrary action or personal whim (often reflecting the representatives of the liberal vanguard within the academy) instead of being a shared concern.

This problem is echoed further by Jean Baudrillard and Henri Lefebvre, who argue that the commodification of mass cultural symbols has created a 'floating stock of meaningless signifiers' which has devalued collective discourse and seriously impeded the struggle over what life means and how it should be lived (Lears 1985: 592). A critical question is therefore raised: how can we get meaning and commitment back into our lives once we have lost grounds for collective practice? What becomes our *point d' appui* for an emancipatory politics?

To the extent that contemporary social science continues to exhibit facets of this postmodern perspective, there is a danger that social theorists will be reduced to mere curators of various discourses, having abandoned a political commitment to making these discourses work in the interest of empowering subordinated groups. To develop a concern for the dispossessed, disenfranchised, and disempowered within the confines of a poststructuralist discourse is no easy matter if, along with Terry Eagleton, we consider that such a discourse 'commits you to affirm nothing' (Eagleton 1983: 145). It could even be argued that in some cases postmodern social theory collapses into a form of a duplicitous avant-gardism 'in which what is really an establishmentarian politics is made to appear radical through the willful inaccessibility of language' (Adamson 1985: 165). In summary, if we accept the view of reality implicit in much of postmodern theorizing, then we will get a reality independent of unambiguous political commitment, independent of a preferential concern for subordinate groups and therefore intrinsically meaningless as the grounds for creating an emancipatory praxis linked to a struggle for democracy. Richard Bernstein skillfully captures the postmodern ethos in the following passage:

> Sometimes it seems as if we are living through a rage against modernity, a total disenchantment with the hopes and aspirations of what is best in our own democratic heritage, and with the type of fallibilistic humanism that Dewey advocated. But perhaps, after the dialectic of fashionable forms of relativism and domesticated nihilism work themselves out, we may return to the spirit of Dewey.

> (Bernstein 1985: 58)

RADICAL PEDAGOGY AND THE POSTMODERN CONDITION

Radical pedagogy has not remained immune to the lush profusion of discourses that have accompanied recent developments in contemporary social theory. In recent years, educational scholars in North America have attempted to usurp the critical potential of new continental thought by relevantly extrapolating from, among other efforts, the deconstructionist assaults of Derrida, the hermeneutical sorties of Gadamer and Ricoeur, Lacan's psychoanalytic reconstitution of the subject, Barthes's anti-subjectivism, Foucault's commentaries on power and historical inquiry, and Deleuze's and Guattari's politics of desire.

In their attempts to 'deconstruct' the curriculum and to read the 'text' of teacher performance, radical educators have drawn upon important insights from the postmodern critique to uncover the mutually constitutive processes of power/ knowledge and how this configuration reproduces itself through particular discourses in school settings. With one foot solidly planted in neo-Marxist traditions and the other posed somewhat hesitatingly over the anti-metaphysical radicalism of post-analytic philosophy and critical social theory, radical pedagogy continues to survey the manifold political dimensions of schooling, pointing out how schools reproduce the discourses, values, and privileges of existing elites.

In effect, burgeoning work in radical educational scholarship has shifted the concept of the politics of schooling from a subsidiary category to a substantive one. Offering an important counter-logic to the positivistic, ahistorical, and depoliticized discourse that informs most conservative and liberal analyses of schooling, radical pedagogy continues to generate categories crucial for interrogating the ideological and material dimensions of schooling. In so doing, it attempts to separate schooling from the social perversions it carries in its very structures and to provide the grounds upon which to launch a politics of refusal. Within this critical perspective, schools are conceptualized as both social and instructional sites made up of dominant and subordinate cultures, each characterized by the power it has to establish particular ways of defining and engaging social experience. On the one hand, a growing engagement with postmodern social theory has provided radical educators with new modes of analysis with which to unravel the logic of capitalist domination, to refuse totalizing narratives that subsume the contingency and situatedness of social relations, to deconstruct radically informed and gendered representations, and to dismantle the colonizing imperatives of the modernist metaphysics of Western logocentrism; on the other hand, little in the corpus of poststructuralist or post-modernist theories has been significantly appropriated for the purposes of educational reform, except by way of critique. (The work of Judith Butler, Giroux and Aronowitz and a few others constitutes an exception.) In short, radical pedagogy still lacks a theoretical and political base from which educators can move beyond critique to a collective formulation of new goals and new strategies designed for building on the imperatives of freedom and democracy.

The establishment of postmodern social theory continues to have pressing implications for critical pedagogy, especially with respect to the conscription of fragmentation and diversity into the development of a unified collective opposi-tional identity that works across a range of public and private levels. As the anti-foundationalist and anti-subjectivist currents of postmodern thought sweep away the last props of metaphysical realism, it becomes clearer that many of these new, post-analytic approaches lack the requisite sociology on which to build a new ethical foundation, what Aronowitz and Giroux (1985), Raymond Williams (1980) and others refer to as a project directed toward possibility. A language of possibility points to 'forms of analysis that move beyond theories of critique to the more difficult task of laying the theoretical basis for transformative modes of . . . practice' (Aronowitz and Giroux 1985: 154) outside of any one normative political project or cultural politics.

The current deconstruction of any privileged ground or transcendental referent with which to guide the task of school reform has been a mixed blessing. On the one hand, it has brought a profound distrust of scientific knowledge, reason and consensus. On the other hand, an understanding of truth as a contingent and shifting set of relations, makes it difficult – although not impossible – to construct the common project necessary to make important political choices. In effect, ludic forms of postmodern social theory have become so hopelessly restrictive in restrategizing the pedagogical as political and in marshalling concerted and sustained attempts at renewing the leftist project of democratic rebirth, that we are hard pressed to argue against Edward W. Said's (1982) prognosis that in America today liberalism and leftist constituencies are in a state of intellectual disarray. Sadly, however, some radical educators have dismissed postmodernism's important criticisms of the humanist subject, aesthetic formalism, and the vanguardism of theory as essentially a problem of inaccessible writing styles and overly theoretical language. Not only does such a defensive position refuse to engage dialectically the important contributions of post- modernism, it also serves to promote a woeful deskilling of those very agents it claims to empower.

One pressing task for a radical pedagogy that takes postmodern criticism seriously is to ensure that the important postmodern perspectives now characterizing the work of various educational theorists are buttressed by the imperative of ethical reflection and subordinated to the creation of a viable, progressive political project. Radical pedagogy must continue to search for a critical language that will stress the primacy of a politics of emancipation and interconnecting oppositional public spheres. For this reason, the work of Paulo Freire provides an important focus of attention.

PAULO FREIRE AND THE PRIMACY OF THE POLITICAL

Viver e lutar

Positioning Freire's work within the foregoing discussion places him in the front ranks of that 'dying class' of modernist revolutionaries for whom liberation remains the banner behind which to fight for social justice and transformation. Freire's dialogic pedagogy, beginning with his goal of empowering oppressed Brazilian peasants, has, over the years, assumed a legendary and epoch-making status. Few educators have strode so knowingly and with such determination along the crossroads of language and culture.

Freire's previous work has been widely cited and evaluated elsewhere and I forbear to pursue a detailed summary of his ideas here (see McLaren and Leonard 1993). I do wish, however, to show how Freire's work constitutes an important contribution to critical pedagogy not simply because of its theoretical refinement, or its arguments against a depoliticization of immanent critique, but because of Freire's success at putting theory into practice within a larger ethics of subversion and transformation. To create such an ethics is no small matter, especially in a First World history-less culture in which hallucination and realism threaten to blur beyond redemption, and where the act of representation and the object represented implode into the brute facticity and hyper-valorization of the image.

Based on a recognition of the cultural underpinnings of folk traditions and the importance of the collective construction of knowledge, Freire's literacy programs for disempowered peasants are now employed in countries all over the world. By linking the categories of history, politics, economics, and class to the concepts of culture and power, Freire has managed to develop both a language of critique and a language of hope that work conjointly and dialectically and which have proven successful in liberating the lives of generations of disenfranchised peoples. It is Freire's language of hope – what Aronowitz and Giroux (1985) refer to as a 'language of possibility' – that will serve as the focus of my discussion as I compare Freire's work with the recent trends in postmodern social theory.

I wish to focus my discussion on one recent book by Freire published in the United States, *The Politics of Education* (1985a). This book constitutes a formidable collection of essays which have been skillfully translated and arranged as a series of complementary themes dealing with such diverse topics as the act of study, adult literacy, the transformative role of the social worker, cultural action and conscientization, political literacy, humanistic education, and liberation theology. These themes are woven into the political design of the book, which attempts to lead the reader to an experience of 'authentic conscientization' – which Freire describes as 'the revelation of the real world as a dynamic and dialectical unity with the actual transformation of reality' (Freire 1985a: 169).

For Freire, speech and language always exist within a social context which, in turn, becomes the critical referent for the transformative possibilities of his work. This social context – which exists for Freire *both in and between language and the social order* – comprises the social relations obtaining among the material conditions of oppression, the exigencies of daily life, critical consciousness, and social transformation. Freire's sensitive grasp of the contradictions and tensions that emerge from such a volatile context is what eventually leads him to posit the need for a radical politics of liberation. As Florence Tager puts it:

> Freire's pedagogy insists on a deep connection between the culture of everyday life and radical politics. For Freire, critical consciousness and the dissection of themes from daily life is an ongoing process that grows out of praxis and leads to further praxis (Freire's term for action with reflection). Ultimately, education for critical consciousness leads to revolutionary politics. For Freire, radical pedagogy integrates culture and politics.

> (1982: 214)

Freire defines culture as a field of struggle over meaning, that is, as a many-sided conversation that is never neutral. For Freire, language and culture are always trace-ridden with a plurality of values, voices, and intentions which are by their very nature dialogical. Such a perspective draws attention to the intensity of social contradictions within linguistic and symbolic systems. Freire's understanding of culture posits it as a terrain where discourses are created and become implicated in the struggle over meaning. Culture is never depoliticized; it always remains tied to the social and class relationships that inform it.

Within the Freirean cosmology, human subjects do not float aimlessly in a sea of signifiers; they are not politically incapacitated even though they may, through conflicting interpellations, be 'decentered'; rather, they are firmly rooted in historical struggle. Human subjectivity is never reduced to a hypothetical or abstract bundle of signs. Consequently, social agents never lose their capacity for suffering or their resoluteness for effecting social transformation. Freirean man and woman are very much alive and anchored materially in a multiplicity of social relations which provide the 'stuff' out of which Freire fashions his particular brand of cultural politics.[2]

In Giroux's terms, Freire's cultural politics combine a language of critique and possibility. This permits his political project to be fundamentally directed toward a struggle over meaning, wherein meaning becomes both a product of and a vehicle for power. In other words, education comes to represent

> that terrain where power and politics are given a fundamental expression, since it is where meaning, desire, language, and values engage and respond to the deeper beliefs about the very nature of what it means to be human, to dream, and to name and struggle for a particular future and way of life.

> (Giroux 1985: xiii)

Becoming part of 'the project'

One of Freire's strongest insights is centered in his analysis of literacy and learning as an underlying political project – which he frequently refers to as 'conscientization' (adapted from the Brazilian term *conscientização*) – a process that invites learners to engage the world and others critically in an act of dialogical transformation; this project implies a fundamental 'recognition of the world, not as a "given" world, but as a world dynamically "in the making"' (Freire 1985a: 106). The ultimate goal of such a process is for learners to 'exercise the right to participate consciously in the sociohistorical transformation of their society' (ibid.: 50). Here Freire emphasizes the fact that human beings 'have the sense of "project," in contrast to the instinctive routines of animals' (ibid.: 44). And, of course, it is Freire's attentiveness to the scope and quality of his political 'project' (i.e. the historical and value dimensions of social life) which illuminates the transformative and emancipatory dimensions of his work. Such a position of political attentiveness is in direct opposition to the critical assault of ludic strands of postmodern anti-foundationalism. In effect, Freire's dialectics of the concrete and his concern with human suffering and social practices have helped him to avoid falling prey to an overwhelming anti-subjectivism.

Rather than constituting a mode of critique devoid of human subjects, Freire's work *begins and ends with the subject*. That is, it begins with a literacy process that grows out of the cultural capital of the oppressed and establishes the condition for forms of consciousness that eventually lead to cultural action and cultural revolution; that is, it grows out of a 'culture of silence' (ibid.: 83) where people are victimized and submerged in 'semi-intransitiveness' (ibid.: 90) to become finally realized as a 'revolutionary project . . . engaged in a struggle against oppressive and dehumanizing structures' (ibid.: 83).

A UTOPIAN PRAXIS

The taking-place of things does not take place in the world. Utopia is the very topia of things.

(Agamben: p. 103)

To be committed to cultural action for conscientization means not only to engage in a vigorous form of ideology critique but also to take part in a praxis which Freire unabashedly and unequivocally refers to as "utopian". Giroux defines the utopian and prophetic foundations of Freire's pedagogy in the introduction to *The Politics of Education*:

The *utopian* character of his analysis is concrete in its nature and appeal, and takes as its starting point collective actors in their various historical settings and the particularity of their problems and forms of oppression. It is *utopian* only in the sense that it refuses to surrender the risks and dangers that face all challenges to dominant power structures. It is prophetic in that it views the kingdom of God as something to be created on earth but only through a faith in both other human beings and the necessity of permanent struggle.

(Giroux 1985: xvii) (my emphasis)

Freire's utopian praxis is pitted against the counter-insurgent relations of domination and privilege of the dominant élite. Freire writes that 'cultural action for conscientization is always a utopian enterprise . . . [which] is what distinguishes it above all from cultural action for domination' (Freire 1985a: 86). He insists that education must always speak to the 'annunciation of a new reality' which becomes not only a temporary 'concrete reality' but a 'permanent cultural revolution' (ibid.: 86).

Freire's utopian project addresses the need for a fundamental faith in human dialogue and community. In this sense, becoming literate is not just a cognitive process of decoding signs, but a critical engagement of lived experience in relation to others. Hence, literacy assumes a form of cultural action for freedom. 'To undertake such a work', writes Freire, 'it is necessary to have faith in the people, solidarity with them. It is necessary to be utopian' (ibid.: 63). The utopian dimension is natural to any revolutionary project dedicated to 'transforming and recreating the world' (ibid.: 82). In fact, it is the very lack of any critically utopian dimension within the praxis of the right that defines the nature of its oppressive regime. According to Freire, authentic revolutionary praxis is utopian in nature, which means that is is dynamic, harmonious, creative, reflective, and dialogical. He writes:

> There ought to be a difference in the praxis of the right and of revolutionary groups that defines them to the people, making the options of each group explicit. This difference between the two groups stems from the utopian nature of the revolutionary groups, and the impossibility of the right to be utopian . . . A true revolutionary project, on the other hand, to which the utopian dimension is natural, is a process in which the people assume the role of subject in the precarious adventure of transforming and recreating the world . . . Revolutionary utopia tends to be dynamic rather than static; tends to life rather than death; to the future as a challenge to [men and women's] creativity rather than as a repetition of the present; to love as liberation of subjects rather than as pathological possessiveness; to the emotion of life rather than cold abstractions; to living together in harmony rather than gregariousness; to dialogue rather than mutism; to praxis rather than "law and order"; to [men and women] who organize themselves reflectively for action rather than [men and women] who are organized for passivity; to creative and communicative language rather than prescriptive signals; to reflective challenges rather than domesticating slogans; and to values that are lived rather than myths that are imposed.
>
> (ibid.: 81–2)

Freire's language of hope and his utopian vision are deeply engrained in his identification with the prophetic new church of Latin America. He assails the traditional church for presenting a world view that 'satisfies the fatalistic and frightened consciousness of the oppressed' (ibid.: 131) while drowning them in a culture of silence. Freire articulates the birth of a new, prophetic church that is at once at odds with both the traditional church and the modernizing church – both of which are characterized by 'do-goodism', a defense of reforms which maintain the status quo, and an ultimate commitment to the power elite.

The prophetic church is occupied by 'a critical analysis of the social structures in which conflict takes place' (ibid.) and demands of its followers 'a knowledge of sociopolitical science' (ibid.) and ultimately 'an ideological choice' (ibid.). Accompanied by a theological reflection which is now commonly referred to as liberation theology,[3] the prophetic church challenges the present historical situation in Latin America. Freire writes that 'such prophetic perspective does not represent an escape into a world of unattainable dreams. It demands a scientific knowledge of the world as it really is' (ibid.).

One important dimension of Freire's utopian vision calls for a restructuring of the nature of existing society in dramatic contrast to the oppressive aspects of everyday life; yet at the same time this utopian vision emerges from a concrete engagement in mundane reality. Freire's utopia does not speak to an idealized 'transcendental signified' that can only be realized in the imagination and therefore is denied historical possibility. Nor is any immutable reference point for emancipation capriciously deconstructed. Rather, Freire's utopia is immanent and realizable, but only in the process of conscientization and revolutionary practice. Suffering, and the historical memories of those who have suffered under the heels of the power elite, become, for Freire, the reference points that ground his revolutionary text. The task of liberating others from their suffering may not emerge from some transcendental fiat, yet it nevertheless compels us to affirm our humanity in solidarity with victims.

Freire encourages individuals to become transformative rhetors, to assume the power to create meanings even as one is created by them. When this happens in the context of the classroom, within historically overdetermined and ideologically inflected institutions such as schools, and in the face of preferred ways of reading culture and history, Freire invites individuals to read the word and the world symptomatically, to give a language and voice to those discourses and social practices, surreptitiously shaping them, and to name the unnameable as they struggle to reintroduce agency and consequence into history. While it is important to recognize that Freire's work does not adhere to a language of freedom that exists outside of human engagement and struggle, it is also important to understand that it nevertheless speaks to an unequivocal and sovereign concern: common, human suffering that must be alleviated and transformed. Whereas the ludic postmodern theorist seeks to deconstruct the semantic space of discourse itself, Freire seeks to unravel the concrete syntax of oppression and transform resistance to material and spiritual suffering into a revolutionary praxis dedicated to the establishment of a discourse of liberation and freedom.

If the sociology of knowledge originated by Karl Mannheim has taught us anything, it is that all theoretical assertions and conclusions are invariably and necessarily shaded by the evaluative preconceptions of the theorist. If values do indeed motivate particular types of research and govern the formulation of theory, then it becomes essential to ask of any social theory or body of research: what is the political project that informs it? What way of life does this theoretical discourse speak to? Freire's project has been and continues to be clear and unambiguous: a life-long engagement in the battle for emancipation and freedom.

Whereas ludic strands of postmodern theory are overwhelmingly conceptual, Freire's struggle is both conceptually oriented and politically motivated. Like Foucault, Freire attempts to illuminate the social and political practices within specific texts. He is less concerned with understanding codes and significations for their own sake; that is, in isolation from their socio-political engagement by social actors. Freire is well aware of the power and peril of discourse, yet he nevertheless understands that discourse alone – that is, in isolation from the social contexts and practices that both construct and 'carry' it – cannot usher in revolutionary change.

While Freire's project has no guarantee of historical possibility, this does not affect the ground of his commitment, which is a preferential option for the oppressed. This commitment is echoed in the words of feminist theologian Sharon D. Welch, who writes:

> Liberation faith is conversion to the other, the resistance to oppression, the attempt to live as though the lives of others matter ... To honestly live and believe as universal the imperative of love and freedom is to hope that suffering can be ended, to hope that all lives without liberation in history were not meaningless, but it is to work for this hope without the guarantee that such meaning is possible.
>
> (1985: 87)

Welch captures the essence of Freire's liberating pedagogy when she speaks of truth as 'conversation' rather than 'reflection of essence'. True liberation, according to Welch, requires that definitions ascertained through one's own experiences of liberation need to be brought into dialogue with other interpretations, without assuming that the dialogue is to be one-sided or rhetorically manipulative.

RESISTANCE POSTMODERNISM AND CRITICAL UTOPIANISM

I want to make clear that my discussion of postmodern social theory is not meant to imply that there exists one unitary postmodern approach to social theory. I am not attempting to dismiss the multiple postmodernist perspectives currently in use. Rather, I am attempting to criticize the ludic variety of postmoderism since it is in my opinion the most politically debilitating. I am encouraging a postmodernist social theory informed by a materialist politics. It is my belief that Freire's work – which stands at the borderline of modernist and postmodernist discourse – can be used as a touchstone for a postmodern materialist politics that is concerned with cultural power as much as cultural politics and aleatory plays of power, and with a logic of necessity as well as a logic of contingency and a critique of the totality of regimes of exploitation in its various guises (race, gender, class, sexual orientation) out of which differences are produced (Ebert, in press).

Freire's work bears a closer affinity to Seyla Benhabib's (1992) position of 'interactive universalism' than to the 'ludic' postmodernist position on ethics, accountability, and social agency. For instance, Freire's work employs a contingently interactive foundationalism that does not dismiss the concrete other as in the case of substitutionalist universalism, and in so doing it acknowledges that every generalized other is also a concrete other (Benhabib 1992: 165).

Freire's work is also based on a commitment to social transformation and justice grounded not simply in the ethics of local narratives (*les petits récits*), everyday social practices or language games that possess their own criteria of legitimization and criticism but rather in assessing the methodological assumptions that guide one's choice of liberating narratives. This is not an act of transcendent criticism, but one that takes into account global forms of oppression, and macro as well as micro analysis.

Freire's concrete utopia can be further revived and deepened by bringing his utopian imagination into conversation with what Teresa Ebert and others have described as 'resistance postmodernism' and what Tom Moylan refers to as 'critical utopianism'.

The kind of postmodern social theory I want to pose as a counter-weight to ludic postmodernism (also known as skeptical and spectral postmodernism) has been referred to as 'oppositional postmodernism' (Foster 1983), 'radical critque-al theory' (Zavarzadeh and Morton 1991), 'postmodern education' (Aronowitz and Giroux 1991), 'resistance postmodernism' (Ebert, forthcoming, 1991a, 1991b), and 'critical post-modernism' (McLaren 1993; Giroux 1992; McLaren and Hammer 1989).

Teresa Ebert (1991b) has proposed a transformative politics based on what she calls a *resistance postmodernism* as a way of forcefully contesting ludic postmodernism. Ebert has described the latter approach as a 'cognitivism and an immanent critique that reduces politics to rhetoric and history to textuality and in the end cannot provide the basis for a transformative social practice' (ibid.: 293). Whether a form of poststructuralism, the 'pastiche' of styles, or the deconstruction of modernist genres, 'ludic postmodernism removes the ground from under both the revolutionary and the reactionary and in the name of difference effectively conceals radical difference' (ibid.). In effect, ludic postmodernism ethicizes politics and criticizes and destabilizes dominant systems of representation through revealing the fragmentary and disruptive play of signifiers in the construction of social life. Yet while it helps to 'clarify the issues from the perspective of representation' (ibid.) and to 'effectively denaturalize and destabilize the dominant regime of knowledge and the naturalization of the status quo [within the logic of] common sense' (ibid.), it fails overwhelmingly to articulate an historical, political differance, or a materialized, resisting differance.

Ebert challenges the ludic notion of difference 'as textuality, as a formal, rhetorical space in which representation narrates its own trajectory of signification' (p. 293) and argues instead that difference is fundamentally social and historical. For instance, a ludic postmodernism criticizes the binary oppositions of logocentric or phallogocentric discourse and, rather than reversing the hierarchy which privileges, for instance, white over black, or male over female, it effectively dehierarchizes or displaces these oppositions altogether by revealing that the binary other is always its suppressed supplement. But a resistance postmodernism goes further than this by demanding that the power relations that are part of such hierarchical arrangements be politically challenged. In other words, differance is situated in social conflict and social struggle. Whereas ludic postmodernism destabilizes meaning by revealing the continuous dissemination of differences within the process of signification and exposing the undecidability of the signified and the non-representational character of language (in that language consists of a system of differences among signifiers), resistance postmodernism locates the sign in the materiality of social struggle. The sign does not float in some panhistorical space 'of eternal ahistorical slippage and excess' (ibid.: 293), but is 'decidable' in the concrete arena of social conflict (Zavarzadeh and Morton 1990: 156).

Resistance postmodernism is geared to understanding totalizing systems of power such as patriarchy and capitalism as well as global structural relations of domination and the systemacity of regimes of exploitation. In this way it redresses some of the shortcomings that result from the emphasis ludic postmodernism places on detotalizing, Foucauldian micropolitics (Ebert 1991). Ebert points out that difference is not adventitious or capricious but always linked to social contradictions. Difference is always *difference in relation*, while totality must be seen as an *overdetermined structure of difference*. This emphasis on totality enables educators, like Freire, to challenge systems of difference that are organized into concrete patterns of domination and subordination. It enables them to challenge directly the imperial logic of the corporate capitalist marketplace.

CRITICAL UTOPIANISM

Freire's stress on totality, like that of resistance postmodernism, does not preclude a strong role for human agency in developing forms of liberatory praxis. On the contrary, as Abdul R. JanMohamed (1993) notes, Freirean praxis essentially calls for a relationship of non-identity with one's social position or the creation of an antagonism with oneself. Further, such a praxis calls for the identification, tacitly or deliberately, with another nascent or fully formed position. JanMohamed writes that

> such a procedure simultaneously requires disidentification and identification: it demands a shift away from the deeply cathected inertia of fixed, sedimented identities and toward an engagement in the process of re-identification. It is therefore also a process of forming affiliations with other positions, of defining equivalences and constructing alliances. To the extent that non-identification is impossible without simultaneous alternate identification, such a process then becomes crucial for the possibility of forming counter-hegemonic organizations.
>
> (ibid.: 111)

Drawing on Giroux's analysis of Freire as a border intellectual, JanMohamed (1993) underscores Freire's insistence that subjects cross borders from the social into the political and transgress the prescribed boundaries of domestication in order to become heterotopic, specular, and transgressive border intellectuals. JanMohamed's discussion of the concept of crossing borders is instructive and fits within the scheme of resistance postmodernism discussed earlier. According to JanMohamed, the act of self-reflection entails the crossing of borders and the development of strong antagonisms. Examining the borders that confine them, subjugated groups 'in effect become archaeologists of the site of their own social formation' (1993: 113). As oppressed peoples begin the process of developing strong antagonisms and crossing borders, their new subject positions begin to cathect around the project of excavating and reading their own social and physical bodies, which are in fact texts of the history of their oppression. Thus their new subjectivity emerges in the process of drawing borders around their old subject positions, a process that constitutes them as nascent specular border intellectuals. Their contemplation of the condition of their lives represents a freedom, or at least an attempt to achieve freedom, from the politics of Imaginary identification and opposition, from conflation of identity and location, and so on – in short, from the varied and powerful forms of suturing that are represented by and instrumental in the construction of their sedimented culture. The process of decoding as well as the emerging command of literacy permits them a gradual shift from the confines of the Imaginary to the outer edges of the Symbolic realm.

(ibid.: 113–14)

Borders, claims JanMohamed, are never simply transgressed or passed over; rather, they are 'reactivated'. As 'digitalized boundaries', borders in principle do not determine the nature of social relations between the oppressors and the oppressed. As oppositional and not binary divisions, borders (defined as either analog or digital differentiations) distinguish between the interests of various groups rather than determine those interests. Consequently, when Freire advocates that oppressed groups understand themselves as the 'antithesis' of the dominant group, he is not simply reconstituting an Hegelian logic but rather, in JanMohamed's terms, is calling for a simultaneous transgression of one border and the establishment of another. In other words, disenfranchised groups 'cross the border of their sedimented social existence, and then introduce, or, more accurately, "reactivate" the border between themselves and the dominant group' (114) as they pass from semi-intransitive to naive transitive consciousness. As oppressed groups 'reactivate' the second boundary, they are changing their relation from passive subjects of history to active social agents of transformation. In other words, 'they are outlining broad differences and antagonisms between the utopian/heterotopian socio-political, economic, and cultural intentionalities of progressive forces and the opposed intentionalities of those who would prefer to confine the peasants to their disenfranchised, sedimented "culture of silence"' (114). However, antagonisms alone do not produce a praxis of liberation. Antagonisms must be accompanied by systematic forms of resistance through social movements and forms of counter-hegemonic struggle. Such a project demands both a 'radical optimism and a realistic caution' – in short, a critical utopianism.

Ernst Bloch (1986) is largely responsible for the current re-evaluation of the meaning of utopia in critical social theory. For Bloch, there exists the 'subjective possibility' of human consciousness and the 'real–objective possibility' which is latent in nature and the dialectic of history. Both these characteristics of the possible produce the creative tension between historical conditions and the utopian imagination. Both mind and matter figure prominently in Bloch's concept of utopia – what he calls 'subjective potency' and 'objective potency'. For Bloch, our collective dreams need to be translated into the material density of everyday struggle through a dialectical process and ontological unfolding in which 'what is' is constantly challenged in the light of what 'might be'.

In many ways, Freire's utopian imagination can be likened to Bloch's process of radical rupture, difference and opposition, in the sense that real, radical democracy is understood by Freire as something latent in the present, something immanently future-bearing that can be grasped in the flickering moment of consciousness. The utopian imagination drives forward the multiple levels of human desire while at the same time it is the result of an unconscious ontological pulling from the 'not-yet' of the still inarticulate future. The utopian imagination has, consequently, a subversive and emancipatory function. Unlike so many other critical social theorists, Freire and Bloch have not dispensed with the utopian impulse in the struggle toward a praxis of liberation; in fact, the utopian imagination and the concept of utopia serve as the centerpiece of their liberatory politics. By seizing from the totalized narratives of social life spaces of emancipatory possibility, both theorists have developed a counter-hegemonic project of creating an historic bloc of liberated collectives.

Tom Moylan's (1986) work has further developed Bloch's concept of utopia in his recent discussion of 'critical utopia'. For Moylan, a critical utopia is manifested in a micropolitics of autonomous social movements – but not the detotalizing micropolitics of ludic postmodernism. Rather, it consists of a political alliance *of the margins without a center* and is directed at creating new, radical, democratic values in both personal and political spheres. The old utopian periphery that so confidently demarcated and separated the past, present and future has been blurred. The utopian vision of change that was underpinned by the articulation of teleological master narratives of a centralized and universal movement toward a prefigured and historically realized state has been fundamentally challenged. With a critical utopia, absolute meaning and sovereign power are jettisoned in favor of the power of a metaphorical engagement with otherness and a displacement of the binary oppositions of current metaphysical thinking responsible for constructing the hegemonic utopias of the past and present. This has been done in order to 'create a yearning for what has not yet been achieved' (1986: 212).

Tom Moylan's (1986) description of 'critical utopia' both reflects and extends many of the characteristics of Freire's emancipatory praxis. Moylan defines critical utopias as 'metaphorical displacements arising out of current contradiction within the political unconscious' (ibid.: 213). Critical utopias are, first and foremost, self-critical, and their formation is designed to resist closure and an imposed totality by stressing 'the contradictory and diverse multiplicity of a broad utopian dialogue' (ibid.: 210). Moylan is worth quoting at length:

> The critical utopias give voice to an emerging radical perception and experience that emphasize process over system, autonomous and marginal activity over the

imposed order of a center, human liberation over white/phallocratic control, and the interrelationships of nature over human chauvinism – and they give voice to the seditious utopian impulse itself. The critical utopias still describe alternative societies, but they are careful to consider the flaws and insufficiencies of these systems. They still draw on the provocative mode of the fantastic, but they also mix in a realism that allows for fuller exploration of the activism required to move toward the better society. But beyond self-criticism at the symbolic level and generic discontinuities which help express the common ideologeme, these texts also call attention to their own formal operations in self-reflective gambits that identify the utopian form itself as a mechanism which makes such anticipations and activisms possible. The critical utopias refuse to be restricted by their own traditions, their own systematizing content; rather, it is their own radically hopeful activity as meaningful proto-political acts which they contribute to the current opposition.

(ibid.: 211)

Freire articulates the 'real–possible' conditions necessary for the utopian function to take root in the concrete materiality of daily struggle, not simply as a negative, denunciatory force that challenges existing systems of intelligibility and relations of power, but as a dehypostatizing project that refuses accommodation to the leadership of an elite vanguard of bourgeois intellectuals and decries the conflation of ideology and utopia. Freire's utopian vision does not speak to a categorical set of blueprints, tactics or strategies for human freedom, but instead remains attentive to the ideological dangers that follow from not challenging the discursive underpinnings of utopian projects that are premised on pre-specified contents and practices. In this way, Freire's pedagogic site is inherently heterotopic in that it can transform its institutional and social space into a counter-site through oppositional forms of agency (JanMohammed 1993).

Freire understands full well that a pedagogy of liberation has no final answers: radical praxis must always emerge from continuous struggle within specific pedagogical sites and among competing theoretical frameworks. Truth has no necessary closure, no transcendental justification. Even the god of history and the oppressed can offer no final solution since history is, for Freire, 'becoming' and is, furthermore, 'a human event' (Freire 1985a: 129).

Freire's ultimate utopian project constitutes a 'counter-discourse' through which contestation stages its struggle and attempts its subversion (Terdiman 1985: 338). And as such, Freire's work reveals the necessary contingency of forms of societal domination – forms which through collective struggle and the exercise of human will can eventually be liberated. In this sense, counter-discourse becomes our necessary hope, and our struggle over domination 'in which something more like authentic democracy might prevail' (Terdiman 1985: 343).

In an era of decentered subjects, in which the schizophrenic has become the 'true hero of desire' and the postmodern auratic symbol *par excellence*, Freire's unwavering and unperturbed focus on politics and empowerment grants critical pedagogy the much-needed respite to gather its critical resources and reshift its momentum away from the celebration of 'the paradoxical self-referentiality of its signifiers', and reaffirm its commitment to the elimination of human suffering and the emancipation of the oppressed. Freire offers a way to break out of the inertia and disciplined mobilizations of everyday life not simply through ideology critique alone but through the development of a critical utopianism that can make and remake what Larry Grossberg (1992: 394) calls 'affective relations' and investments and assist social agents to 'recenter the strategic politics of the social formation' (394).

Freire's refusal to forfeit his political project and language of possibility points to the promise of resisting and perhaps even transforming the current postmodern condition through a pedagogy that can be located at the border of modernist and postmodernist critique. As Andreas Huyssen puts it: 'A post- modernist culture . . . will have to be a postmodernism of resistance, including resistance to that easy postmodernism of the "anything goes" variety. Resistance will always have to be specific and contingent upon the cultural field within which it operates' (Huyssen 1984: 52). I have tried to make the case that resistance postmodernism can be considered an extension of Freire's own project.

Freire's kinship with resistance postmodernism resides in the fact that he is less concerned with the status and validity of epistemological methods for adjudicating the real and empirical than with the way in which existing social practices can be transformed. Freire's is a metaphilosophical move in that he does not look to Western philosophy or the self-appointed intellectual avant garde or their patron saints to resolve the binarisms of representation and reality. Instead, he concerns himself with concrete explanation rather than philosophical speculation. In other words, he is interested in the relation of knowledge and ethics to questions of power and social practices and how these often function to reproduce and legitimate existing economies of production and consumption, structures of intelligibility, social institutions and cultural politics. For Freire, as for Marx (see West 1991), these relationships too often reinforce traditional self-conceptions of citizenship which preclude ways of overcoming capitalist exploitation and oppression.[4]

Freire's work remains uncompromising in its call for revolutionary praxis and the elimination of human suffering. It captures the spirit of hope and the courage of one who remains engaged in an unwavering struggle against injustice. In this light, Freire's work could become, for contemporary social theorists, both a modernist reminder that people still suffer pain, oppression, and abandonment and a postmodernist strategy for destabilizing totalizing regimes of signification. As such, Freirean utopianism seeks to put flesh, bones, and human will back into social theory. It is a politics whose sensibility animates a responsibility to others, and it does so by not dispensing entirely with the concept of totality. Freire works from the metanarrative of liberation and human freedom without allowing such a narrative to become the imposed totality of a categorical utopia. He achieves this by interpreting his concept of liberation and human freedom pragmatically and by employing a pedagogy that is self-critical and that is meant to be reinvented by those groups who choose to practice it, so that the act of knowing is always situated in the context of the life-world concerns of those people who could most benefit from it. However, Freire is careful not to turn to lived experience as a postmodern mode of radical subjectivity or to situate identity outside of the mediations of discursive formations or of historical contexts. Lived experience, even when marshalled in the service of a politics of refusal, is not in itself unproblematic in the sense that its categories of race, class and gender are often determined by what dominant cultures have selectively provided. The text of experience needs diverse and critical readings of its own status as objectification and commodity. Freire's metanarrative does not, then, become a master narrative in the modernist sense of claiming universality, because Freire is not using his pedagogy of liberation as a way of testing arguments for their truth value, but rather is asking whether his provisional and situated pedagogy based on a narrative of liberation can help to stimulate the associative energies and practices of oppressed groups. Certainly Freire stresses universal goals, such as human rights and self-determination, but he does so in the knowledge that such rights and determinations are always provisional, contextual, and the result of a material struggle over meaning and that they should not be situated transcendentally within a project of liberation but engaged in their historical specificity. One could perhaps invoke on behalf of Freire the term 'contingent universalities' (see Butler 1992). Freire's pedagogy is designed to offer a reasonable and practical context for rebuilding democracy and for living and struggling for a qualitatively better life for the oppressed, the non-oppressed, and generations to follow. His pedagogy poses the postmodern challenge of finding new ways of facing up to our own frailty and infinitude as global citizens while at the same time searching for the strength of will and loyalty to hope that will enable us to continue dreaming of utopia.

As we search for a politics of liberation outside of the modernist constraints of consensus and epistemological certainty, for a politics inclusive of the multiple experiences and voices of groups oppressed within and outside of the developed world, Freire's work can continue to be instructive. Especially at this historical juncture in which we are witnessing a political factionalization of the left amidst a conservative restoration, one in which the legitimacy of one's identity papers must be established in advance. Freire's ideas can help to produce the constitution of possibility as a precondition for new forms of historical agency.

Here I would follow Judith Butler (1992) in claiming that since there is no 'ontologically intact reflexivity to the subject' (p. 12), we need to question the conditions of possibility for creating subjects capable of struggling against multiple forms of race, class, and gender domination. Chantal Mouffe (1992) has charted out the beginnings of a liberation politics that moves beyond the current enchantment with interest group pluralism. In her discussion of the importance of establishing a radical democratic citizenship, Mouffe argues that what is crucially needed at this present moment is 'a common political identity that would create the conditions for the establishment of a new hegemony articulated through new egalitarian social relations, practices, and institutions' (p. 380). Such a position would enable new forms of liberation struggle against multiple forms of oppression while at the same time facilitating the disarticulation of essentialist identities of oppressed groups. It is to these new articulatory practices that Freire's work holds out its promise of possibility in these 'new' times.

The politics and pedagogy of Paulo Freire constitute the voice of a great teacher who has managed to replace the melancholic and despairing discourse of the ludic postmodern left with possibility and human compassion and to instill a passion for freedom. Unlike those who dismiss critical pedagogy and liberatory politics as simply a 'repressive myth', Freire's pedagogy remains rooted in the faith and dreams of those who long for freedom and justice. This moves us beyond the futility of self-fashioning through the act of will alone and into the realm of transforming the regimes of discourse that hold us captive. The transformative praxis that informs Freire's work will undoubtedly play an increasing role in developing the moral conscience of social theorists, teachers, and cultural workers of the future. Whether or not they heed such a conscience will undoubtedly influence the next decade of social and educational theory and the practices of the self and the social that will follow in their wake.

NOTES

This chapter is a revised version of an essay that appeared as Peter McLaren (1986) 'Postmodernity and the death of politics: A Brazilian reprieve', *Educational Theory* 36, 4, 389–401. Some sections have drawn from Henry A. Giroux and Peter McLaren (in press), 'Paulo Freire, postmodernism and the utopian imagination: a Blochian reading', in T. Moylan and J. Owen Daniel, eds, *Bloch in our Time*, London and New York: Verso.

1 While I agree with Hal Foster (1983) that there exists an oppositional postmodernism, I would argue that it is an opposition couched in a language of critique, devoid of utopian possibilities. My critique of postmodernism is directed mainly against what Foster refers to as the reactionary postmodernism of the neo-conservatives and not explicitly against the postmodernism of resistance. The former calls for a return to the verities of tradition, while the latter refers to a deconstruction of tradition and dominant regimes of power. But even the postmodernism of resistance fails to incorporate a language of possibility or the capacity for utopian thinking. It is one thing to deconstruct representations, it is quite another to reinscribe them in a language that takes seriously the discourse of democracy and emancipation. However, in recent years the works of Donald Morton, Mas'ud Zavarzadeh, Teresa Ebert, Henry Giroux, and Stanley Aronowitz have significantly contributed to developing a resistance postmodernism.

2 Freire's concept of pedagogy and culture is not entirely unproblematic, and Freire's work has certainly been criticized on a number of accounts. Not surprisingly, many of the arguments used to criticize Freire's work have had strong cultural-conservative instincts. C.A. Bowers's review of the *The Politics of Education* (1986) is a case in point. In his review, Bowers attacks Freire for contributing to the reproduction of basic root metaphors or epistemes embedded in Western thinking, especially around the issues of individualism, critical reflection, and the progressive nature of change. Bowers's critique is not new, and he appears to have used his review as a pretext for discussing his own previous criticisms of Freire, as well as for resurrecting his tired and

worn (and conceptually misguided) criticisms of Giroux. Bowers's critique of Freire is informed by an understanding of Enlightenment rationality which lacks the benefit of being dialectical. To suggest that Freire's work celebrates an uncritical endorsement of Enlightenment rationality sets up a false dichotomy around Freire's work that places individual judgement against communal wisdom, agency over collective action, and a nihilistic relativization of values over the time-tested truth of tradition. Furthermore, to claim that Freire possesses an oversimplified understanding of tradition, collective action, or the cultural assumptions inherent in his own pedagogy is to discredit the very strengths of Freire's pedagogy.

Certainly we are 'positioned' as readers by language, as discourse theorists and thinkers such as Barthes, Bakhtin (Vološinov), Lacan, and Kristeva have taught us. But to criticize Freire for not deconstructing the text of his own pedagogy around this issue by engaging the ideas of Ong, Shils, Nietzsche, Heidegger, Vygotsky, Foucault, and others is to suggest that Freire remains unaware of the relationship between language and power. I would argue that Freire's position on language, culture, and power is as perceptive as that of Foucault.

3 Freire's position on the role of literacy training, consciousness raising, and the prophetic church shares similarities with numerous liberation theologians. See Segundo (1980), Gutierrez (1973, 1983). Brazilian theologian Leonardo Boff (1985) discusses Freire in relation to liberation theology. Freire's celebration of the prophetic church also shares much in common with the political theology of Johannes Baptist Metz. (See Metz (1980.) In the case of political theology, theological reflection attempts to turn critical reasoning into practical action.

The current Vatican position on liberation theology is confusing, to say the least. On the one hand we have witnessed the Latin American Bishops' Conference meeting at Medellin, Colombia, in 1968, and at Puebla, Mexico, in 1979, where Christians were called to a radical commitment in the struggle for social justice. This new orientation of Catholic social teaching, often termed the 'preferential option for the poor', was given amplification in John Paul II's encyclical, *Laborem Exercens*, with the qualification that liberation was to be understood in more than purely economic and political terms. On the other hand, there are the actions of the Roman Congregation of the Doctrine of Faith (the former Holy Office) against Gutierrez and Boff, and the 1984 Instruction of the Holy Office, which warns Catholics of the Marxist threat within liberation theology.

It is significant here to remark that Bishop José Iro Lorscheiter, president of the Brazilian Conference of Bishops, recently offered a dramatic defense of liberation theology at the Extraordinary Synod of Bishops in Rome, 1985, one which 'ranks as one of the most challenging statements made publicly to the Vatican by a high-ranking defender of liberation theology' (Pasca 1986: 115). Such a recent statement of support surely attests to the continuing desire among many Third World Catholics for the form of empowerment which Freire links to the role of the prophetic church.

4 Cornel West (1991) makes a similar argument with respect to Marx's metaphilosophical move. I have applied West's arguments to Freire's position.

REFERENCES

Adamson, W. (1985) *Marx and the Disillusionment of Marxism*, Berkeley: University of California Press.

Agamben, G. (1993) *The Coming Community*, Minneapolis: University of Minnesota Press.

Aronowitz, S. (1985) 'Technology and culture', *Canadian Journal of Political and Social Theory* 9, 3, 126–33.

Aronowitz, S. and Giroux, H.A. (1985) *Education Under Siege*, South Hadley, MA: Bergin and Garvey.

—— (1991) *Postmodern Education*, Minneapolis: University of Minnesota Press.

Benhabib, S. (1992) *Situating the Self: Gender, Community and Postmodernism in Contemporary Ethics*, London and New York: Routledge.

Bernstein, R.J. (1985) 'Dewey, democracy: the task ahead of us', in J. Rajchman and C. West, eds, *Post-Analytic Philosophy*, New York: Columbia University Press.

Bloch, E. (1986) *The Principle of Hope*, 3 vols (Neville Stephen Plaice and Paul Knight, trans.), Cambridge, MA: MIT Press.

Boff, L. (1985) *Church: Charisma and Power*, New York: Crossroads.

Bowers, C.A. (1986) 'Review article – "Education Under Siege" by Stanley Aronowitz and Henry A. Giroux', *Educational Studies* 17, 1, 147–59.

Butler, J. (1992) 'Contingent foundations: feminism and the question of "postmodernism"', in J. Butler and J.W. Scott, eds, *Feminists Theorize the Political*, London and New York: Routledge.

Eagleton, T. (1983) *Literary Theory*, Minneapolis: University of Minnesota Press.

Ebert, T. (1991a) 'Political semiosis in/of American cultural studies', *The American Journal of Semiotics* 8, 1/2, 113–35.

—— (1991b) 'Writing in the political: resistance (post) modernism', *Legal Studies Forum* XV, 4, 291–303.

—— (in press) 'Ludic feminism, the body, performance and labor: bringing materialism back into feminist cultural studies', *Cultural Critique*.

Foster, H. (ed.) (1983) *The Anti-Aesthetic: Essays on Postmodern Culture*, Port Townsend, WA: Bay Press.

Freire, P. (1985a) *The Politics of Education: Culture, Power, and Liberation*, South Hadley, MA: Bergin and Garvey.

—— (1985b) 'Reading the world and reading the word: an interview with Paulo Freire', *Language Arts* 62, 1, 15–21.

Giddens, A. (1984) *The Constitution of Society*, Berkeley and Los Angeles: University of California Press.

Giroux, H.A. (1985) 'Introduction' in *The Politics of Education: Culture, Power and Liberation*, South Hadley, MA: Bergin and Garvey.

—— (1992) *Border Crossings: Cultural Workers and the Politics of Education*, New York and London: Routledge.

Grossberg, L. (1992) *We Gotta Get Out of This Place: Popular Conservatism and Postmodern Culture*, New York and London: Routledge.

Gutierrez, G. (1973) *A Theology of Liberation*, New York: Orbis.

—— (1983) *The Power of the Poor in History*, New York: Orbis.

Habermas, J. (1985) 'A philosophico-political profile', *New Left Review* 151, 75–105.

Huyssen, A. (1984) 'Mapping the postmodern', *New German Critique* 33, 5–52.

JanMohammed, A.R. (1993) 'Some implications of Paulo Freire's border pedagogy', *Cultural Studies* 7, 1, 107–17.

Lears, T.J.J. (1985) 'The concept of cultural hegemony: problems and possibilities', *American Historical Review* 90, 3, 567–93.

Lyotard, J.-F. (1984) *The Postmodern Condition: A Report on Knowledge* (G. Bennington and B. Massouri, trans.), Minneapolis: University of Minnesota Press.

McLaren, P. (1993) 'Multiculturalism and the postmodern critique: towards a pedagogy of resistance and transformation', *Cultural Studies* 7, 1, 118–46.

McLaren, P. and Hammer, R. (1989) 'Critical pedagogy and the postmodern challenge', *Educational Foundations* 3, 3, 29–62.

McLaren, P. and Leonard, P. (eds) (1993) *Paulo Freire: A Critical Encounter*, London and New York: Routledge.

Metz, J.B. (1980) *Faith in History and Society* (D. Smith, trans.), New York: Seabury Press.

Mouffe, C. (1992) 'Feminism, citizenship and radical democratic politics', in J. Butler and J.W. Scott, eds, *Feminists Theorize the Political*, London and New York: Routledge.

Moylan, T. (1986) *Demand the Impossible: Science Fiction and the Utopian Imagination*, London and New York: Methuen.

Pasca, T.M. (1986) 'The three churches of Catholicism', *The Nation*, 1 February.

Said, E. (1982) 'Opponents, audiences, constituencies, and community', *Critical Inquiry* 9, 1, 1–26.

Segundo, J.L. (1980) *Our Idea of God*, Dublin: Gill and Macmillan.

Tager, F. (1982) 'The relation between politics and culture in the teaching of working class students', *Curriculum Inquiry* 12, 2, 209–19.

Terdiman, R. (1985) *Discourse/Counter-Discourse*, Ithaca, NY: Cornell University Press.

Welch, S.D. (1985) *Communities of Resistance and Solidarity: A Feminist Theology of Liberation*, New York: Orbis.

West, C. (1991) *The Ethical Dimensions of Marxist Thought*, New York: Monthly Review Press.

Williams, R. (1980) *Problems in Materialism and Culture*, London: Verso Editions and New Left Books.

Zavarzadeh, M. and Morton, D. (1990) 'Signs of knowledge in the contemporary academy', *American Journal of Semiotics* 7, 4, 149–60.

Afterword

Joe L. Kincheloe

What an interesting development this volume heralds. Radical pedagogy and social theory can no longer be contemplated outside the parameters of postmodernism. Indeed, even our most revered proponent of critical pedagogy must be reconsidered in light of the *Zeitgeist* of the New Times. Moving postmodernism beyond the text to gritty reality – while pushing Freire into the fray of textual analysis – the authors here initiate the quintessentially critical project of deconstructing the classic texts (the canon?) of liberatory pedagogy. Allan Bloom can take posthumous comfort in the realization that the arrows of deconstructionism were not reserved for only the Western tradition. If a barometer of democracy involves the degree of self-reflection it allows, then the critical educational tradition must be flourishing.

Contrary to our fear that postmodernism in its ludic guise would negate the emancipatory project, would extinguish the passion of Freire's radical love, the poststructural analysis of McLaren and Lankshear and the authors assure us that the critical project will be fortified through its encounter with recent innovations in social theory. Emancipation can never be addressed as innocently as it once was: we must now hesitate and maybe exchange a furtive glance before invoking the word. The postmodern emancipatory discourse forces us to think about our positionality, our place, in the multi-dimensional web of reality. We can no longer employ the word without a consciousness of who has used it in the past and who they 'used it on'. Because of feminism and the 'post- discourses' we are more conscious, more critically aware of power relations and the construction of the subject – both central features of the way, at least, I read the historical purposes of the critical tradition. Indeed, instead of sabotaging the praxiological quest, the new discourses have produced a critical synergism that extends the human vocation of becoming more fully human.

Refusing to deify Freire and in the process destroy the living vibrancy of his work, the authors take seriously his call to become more fully human and thus critique him in light of what they have learned in the last couple of decades. This book is a testament to Freire's critical pedagogy – it is an example of what happens when students are empowered. As many of us have witnessed in those times we are successful in our own teaching, our students go beyond us. Their deconstructions know no limits as they apply their semiotics to us, our own teaching, our comfortable assumptions, and even the power dimensions of our relationships with them. Such actions represent our highest form of affection – indeed, they are expressions of a radical love.

As our wake-up call from the Third World, Freire's work continues to hold the possibility of new readings depending on the spatial and temporal positioning of the reader. Over two decades ago Freire helped us name the intuitions we had developed concerning the inadequacy of traditional pedagogies. As we came to understand the concept of 'banking education', we began to analyze the nature of the deposits we had stored in our own mental vaults. Empowered by our new metaphors we began our teaching careers in search of generative themes and emancipatory moments in the lived worlds of our students. In the 1990s our reading of Freire provides an ethical bass line to our postmodern improvisations revolving around the escape from modernity. In a cosmos full of decentered subjects, hypertexts, crumbling foundationalism, and revolts against totality, Freire will not let us forget the children of the damned, the victims of the culture of silence. It is through the kaleidoscope eyes of these victims that we formulate a critical (post-) epistemology for a radical pedagogy, that we ethically ground a postmodern education.

While the destabilization of meaning is an important feature of any postmodernism, a more critical postmodernism draws upon the Freirean notion of power relations as it analyzes the sign. Along with feminism, Freire's work provides a sharp political edge to postmodern analysis. Here again we find evidence of the synergism formed by the intersection of Freirean ethics and postmodernism. Constantly self-reflective, this critical synergism opens new ways of knowing, new modes of inquiry which expose the insidious ways that oppression operates. As class, race, and gender forms of oppression mutate in the fallout of postmodern hyper-reality, these synergized modes of inquiry become essential devices in our efforts to expose the new forms of subjugation. In a world that is blind to the political but hypersensitive to the cultural, inhabitants of the postmodern West cannot understand or be understood via traditional forms of critical analysis. For this and many other reasons, we must move on. If we cannot travel with Freire, we will certainly keep a copy of *Pedagogy of the Oppressed* or *The Politics of Education* in our luggage.

The editors and the authors have called for the reinvention of revolutionary praxis. In a time when the power of the United States is unchallenged, such a reinvention becomes particularly important. Even when *Pedagogy of the Oppressed* was written, the tendency to ignore the suffering of the subjugated was not as great as it is in the 1990s. The proponents of this reinvented praxis have the responsibility for engaging teachers and other cultural workers in the critical task. By no means will this be easy. For a plethora of reasons – the success of right-wing forms of cultural co-option being only one among them – educators are blinded to the urgency of the project. Is it possible to translate the complexity and ambiguity of this reinvented praxis into a public awareness of the insidious nature of postmodern oppression? There is evidence of the disintegration of the precarious right-wing coalition of the Reagan–Bush era. We must draw upon Freire's passion and the power of the reinvented praxis to take advantage of this long-awaited opportunity.

Name index

Abelenda, Fr S. 166
Adams III, H.H. 75, 90
Adamson, W. 196
Agamben, G. 201
Allende, Salvador 8
Allman, P. 72
Amin, S. 157
Anderson, S.E. 80, 89
Apel, K.-O. 187–8
Apple, M. 59
Arbens, J. 126
Aronowitz, S. xiv, xviii, 59, 195, 197–9,
    205
Ascher, M. 77
Ascher, R. 77

Bacon, Francis 68
Barthes, R. 7, 197
Baudrillard, J. 135, 196
Bauman, Z. 174
Beaty, J. xiv
Bell, Daniel 2
Benhabib, S. 204
Berlak, A. 14
Berman, M. 3
Bermudez, F. 49, 57
Bernal, M. 89
Bernstein, R. 196
Betto, Frei xiv, 123
Biko, Steve 93
Bimbi, L. xiv
Bishop, A.J. 85
Bloch, E. 207–8
Bloom, A. 216
Boggs, C. 109
Borba, M.C. 79
Boxer, M. 22
Bourdieu, P. 156, 170

Brady, Jeanne 10, 142–53
Brandao, C.R. 100
Braungart, R.G. 110
Bredo, E. 75
Britzman, D. 12, 14
Brown, C. 76, 100
Brunt, R. 146
Buber, M. 175
Bunch, C. 26
Butler, J. 211

Camara, Msgr Hélder 155
Cameron, D. 112–13
Carmichael, Stokely 21
Carraher, D.W. 85
Carraher, T.N. 85
Cauchy, A.L. 87
CEDI 102
Cerda, A. 126
Cerezo, V. 42, 55
Cherryholmes, C. 12
Collins, D. 55
Coraggio, J.L. 54
Cortázar, J. 164
Cortella, M.S. 102
Crick, B. 62–3
Culley, M. 13, 24
Cunha, L.A. 102
Cunningham, F. 112, 115, 117
Cunningham, J. 70

D'Ambrosio, U. 77–80, 82
da Silva, L.I.L. 101
Davis, B. 24
de Alba, Alicia 10, 123–41
de Ataíde, T. 167
de Chardin, T. 175
de Chungara, D.B. 120

de la Garza, T. 131–2
de Lauretis, T. 13
Deleuze, G. 197
de Lima Pe Vaz, H. 175
de Melo, F.C. 101
Deprew, P.J. 187
Derrida, J. 196
Descartes, R. 184
Dewey, J. 66, 100, 171, 196
Dewey, John 100, 171
Dewey, T. 196
Dilthey, W. 173, 182
Diop, C.A. 75, 89
Dirac, P.A.M. 79
Dostoevsky, F.M. 182
Drache, D. 112–13
Dussel, E. 48–9, 57–8
Dyson, J. 70–1

Eagleton, T. 196
Ebert, T. 204–6
Echeverria, E. 42–5, 50, 53, 56, 58
Ellsworth, E. 14
Ermarth, M. 182
Esquivel, A.P. 54, 59
Euclid 89

Fanon, F. 155
Fasheh, M. 75, 80
Feinberg, W. 75
Ferrer y Guardia, F. 171
Findlay, Peter 9, 108–22
Fisher, B. 22, 25–6, 28–9
Flax, J. 32
Fonseca, C. 125
Ford-Smith, H. 31
Foster, H. 205
Foucault, M. 29, 50, 54, 197, 203
Frankenstein, Marilyn 9, 74–99
Friedman, S. 24, 25
Freire, Paulo xiii–xiv, xvi–xviii, 216–18;
    actions and political skills 66–8;
    'being' and 'time' in philosophy of
    175–81; British encounter with 62–73;
    and Crick 62–3; critical pedagogy
    143–5; critical thinking 41, 143; on
    conscientization 117–21; on conscious
    partiality 56–8; education for critical
    consciousness 50–3; and educational
    challenges 134–6; on educational
    theory 123–41; epistemology of 75–6;
    and ethnomathematics 74, 80–90;
    feminist critique of thought 145–9; on
    hegemony and neutrality 55; and
    hermeneutics 173–92; on issues 65;
    and liberation 154–72; and moral
    imagination 46–8; and new movements
    69–71; North American critical
    thinking, challenge to 53; and
    oppression 1–11 passim; pedagogical
    roots 124–7; pedagogy of 13–19,
    127–34, 143; and postmodernism
    193–215; primacy of the political
    198–201; and Torres 100–7;
    utopianism of 201–4, 206–12
Furter, P. 100
Fuss, D. 30

Gadamer, H.-G. 10, 173–5, 184–8, 196
Gadotti, M. xiv, 100–1
Galeano, E. 128
Gasset, Ortega y xvii
Gattegno, C. 85
Gerdes, P. 87
Germain, S. 89
Giddens, A. 174, 195
Gillings, R.J. 83
Giroux, H. xv, 59; on border pedagogy
    171; on critical literacy 145, 149–50;
    on domination 118; epistemology of
    Freire 75; and feminist pedagogy 12,
    35, 145; on politics 199–200; on
    radical pedagogy 197–200; on utopia
    201, 205–6
Glick, J. 83
González Gaudiana, Edgar 10, 123–41
Gordon, L. 19
Gordon, M. 80–1
Goudvis, P. 46, 54
Goulart, J. 166
Graff, H. 143
Gramsci, A. 13, 55, 120, 136, 136, 137
Grant, D. 72
Grossberg, L. 210
Guattari, F. 197

Habermas, J. 1, 187–8, 194
Hall, Stuart 2–3, 6, 7
Hammer, R. 205
Haraway, D. 32
Harris, M. 82, 89
Harvey, F. 90
Haug, F. 30–1, 35
Hawley, N. 20

Hegel, G.W.F. 182
Heidegger, M. 173, 175, 182–5, 187
Henderson, D.W. 90
Henriot, SJ P. 55
Hernon, D. 55
Hesse, M. 174
Hinkelammert, F. 47
Hinton, W. 21
Hirsch, E.D. Jr 71
Holland, J. 55
hooks, b. 24, 146
Howe, F. 22
Husserl, E. 176, 182–3
Huyssen, A. 210

Illich, I. 62, 68
Ingenieros, J. 124

Jackson, Jesse 109
Jameson, F. 135
JanMohamed, A. 145, 149–50, 206–7, 209
Jaspers, K. 175
Jeffries, D.A. 91
Johnson, D.K. 87
Joseph, G.C. 83, 88, 90

Kautsky, K. 124
Kierkegaard, S.A. 182
Kincheloe, J. 1–11, 216–18
Kintz, L. 146
Kisiel, T. 183, 185
Kline, M. 88
Knijnik, G. 91
Kosik, K. 128, 189
Kuhn, T. 174

Lacan, F. 196
Laclau, E. 158, 164, 168
Lange, B. 92
Lange, J. 92
Langille, D. 113–14
Lankshear, Colin 3, 10, 173–92, 216
Lauter, P. 22
Lave, J. 75, 86, 92
Láinez, Sen M. 160
Lears, T.J.J. 195–6
Lefebvre, H. 196
Leonard, P. 145, 198
Levett, A. 3
Lipman, M. 41–2, 44, 50
Lister, Ian 9, 62–73, 70
Lorde, A. 14, 28–9, 30

Lovett, T. 72
López, J.A. 91
Luke, A. 3
Lumpkin, B. 88–9
Lyotard, J.-F. 194

Macedo, D. xiii–xviii, 100–1, 143
Machel, S. 92–3
McCarthy, C. 16
Mackie, R. 81, 175
McLaren, Peter 6, 8, 10, 216; on critical pedagogy 144–5; on feminism 148; on Freire 120, 133, 146; on liberation 154; on pedagogy of Freire 18; on postmodernism 150, 193–215; on ritual 163
Macquarrie, J. 182
Majka, L.C. 110
Majka, T.J. 110
Malcolm X 21
Maldonaldo, F.M. 42
Malone, B. 55
Mann, Horace 160
Mannheim, K. 203
Mao Tsetung 21
Marcel, G. 167, 175
Mariategui, J.C. 124–6
Maritain, J. 167
Marshack, A. 89
Martin, B. 34, 35, 86, 88
Martin, D. 119
Martí, F. 124–5
Marx, K. 1, 87, 178, 187
Megill, A. 7
Mehlinger, H. 69
Mejía, J.M.R. 160
Mella, J.A. 124–5
Mendes, C. 129
Menem, Saúl 165
Micheli, J. 129
Milner, H. 110
Mitchell, J. 34
Mohanty, C. 34, 35
Morton, D. 205–6
Mouffe, C. 211
Mournier, E. 167
Moyana, Dr T.T. 120
Moylan, T. 205, 208
Mtetwa, D. 79

Navarro, V. 109
Neill, A.S. 171

Nietzsche, F.W. 182
Nteta, C. 93

Omolade, B. 33
Osen, L.M. 89
Outhwaite, W. 174

Passeron, J.-C. 156–7
Perelia, O. 101
Perón, Juan 163
Peslikis, I. 22
Peters, Michael 10, 173–92
Pietri, U. 124
Pinochet, General A. 8
Pinxten, R. 90
Ponce, A. 124–5
Porter, A. 64
Portuges, C. 13, 24
Powell, A.B. 9, 74–99, 87, 91
Ptolemy 89
Puiggrós, Adriana 10; on Freire's roots
    124, 126, 133–4; on liberation 154–72
Puiggrós, Rudolpho 154
Puiggrós, Sergio 154
Puchalska, E. 82

Rabinow, P. 174
Ramnauth, M. 91
Reagon, B. 35
Rega, Lopez 154
Rich, A. 30, 32
Richter, R. 46, 54
Rickert, H. 182
Ricoeur, P. 173, 196
Rivage-Seul, Marguerite 9, 41–61
Rivage-Seul, Michael 9, 41–61
Rodríguez, S. 124, 171
Rogers, C. 70
Rorty, R. 174
Rose, E. 21
Rose, M. 83
Rosenblum, S. 110
Rothschild-Whitt, R. 110
Russell, M. 21, 33, 35

Said, E.W. 198
Sandino, A.C. 124–5
Sarachild, K. 20–2, 30
Sarmiento, D.F. 160
Sartre, J.P. 175

Schleiermacher, F. 173, 182, 184
Schliemann, A.D. 85
Schniedewind, N. 19
Scribner, S. 86
Selby, A.E. 91
Semadeni, Z. 82
Shannon, P. 143
Shor, I. 15, 17, 100, 143–4
Simard, M. 116
Simon, J.-M. 49
Simon, R. 12
Sitton, N. 129
Smith, B. 35
Somoza, A. 127
Spivak, G.C. 17
Spradbery, J. 82
Stradling, R. 64
Struik, D.J. 89
Stygall, G. 144
Sullivan, W.M. 174

Tager, F. 199
Taylor, C. 173
Terdiman, R. 209
Thompson, A.G. 42–5, 50, 53, 56, 58
Torres, Carlos Alberto 9, 100–7
Torton Beck, E. 24
Touraine, A. 2

Vandenberg, D. 174
van Dooren, I. 90
Vargas, G. 158, 165
Vasconcelos, J. 124–5

Walkerdine, V. 83–4
Walton, C. 3
Webb, K. 67–8
Weedon, C. 31, 34
Weiler, Kathleen 9, 12–40, 57, 145–7
Weizenbaum, J. 90
Welch, S.D. 18, 204
West, C. 151
Williams, R. 197

Youngman, F. 81, 92
Yrigoyen, H. 162, 164
Yudice, G. 7

Zavarzadeh, M. 205–6
Zimmerman, M. 187

Subject index

activity-based teaching in political education 66–7
agriculture, and mathematical knowledge 89–90
Alexandria, and mathematical knowledge 88–9
Amnesty International 67
annunciation 15; of new reality 201
antagonisms, and crossing borders 207
anticipatory moral imagination 44
Argentina: centralized education in 162; educational reforms in 165–6; Freire in 165–6; Freire's influence in 159–60; Freire's pedagogy in 155; liberation pedagogy in 159; migration to 160–1; public education in 161–2; ritualization in education, Puiggrós on 163; school system in 160–1
authority: emancipatory, in feminist thought 148–9; in feminist pedagogy 23–6; and feminist pedagogy of place 148–9; in Freirean thought, feminist critique of 146–9; in *Pedagogy of the Oppressed* (Freire) 17–18; and teachers in Freirean thought 148–9

becoming: being as 177, 179; and consciousness, Freire on 179–80; as human event 209
being: as becoming 177, 179; Freire and Gadamer on 187; in Freire's philosophy 175–80; in hermeneutics 182–6
Being and Time (Heidegger) 183–4
black women *see* women of color
borders: crossing 206–7; defined 207
bourgeoisie, Latin American, Puiggrós on 158

Brazil: children's mathematics 85–6; Freire in 14, 50, 100, 143; public education, Puiggrós on 158–9, 165
Britain: national curriculum in 72; political education in 63; young's views of 72–3
British Programme for Political Education: achievements and limitations 68–9; criticisms of 68; and Freire 69–71; issue-based groups in 67–8; issues in 64–5; and modern citizenship 72–3; political skills in 66–8
Business Council on National Issues (BCNI, Canada) 113–14

Cabo verde 100
calendars 89
Canada: as binational society 110–11; conscientization and social movements in 108–22; post-socialist social movements 115–17; Pro-Canada Network 112–17; trade agreements with United States 110–11, 112
Canadian Centre for Policy Alternatives 116
Capital (Marx) 162
CEDI 102
Chile: Freire in 14, 50, 100, 143
Chilean Popular Front 126
Christianity, and Freire 14–15
citizenship, and political education 72–3
class: and ethnomathematics 78, 82–3; and Marxism in Latin America 167; and oppression, Freire on 14; and racism and sexism 109
class-neutral critical thinking 55–6
class struggle, in Freire's work 109–10, 143

codification of student experiences 51–2
collective memory work, of women 30–1
colonialist pedagogy, Puiggrós on 155, 158
Combahee River Collective 32–3
conceptual imagination 47
conscientização (critical perception of
    reality) 46, 50, 200
conscientization: Freire on 15; and
    knowledge, sources of 27; in *Pedagogy
    of the Oppressed* (Freire) 17; and
    political literacy 63–4, 200–1; in
    Pro-Canada Network 114; social
    movements and social change 117–21;
    and social movements in Canada
    108–22; and utopian praxis of Freire
    201–3
conscious partiality in education 56–8
consciousness: and becoming 179–80;
    Freire on 176; in postmodernism 194
consciousness raising: in feminist
    pedagogy 19–23; and political
    education 63
consciousness-raising groups: among
    women 20–3; and feelings 28, 30
Council of Canadians 115
creation and re-creation of knowledge
    75–6; in mathematics 81
critical consciousness: and becoming
    179–80; Freire's education for 50–3;
    and hermeneutics 189; and time 180–1
critical literacy 142; and Freirean thought,
    feminist critique of 146
critical pedagogy 216; and critical
    utopianism 209–10; extending 143–5
critical perception of reality
    (*conscientização*) 46, 50
critical thinking: American, challenges to
    53; class-neutral 55–6; dialogue focus
    in 52; evaluation in 52–3; and
    Guatemalan education 42; and moral
    imagination 44–8; social analysis in
    52; time in 181
critical understanding *see* critical
    perception of reality
critical utopianism 206–12; conditions
    necessary for 209; Moylan on 208–9;
    and resistance postmodernism 204–6
Cultural Action for Freedom 8
cultural colonialism, Puiggrós on 155, 158
cultural diversity: between educators and
    educatees 171; in Latin America 129
cultural literacy, and political education 71

culture: creation of 84–5; Freire's
    definition 200; interactions with
    mathematics 84–8; and mathematics
    78–80

Dasein 173; in hermeneutics 182–5
decision making and democracy 54–5
deconstruction 216–17; in postmodernism
    193–4; and radical pedagogy 197–8
dehumanization 15
democracy 53–8; and decision making
    54–5; formal 54; Freire's definition 53;
    in Guatemala 44–5; real 54; and social
    justice 55; US model of 53
democratic learning: dialogue focus in 52;
    evaluation in 52–3; as praxis 53; social
    analysis in 52
Democratization Observation Test (DOT)
    42–3, 50, 55
denunciation 15
dialectics, and mathematics 87
dialogue: between educators and
    educatees 171; Freire on 15; Gadamer
    on 188; and hermeneutics 175; and
    utopian praxis of Freire 201–2; and
    word in Freire's philosophy 178–9
dialogue focus in critical thinking 52
Dictionary of Cultural Literacy (Hirsch) 71
difference: among women 30–4; and
    authority in Freirean thought 147;
    between educators and educatees 171;
    in Freirean thought, feminist critique of
    146; in resistant postmodernism 206;
    and utopia 208
differential calculus, Marx on 87
discourse: and literacy, Puiggrós on 168;
    and utopian praxis of Freire 203–4
domination: and crossing borders 207; in
    pedagogical relationship, Freire on
    170; in pedagogy of Freire 143; and
    postmodern society 134–5; in social
    movements 118, 120; and utopian
    praxis of Freire 201–2, 206

East–West binarism of world politics
    135–6
economic power and political power 55–6
educatees: and cultural difference of
    educators 171; dialogue with educators
    180; as empty subject 170; roles, Freire
    on 169–70
education: after Péron (Argentina) 164–5;

as an activity 66; centralized, in Argentina 162; conscious partiality in 56–8; crisis in 134–6; for democracy in Guatemala 45–6; Freire on 104; and hermeneutics 173–92; Latin American, Puiggrós on 156; limitations of, Freire on 106; of native peoples in Mexico 130–1; Peronist control (Argentina) 163–4; and Philosophy for Children (P4C) in Guatemala 42–3; and politics, Freire on 102–6; and postmodernism 196–8; public, in Argentina 161–2; of refugees 131–2; reproduction theory in 170; and revolutionary struggle, Freire on 14; *see also* political education, schooling

Education, Liberation and the Creative Act (Moyana) 120

Education: the Practice of Freedom (Freire) 124, 135, 155, 168, 189

Education for Critical Consciousness (Freire) 100, 143

educators: and cultural difference of educatees 171; and dialogue with educatees 180; and educatees as empty subject 170; in postmodernism 197; roles, Freire on 169–70

Egyptian mathematics 77, 83, 88–9

elitism, and mathematical knowledge 83–4, 88

emotion, and political action 27–8

Enlightenment rationality 193–4

epistemology of Freire 75–6; and ethnomathematics 80–90

erotic, power of 29

ethnic minorities, in postmodern society 134–5

ethnocentrism of Western society 134–5

ethnomathematics: and culture, interactions between 84–8; and epistemology of Freire 80–90; and knowledge 77–80; and mathematical knowledge 90

Eurocentrism: in Latin American education 127; in mathematics 77, 83, 89

evaluation in critical thinking 52–3

exile, Freire as 102

existentialism in Freire's thinking 175, 178

existentiality in hermeneutics 183–4

Existenzphilosophie (Jaspers) 182

experience, as source of knowledge 27–30

facticity, in hermeneutics 183–4

Fanshen (Hinton) 21

feeling, as source of knowledge 27–30

feminism: and *Pedagogy of the Oppressed* (Freire) 16–19; and teachers, role of 23–6

feminist critique of Freirean thought 145–9; authority in 146–9

feminist intellectual, authority of 25–6

feminist pedagogy: and consciousness raising and women's liberation 19–23; empowerment of students in 149; and knowledge, sources of 27–30; of place 148–9; and teachers' role 24; and women's differences 33–4

Feminist Studies (journal) 22

formal democracy 54

Free Trade Papers, The (Drache and Cameron) 112

Freire for the Classroom (Shor) 144

fundamental democratization *see* real democracy

generative word, in Freirean thought 168

government and formal democracy 54

Greek mathematics 77, 83, 88–9

Grenada 50, 100

Guatemala: democracy in 49; Philosophy for Children (P4C) in 42–3; refugees in Mexico 131–2; unemployment in 49

Guinea-Bissau: Freire in 14, 50, 100, 144

Harry Stottlemeier's Discovery (Lipman) 42, 50

hegemony: and political power 55–6; Puiggrós on 156–8

hermeneutics: and *Dasein* 182–3; developments in 173–4; and education 173–92; and existence 182; of Freire 188–9; and interpretation 183; and phenomenology 182–3; in postmodernism 194

hierarchy, and teachers and feminism 23–6

history, Freire and Gadamer on 187

human being *see* being

human consciousness, and knowledge 76

human interactions with world 176, 178

human relationships, in Freire's philosophy 176

human rights in political education 71

humanization 15, 175

ideology: in Latin American education
127–8; and mathematics 87; in
post-colonial politics 149–50
In Defence of Politics (Crick) 63
interactive universalism 203
international issues in political education
65
International Monetary Fund (IMF) 136
interpretation, in hermeneutics 183
issue-based teaching: groups in political
education 67–8; problems of 69
issues in political education: identification
and formulation 64–5; teaching of 65

knowledge: creation and re-creation of
75–6; in epistemology of Freire 75–6;
and ethnomathematics 77–80;
experience as source of 30; feeling as
source of 27–30; and hermeneutics
173–4; mathematical *see* mathematical
knowledge; mathematics as 80, 82–4;
non-neutrality of 75–6; in
postmodernism 193; praxis,
non-neutrality of 76; and relationship
of educator to educatee 170; and
utopian praxis of Freire 203
knowledge content in political education
69, 70–1

language: Freire and Gadamer on 187–8;
Gadamer on 186; in literary programs
199; in postmodernism 194–6; social
context of 199–200; and utopian praxis
of Freire 202–3
Latin America: bourgeoisie, Puiggrós on
158; central and peripheral schooling
in 156–7; cultural colonialism,
Puiggrós on 155, 158; cultural
diversity in 129; education, Puiggrós
on 156; education in, and Freire 124–6;
native peoples and public schooling
156; pedagogy, Freire's effect on
169–70; socialist thought in 124–5;
unequal and unjust development of
157–8
learning: in epistemology of Freire 75–6;
as political project 200–1; as process in
political education 70; *see also*
democratic learning
lesbian women: and differences in social
identity 30–2; in Freirean thought,
feminist critique of 146

Let Me Speak (de Chungara) 120
liberation, women's, in feminist pedagogy
19–23
liberation pedagogy: in Argentina 159;
and critical utopianism 209; and
education of refugees 133; of Freire 15,
168–9; in mathematics 81; Puiggrós on
155, 159, 168
liberation politics 211–12
liberation theology, Puiggrós on 155
limit situations: in learning 51–2; in
political education teaching 65
Lionheart Girl 31
literacy: Brazilian, Freire on 105; as
cultural politics 101; and discourse,
Puiggrós on 168; and Freire in modern
society, Puiggrós on 165, 168; of
native peoples in Mexico 131; in
Nicaragua 127; as political project
200–1; and utopian praxis of Freire
201–2; *see also* critical literacy;
political literacy
lived experience 211
local issues in political education 64;
absence of 65
ludic postmodernism 204–6

March 8th Coalition (Canada) 116–17
marginalized people: education for 128–9;
and Freirean thought, feminist critique
of 148–9; in Latin America 124–5; and
moral imagination 48–9
Marxism: and Freire 166–7, 178; in Latin
America 125
mathematical knowledge 80; content of,
reconsidering 82–4; context of 86; and
ethnomathematics 90; history of,
uncovering 88–90; of women 82–3, 88,
89–90
mathematics: alienation from 80; as
cultural product 85; and culture *see*
ethnomathematics; unschooled learning
of 85–6; value-free concepts in 86–7
Maya culture, refugees 131–2
mental structures and mathematics 85
Mesopotamian mathematics 83, 88
Mexican Commission for Assisting
Refugees (COMAR) 131
Mexico: educational studies in 124; forest,
destruction of 129–30; and pedagogy
of Freire 127–34; socialist education
project 126

moral imagination: and critical thinking 44–8; Freire on 46–8; and Third World critical theory 48–50
MOVA-São Paulo 102, 105
myth: Freire as 100–1; institutions as 47; and mathematical knowledge 88–9; in postmodernism 193, 212; of social conditions 52

National Endowment for Democracy 57
national issues in political education 64
nationalism: in Argentina, Puiggrós on 163; and *pueblo* 168
native peoples: education of 130–1; in Latin America 129; in Mexico 129–30; in Pro-Canada Network 112; and public schooling in Latin America 156
neutrality: of knowledge 75–6; and political power 55–6; *see also* class-neutral
New Jersey Test of Reasoning Skill (NJTRS) 42, 50, 56
Nicaragua 50, 100; educational reforms in 127
non-literate peoples, and ethnomathematics 77–8
North American Free Trade Agreement (NAFTA): and BCNI 113–14; proposed 113
North–South world relations 135–6

objectivity: and learning mathematics 80; and subjectivity, Freire on 75–6
objects, and epistemology of Freire 75–6
opposition, and utopia 208
oppressed, pedagogy of: and education of refugees 133; Freire on 102–4; and moral imagination 48–50
oppression: class terms of, Freire on 14–15; and critical perception of reality 46–7; and crossing borders 207; in Freirean thought, feminist critique of 145–6; interlocking systems 33; and mathematical silence 88; nonsynchrony of 16; in *Pedagogy of the Oppressed* (Freire) 16–17; and utopian praxis of Freire 202–3
oppressor, pedagogy of 103; in Latin American education 128
Other MacDonald Report (Drache and Cameron) 112

Parliament (British) 63

peace education in Freirean perspective 41–61
pedagogy: dominant, in Latin America 128; feminist *see* feminist pedagogy; liberation *see* liberation pedagogy; of the oppressed *see* oppressed, pedagogy of; radical, and postmodernism 196–8
Pedagogy and Process 8, 100, 143, 145
pedagogy of Freire 14–19; Argentina, influence in 159–60; feminist critique of 145–9; in Mexico 127–34; misuse of 144–5; personal experience in 148; in post-colonial and postmodern politics 149–51; roots of 124–7; strengths and weaknesses, Puiggrós on 168–9; and twenty-first century challenges 134–6; weaknesses in 143–4; women ignored in 143–4
Pedagogy of the Oppressed (Freire) 2, 4, 8, 9, 217; and critical pedagogy 143, 145; and feminist pedagogy 13–18, 23; pedagogical roots of Freire 124, 135; Torres, conversation with 100, 102–4
people (*pueblo*) as category in Freire's conceptualization 167
perception, categorical limits of 47
Peronism (Argentina) 155, 159; education after 164–5; in power 163–4
phenomenology 182–3
philosophy, and mathematics 87
Philosophy and the Mirror of Nature (Rorty) 174
Philosophy for Children (P4C) 41–2; as counter-productive measure 48–9; in Guatemala 42–3, 49–50; inappropriateness of texts selected 50–1
political education: abilities acquired through practice 68; as activity-based teaching 66–7; application of 67–8; and citizenship 72–3; immaturity of students 68; issue-based groups 67–8; issues in 64–5; knowledge content in 69, 70–1; and political literacy 63; teacher closure in 65
political literacy: and conscientization 63–4; movement in Britain 62–73
political power and hegemony 55–6
political project (Freire's): and critical utopianism 210; literacy and learning in 200–1
political skills in political education 66–8
politics: as an activity 63–4, 66; and

education, Freire on 102–6; of
post-colonialism 149–51; and
post-socialist social movements
116–17; in postmodernism 149–51,
194–6; social movements in 109
Politics of Education, The (Freire) 199,
201, 217
positivism 75–6
post-colonialism, politics of 149–51
post-socialist social movements 115–17;
problems of 116, 119
post-structuralism 194
postmodern society, and Freire 134–5
postmodernism: description of 194; ludic
204–6; politics of 149–51, 217; and
radical pedagogy 196–8; resistance,
and critical utopianism 204–6; 'retreat
into the code' 195–6; shortcomings of
194–6; social theory in 193–6
practicism, Puiggrós on 169
praxis: in critical utopianism 206;
democratic learning as 53; and
education of refugees 132–3; and
hermeneutics 175, 177; in history,
Freire and Gadamer on 187; in
mathematics learning 81, 83;
non-neutrality of, and knowledge 76;
in postmodernism 193; in Pro-Canada
Network 114; of utopia 201–4
Principe 100
Pro-Canada Network 112–17; aims 114;
development of 114

racism 15; in Freirean thought, feminist
critique of 146; and mathematical
knowledge 82–3, 88; and post-socialist
social movements 116–17; and unitary
concept of women 31
radical pedagogy 216; and postmodernism
196–8
radical rupture, and utopia 208
real democracy 54
reality: and hermeneutics 177–8, 190; and
knowledge 76; in postmodernism 193
Redstockings 21
reductionism, Puiggrós on 167
reflection, and word, Freire on 178
religion and science, separation of 90
representation, in postmodernism 195
reproduction theory 170
revolutionary praxis, Freire on 210
revolutionary struggle and education,

Freire on 14
ritualization in Argentina, Puiggrós on 163

São Paulo 101; Freire as Secretary of
Education 101–2
São Tome 100
schooling: in Argentina 160–2; and
authority in Freirean thought 147;
central and peripheral in Latin America
156–7; demands in multiple society 128
Schooling as a Ritual Performance
(McLaren) 163
science and religion, separation of 90
secularism in Argentina, Puiggrós on 163
sexism 15; in Freirean thought, feminist
critique of 146; and mathematical
knowledge 82–3, 88; and post-socialist
social movements 116–17
Shelter 67
signification, in postmodernism 195–6
Signs (journal) 22
Sistern (group) 31
social action, and political education 70
social analysis in critical thinking 52
social antagonisms and social movements
117–18
social change and social movements 117–21
social class *see* class
social groups, and ethnomathematics
78–9, 82–3
social justice, and democracy 55
social movements: in Canada 108–22;
cross-class character 119; and Freire
118–19; post-socialist in Canada
115–17; and Pro-Canada Network
112–17; and social change 117–21
Social Movements and Social Change
(Cunningham) 112
social reality, in postmodernism 195–6
social systems, specific, in society 128
social theory in postmodern age 193–6,
216; and critical utopianism 204–6;
Freire's impact on 210–11
socialist education project (Mexico) 126
socialist thought, in Latin American
education 124
socialization 175
Sorge (care), in hermeneutics 183–4
speech, social context of 199–200
state, and post-socialist social movements
116–17
structural perception 47–8

students: Freire on 103; immaturity of, in political education 68; mathematical knowledge of 90–2; *see also* educatees
subjectivity: and authority in Freirean thought 147; Freire on 103–4; and learning mathematics 80–1; and objectivity, Freire on 75–6
substitutionalist universalism 203

Tanzania 100
teacher closure in political education 65
teachers: conscious partiality for 57; in Freirean thought, feminist critique of 148–9; mathematical knowledge of 90–2; in *Pedagogy of the Oppressed* (Freire) 17–18; in post-colonial politics 149–50; role and authority of 23–6; women, pedagogy of 19–20; *see also* educators
teaching: Freire on 103
temporality, in hermeneutics 184
texts selected for teaching: conscious partiality in 57–8; inappropriateness of P4C 50–1; roots of 51
Third World: critical theory and moral imagination in 48–50; democracy, meanings in 53–4; studies of, in political education 70; technology transfers to 136; texts selected for, inappropriateness of 50–1; and United States, in postmodern society 135–6
time: in critical thinking 181; Freire and Gadamer on 187; in Freire's philosophy 180–1; in hermeneutics 182–6
trade agreements: United States and Canada 110, 112–13; coalition of popular groups opposed to 112–13; social movements in opposition to 111–12

tradition: Freire on 189; Gadamer on 188
transcendental imagination 47

understanding: Freire and Gadamer on 186; in hermeneutics 185–6
unemployment, and oppression 49
United States: challenges to critical thinking 53; mathematical context of knowledge 86; model of democracy 53–8; and Third World, in postmodern society 135–6; trade agreements with Canada 110–11, 112
utopia: and postmodern society 134–5; praxis of 201–4; re-evaluation of 207–8; *see also* critical utopianism

Warisata project (Bolivia) 126
women: and authority in Freirean thought 147–9; and collective memory 30–1; consciousness-raising groups 20; differences among 30–4; feeling as source of knowledge 27; ignored in pedagogy of Freire 143–4; liberation in feminist pedagogy 19–23; and mathematical knowledge 82–3, 88, 89–90; role of, in Freirean thought 146; social movements in Canada 116–17; unitary concept of 30
women of color: and differences in social identity 30–3; in Freirean thought, feminist critique of 146
word, Freire on 178–9
Workers' Party (Brazil) 101–2, 126
working class, in social movements 118–19
World Bank 136

Youth and Adult Education Campaign (Brazil) 158